IMAGES
of America

AFRICAN AMERICANS OF HENRICO COUNTY

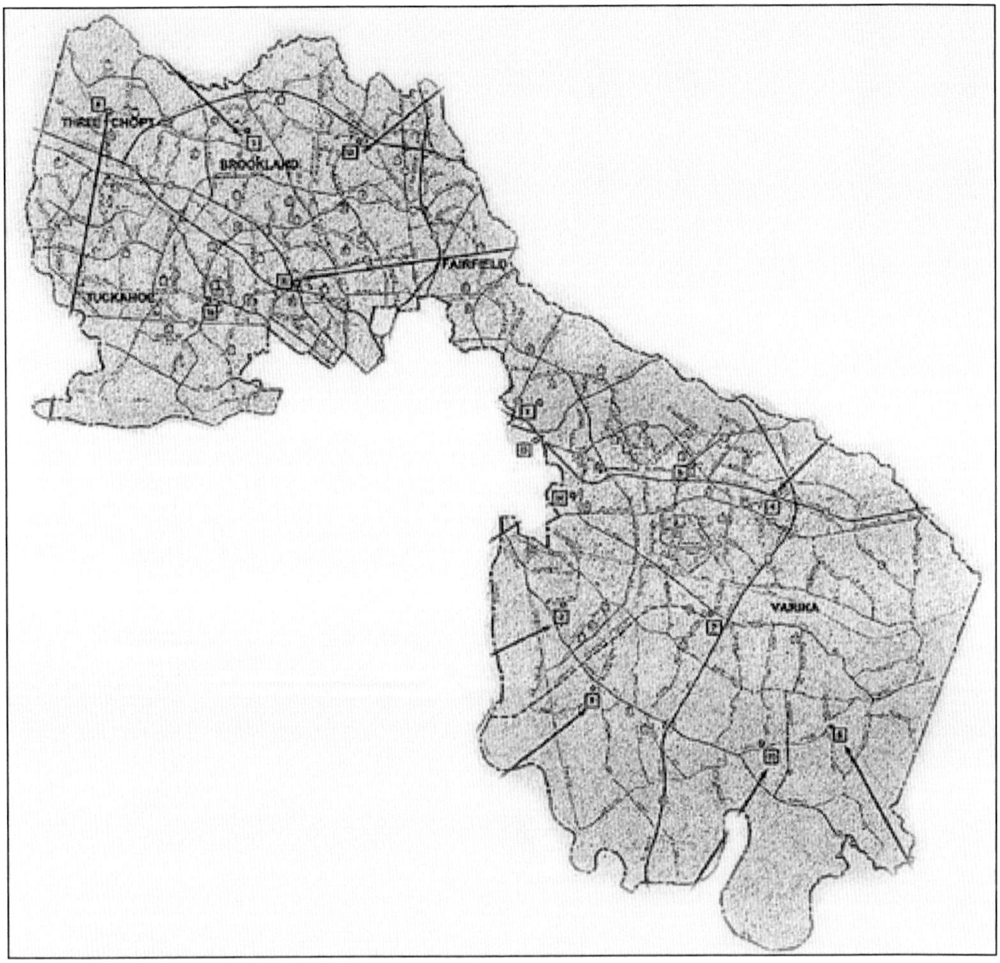

This geographical depiction shows the present-day outline of Henrico County. (Henrico County Virginia Historical Society.)

On the Cover: This is the family of Clarence (Eddie) and Evelyn Juanita Jones Morse, who lived on lower Ridge Road, enjoying Echo Lake around 1930. From left to right are Morse family members Juanita, Louise Morse Fountain, Eddie Jr. (Stony), and Emily. Eddie and Juanita owned Evelyn's Place (a dinner and night spot across the street from their home) and C. E. Morse and Sons Music Amusement for 34 years. (Gertrude Morse.)

IMAGES
of America

AFRICAN AMERICANS OF HENRICO COUNTY

Brenda Dabney Nichols

ARCADIA
PUBLISHING

ISBN 978-0-7385-6650-4

Published by Arcadia Publishing
Charleston, South Carolina

Printed in the United States of America

Library of Congress Control Number: 2009930980

For all general information contact Arcadia Publishing at:
Telephone 843-853-2070
Fax 843-853-0044
E-mail sales@arcadiapublishing.com
For customer service and orders:
Toll-Free 1-888-313-2665

Visit us on the Internet at www.arcadiapublishing.com

To my late husband, Dr. Paul Nichols, who first encouraged me to follow my dreams to write a book. Now, 19 years later, I am fulfilling the dream that he inspired.

Contents

Acknowledgments

It is with great humbleness that I thank my heavenly Father and the people who have helped to make this book a reality. As a native of Henrico County, the many, many hours that I spent gathering pictures, keeping appointments, and conducting interviews have occurred over a two-year period. I appreciate how most embraced this research project and caught my vision to highlight the accomplishments of African Americans in Henrico County. Dr. Roy West, Mary Frances W. Lambert, former state senator Dr. Benjamin J. Lambert III, Leonard Lambert, Esq., Frances Watson, Ocie J. Walker, Emma J. Truman, Carol Dabney, H. Clay Jones Jr., Leland Cauthorne, Gloria Nash, Frances Trent Hughes, Laverne Dean Woodson, Bernice W. Cousins, Anne Hamlette Johnson, Douglas Houston, Adelaide Warren, Jean V. Carter, and Richard Peebles provided pictures and oral histories that were so valuable. Also, there were persons who contributed pictures and narratives such as Aubrey Fountain Jr., Dr. Lloyd Jackson, and Hilda Cosby, curator of the Virginia Randolph Museum in Glen Allen. I also thank M. Delores Williams Keyes, neighbor, advisor, and confidant.

My father, Ernest Dabney, and aunt, Mable Dabney Hubbard, are thanked for their enthusiasm and encouragement. A heartfelt thanks to my children; Dr. Colita and her husband, Anthony E. Fairfax, for typing, editing, and scanning materials; and Kimberly N. (Rudolph) McKissick and Camilla and Paul Brandon Nichols for listening and reading. I must mention my late mother, Lavinia Holmes Dabney, who was a daughter of Henrico and a life student of history. She would have marveled at all that has been uncovered. As the project unfolded, I lost my only sister, Wanda Dabney Zanders. My sister sacrificed the comforts of her childhood to integrate Henrico County schools so that Henrico would truly be considered a home to all. In their memories, this text exemplifies that African Americans are an integral element in Henrico.

INTRODUCTION

Although the history of Henrico County has been predominantly told from the perspective of English development within the Virginia colony, historians also acknowledge that Native Americans were its first inhabitants. The Algonquin Nation, also referred to as the Powhatan Confederacy, was ruled by Chief Wahunsenacawh (Powhatan). The Algonquin Nation was among those first peoples settling at the head of the Chickahominy River where Powhatan lived. After Wahunsenacawh's death, his brother Chief Opechancanough ruled. Failed treaties between the Algonquin Nation and English settlers resulted in different tribes being forced onto reservations. The English arrived in Jamestown in 1607 and Elizabeth City County (now the city of Hampton) in 1610, and they eventually settled in Henrico County in 1634. Henrico County surrounds the city of Richmond on three sides.

Africans arrived in 1619 in Elizabeth City County and Jamestown, and some African American communities evolved before the Civil War throughout Virginia. They were not all enslaved. Those who were enslaved were owned by prominent Henricoans, were considered personal property, and lived on huge plantations throughout Henrico County (such as Paradise and Ravenswood). An enslaved person had little to no rights, could not own property, worked from sunrise to sunset, and could not exercise any right or authority over his or her own family and own life. Under the laws of the state, slaves were denied basic human rights. Even the rights of free blacks were severely restricted. Plantation life was dehumanizing, atrocious, and appalling. Treated like cattle, enslaved persons experienced daily loss, as families were sold apart without provocation. Husbands, wives, children, and other relatives were separated at the will of owners. Enslaved persons were whipped, branded, sexually violated, economically exploited, and vulnerable to violence and emotional cruelty. Men could not protect their wives and daughters from rape or violations, for they would be whipped or killed. Often, children were born as a result of rape, which created a labor base for owners. Young men were considered bucks or studs. These bucks or studs were forced to impregnate women to sire more slaves as workers in the tobacco fields to profit the lives of masters. These fields were a major source of revenue in Virginia, as evidenced by the English-sponsored Virginia Company of London, the company charged with settling Virginia.

With the Emancipation Proclamation of 1863 and the end of the Civil War in 1865, African American communities burgeoned. The Civil War was over, enslavement was over, and families traveled to find lost relatives and live as free people. Many were able to purchase land close to the plantations they had been born on and worked all of their lives. There are land deeds verifying that property was sold to newly freed men who had worked on adjacent plantations. Under segregationist laws, these neighborhoods blossomed, and many still exist with single-family dwellings built of wood or brick. Spiritual and religious life is central in the African American psyche, and these neighborhoods soon established churches. Many of these churches were built as early as 1850. These churches were the epicenters of sustained and organized activities that not only underscored the value, beauty, and culture of African Americans but also advanced leaders who have contributed immensely to Henrico.

The creation of community schools, as depicted in this book, is a testimony to the importance of education as a means of upward mobility and community progress. All of these community schools would prepare children for the Virginia E. Randolph Training School, later renamed Virginia E. Randolph High School, the only black high school in Henrico. African American children of Henrico would become household names in the county, the city of Richmond, and the state of Virginia. The strong entrepreneurial spirit is also a pervasive feature in these communities, as creative talent and ingenuity would be showcased in the diverse businesses that would add to community life. Future generations would benefit from these communities and maintain their inheritance by passing the rich oral history to those staunchly remaining in Henrico County, continuing traditions as African Americans.

One

New Bridge Fair Oaks Bungalow City

In the mid-1800s, black and white residents organized the historic New Bridge community, which derived its name from a new bridge built over the Chickahominy River. Both the black and white communities attended the New Bridge Baptist Church in 1834. Although people of color worshipped at the white New Bridge Baptist Church, they were seated separately. They eventually left and began worshipping at the First African Baptist Church at Fourteenth and Broad Streets. That church donated the money for them to purchase land on which to build the black New Bridge Baptist Church in 1864. The first pastor was Rev. John Fauntleroy. Succeeding pastors were Rev. J. H. Binford, W. H. Spurlock, A. L. Anderson, Augustus McHerrin, George D. Hill, William Beard, Cessar Scott, and William A. Jenkins. To this day, the separate white and black New Bridge Baptist Churches still exist, side by side.

Fair Oaks' roots date back to the late 1800s. The community was originally called Fair Oak, but residents began referring to their neighborhood as Fair Oaks (with an *s*) because of the abundance of oak trees. Rev. J. R. Vaughan became the first minister of Fair Oaks Baptist Church, founded around the same time as the community. The teachers at the one-room schoolhouse were Lillie John and Louise Williams Hardy Moore, with Ora Wingfield as principal. Noted family names in Fair Oaks are Sampson, Trent, Gaines, and Robinson.

Matthew Robinson Jr. tells the intriguing family story of his grandfather, George Robinson, who learned the art of broom making in England. He arrived in America as an indentured man and later migrated to Henrico from West Point with his wife Effie and son Matthew Sr., who was born in the city of West Point in 1898. A deacon and trustee of New Bridge Baptist Church, he joined the faculty at Virginia Randolph High School in 1941 and taught there until 1964. George Robinson and his son started the Imperial Broom Company.

Bungalow City was located within the Fair Oaks community. Much of Bungalow City has disappeared, but it still lives in the memory of many African Americans in Henrico County, for there are still descendants very connected to that geographical area.

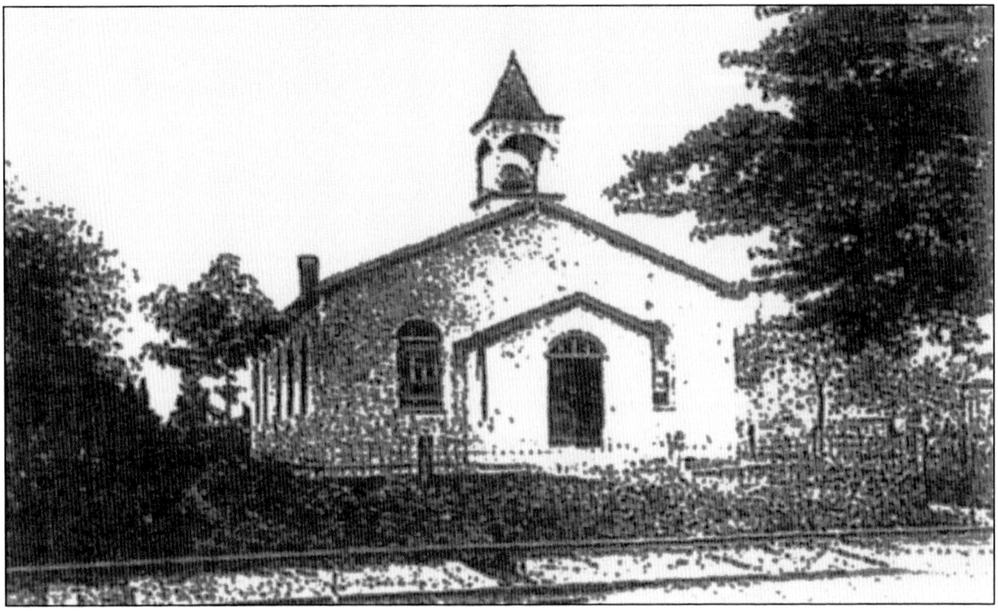

This picture is of the original New Bridge Baptist Church, founded in 1834. (Burnette DePriest Burgess.)

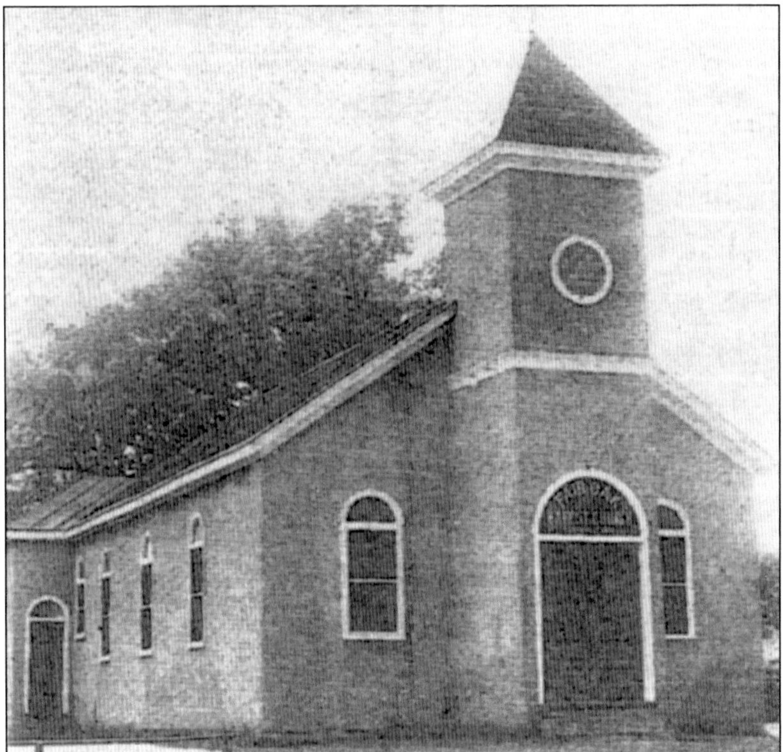

This picture shows the original Fair Oaks Baptist Church, founded around 1923. (Shirley Carter.)

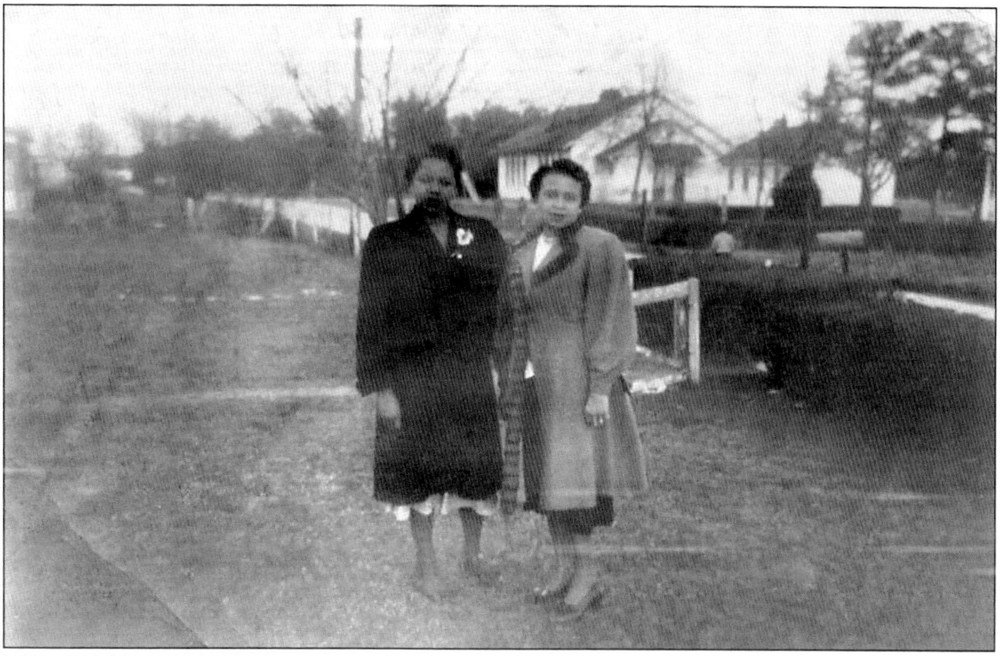

Lillian (left) and Elizabeth Sampson pose in front of the original Fair Oaks Elementary School, which is still in operation today. Elizabeth Sampson Johnson was one of the first African American food services managers for Henrico schools. She was employed at Fair Oaks from September 1951 to June 1986. (Elizabeth S. Johnson.)

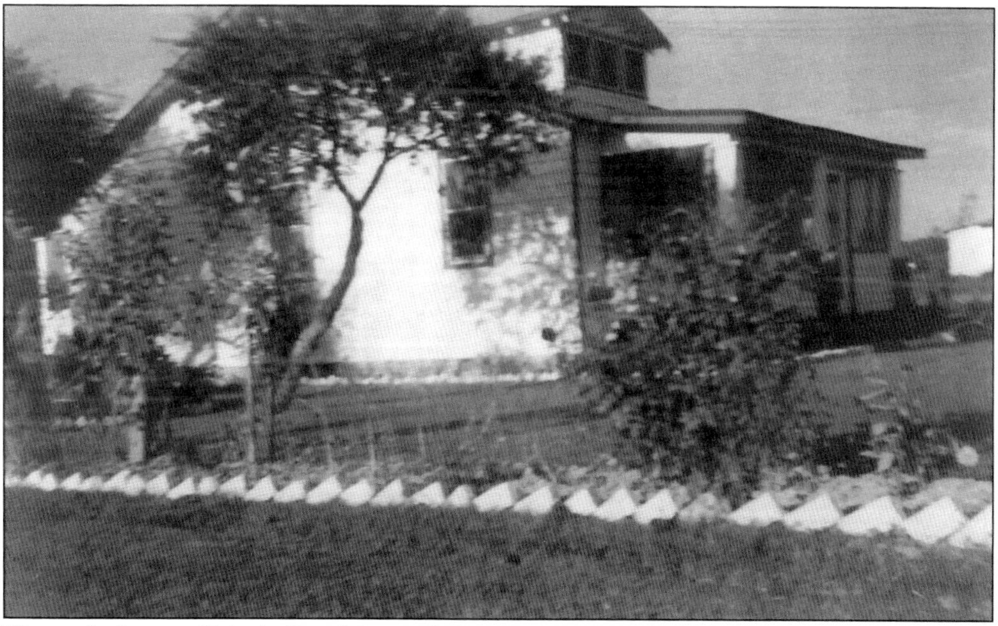

This is the home of Mitchell and Cora Claiborne Sampson, which was located across the street from the school. Mitchell Sampson was born in the Westwood community in 1897 and died in 1958. Cora Claiborne Sampson was born 1899 in Powhatan County and died in 1985. Cora took pride in caring for her flowers and was a member of the Henrico Home Demonstration Club. She often won prizes in the club for her beautifully arranged, colorful flowers. (Elnora S. Hubbard.)

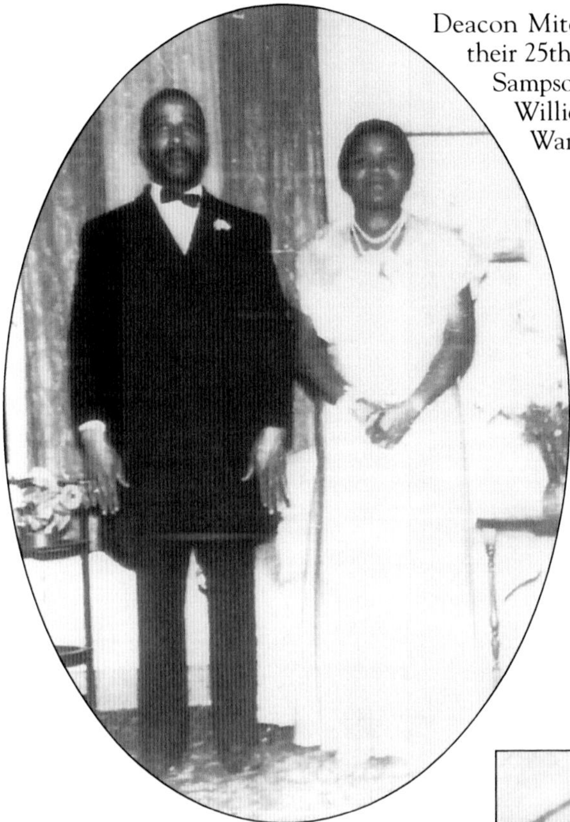

Deacon Mitchell and Cora C. Sampson celebrate their 25th wedding anniversary in the early 1940s. Sampson left the Westwood home of his parents, Willie and Mary Sampson, to fight in World War I. (Elnora S. Hubbard.)

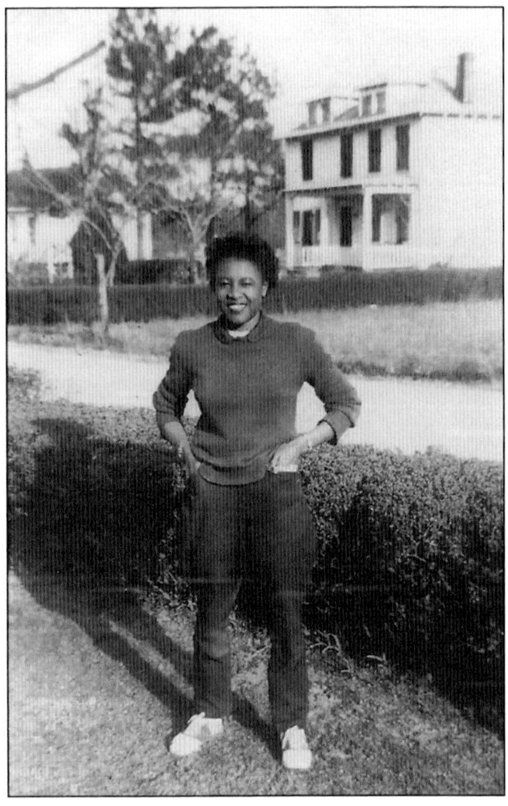

Elnora Sampson Hubbard poses in front of the Trent family store. Morris and Betty Trent operated the store, which sold bread, milk, eggs, bacon, and other essentials. The Trents also raised strawberries, which they allowed the schoolchildren to pick after school for pocket money during summer vacation. (Elnora S. Hubbard.)

This picture is of Matthew Robinson Jr. and his son Carlton. They are standing in front of the Imperial Broom Company, a long-standing family business started by Matthew's grandfather. (Matthew Robinson Jr.)

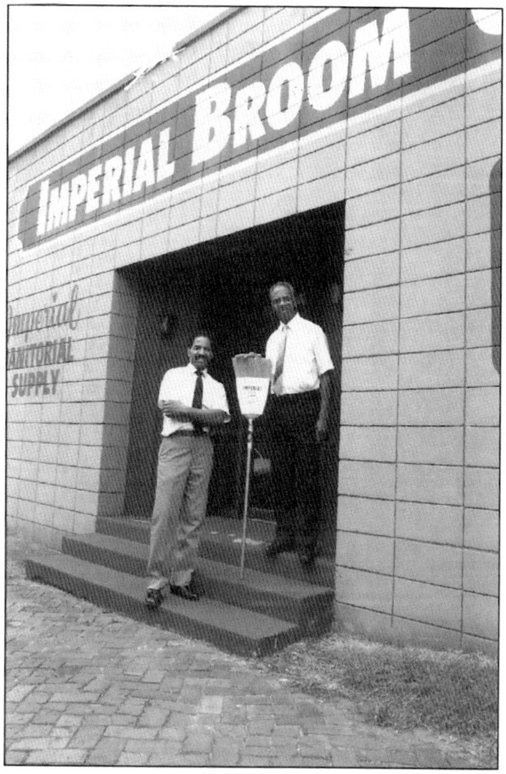

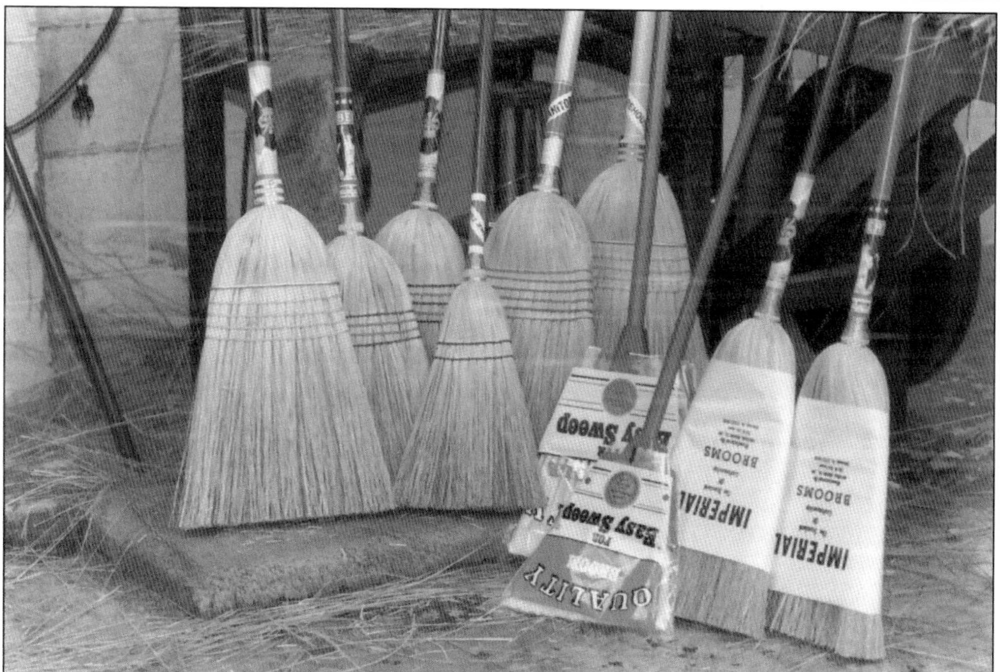

These are brooms manufactured by the Imperial Broom Company. The company was relocated to the East End community in Richmond after a fire. The company expanded sales from Buffalo, New York, to Atlanta, Georgia. (Matthew Robinson Jr.)

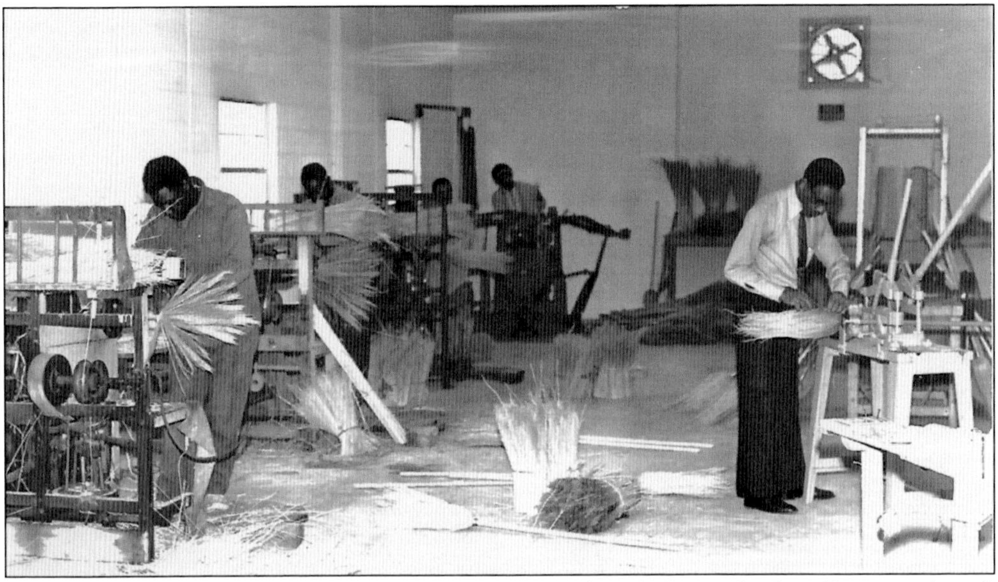

This picture shows the art of broom making. Raw materials include wooden handles, wire, thread, and top grades of corn or yucca grown in Mexico. The wire is passed systematically through a hole at the end of the wooden handle and wound securely. A machine then rotates the handle while the operator assembles stalks of broomcorn. The work is trimmed with a knife, shaped, and built up in layers. In addition to regular household brooms, the Imperial Broom Company also made brooms for the ritual of jumping the broom. This West African ritual was used in weddings, when newly pronounced couples would jump over a broomstick. (Matthew Robinson Jr.)

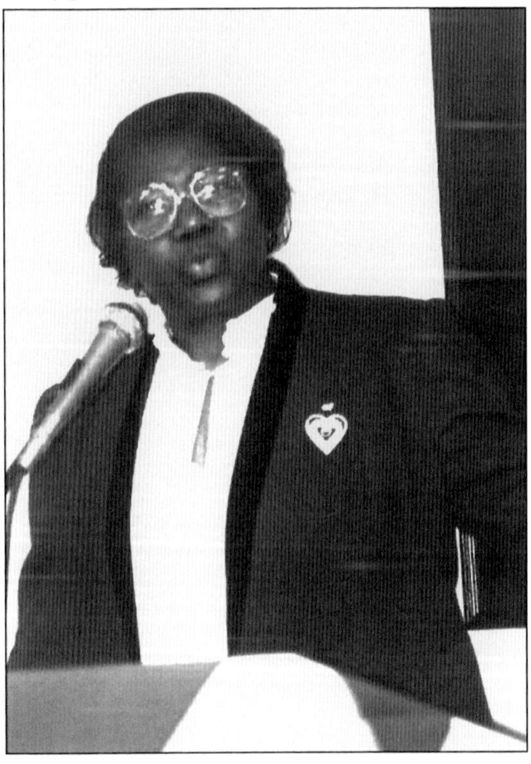

Elsie Gaines Dabney, a lifelong resident of Fair Oaks, was the church secretary at Seven Pines Baptist Church for 30 years. She is pictured here making announcements at the 11:00 a.m. worship service. (Elsie G. Dabney.)

Two

SANDSTON

The community of Sandston had its early beginnings around 1861 to 1862. There were several little neighborhoods within this community, namely Seven Pines, Boar Swamp, Whiteside, and White Oak. There were also smaller pockets of neighborhoods throughout Sandston such as Poplar Springs. Seven Pines is named from the cluster of the seven stately pine trees standing side by side in front of Seven Pines Cemetery. This area also bears a landmark where the Battle of Seven Pines, also known as the Battle of Fair Oaks or Fair Oaks Station, was fought. This Civil War battle took place May 31–June 1, 1862.

After the Civil War, the families who settled in these neighborhoods formed several churches: Seven Pines Baptist, Rising Mount Zion Baptist, and Bethany Baptist. Seven Pines Baptist Church was organized in May 1872 on a spot between the Southern Railroad track and Williamsburg Road. The church purchased one acre, triangular in shape, on the south side of Williamsburg Road. The deed dated August 10, 1872, was sold for the price of $15 by Mahala Ann Christian to the church trustees: Peter Anderson, Essex Hill, Benjamin Goode, and Robert Laws. In 1937, the church was destroyed by fire. The congregation worshipped temporarily in the Dry Bridge School, located in the lower section of the Seven Pines neighborhood. The congregation later relocated to the Rising Mount Zion Hall, a chapel that was a portion of a military installation, which they later purchased for $750. Rising Mount Zion Baptist, located in Boar Swamp, was organized in 1910. Throughout the development of Rising Mount Zion, Deacons Louis Marrow, Maxwell Lightfoot, and Melvin Marrow gave of their expertise to make plans for expansion to include a fellowship hall. Lastly, Bethany Baptist Church was organized in 1914, in the Whiteside community, and its first pastor was Rev. George Carter.

These neighborhoods in Sandston built the Dry Bridge School to educate the black children from all of these communities. A Mrs. Houston was one of the teachers in the school. When money and circumstances permitted, students would complete the lower grades at Dry Bridge, travel to Fair Oaks School for the middle grades, and enter Virginia Randolph School when high school became available for black students. These students had to secure their transportation, because school was 25 miles, too far to walk. Finally, buses were purchased due to the efforts of Virginia Randolph.

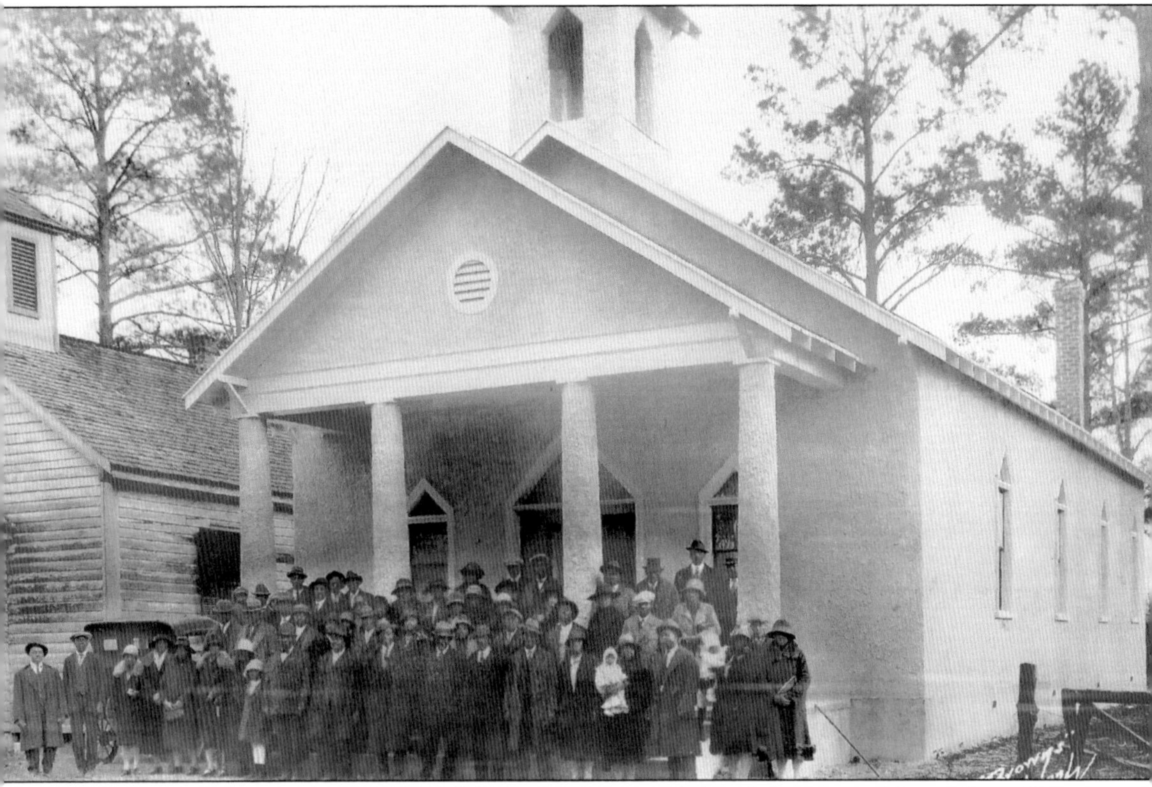

This picture was taken in 1926 of the parishioners and church building of Seven Pines Baptist Church. (Virginia Sorrell.)

This picture is of the Dry Bridge School in Sandston. Very similar to Fair Oaks, it served as a community school and held grades one through four in a one-room building. Emma Skipper Jones taught all four grades and was also counselor and principal. (Virginia Sorrell.)

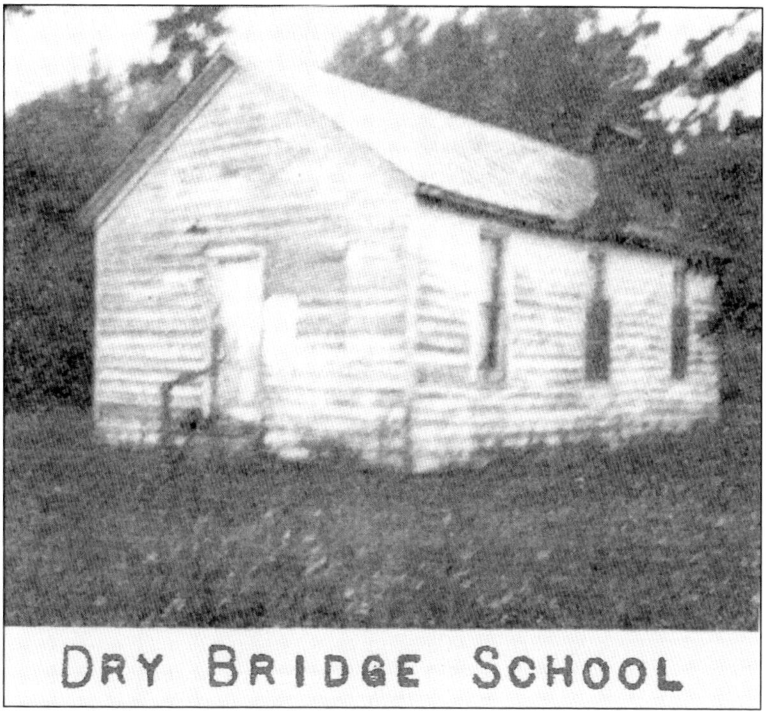

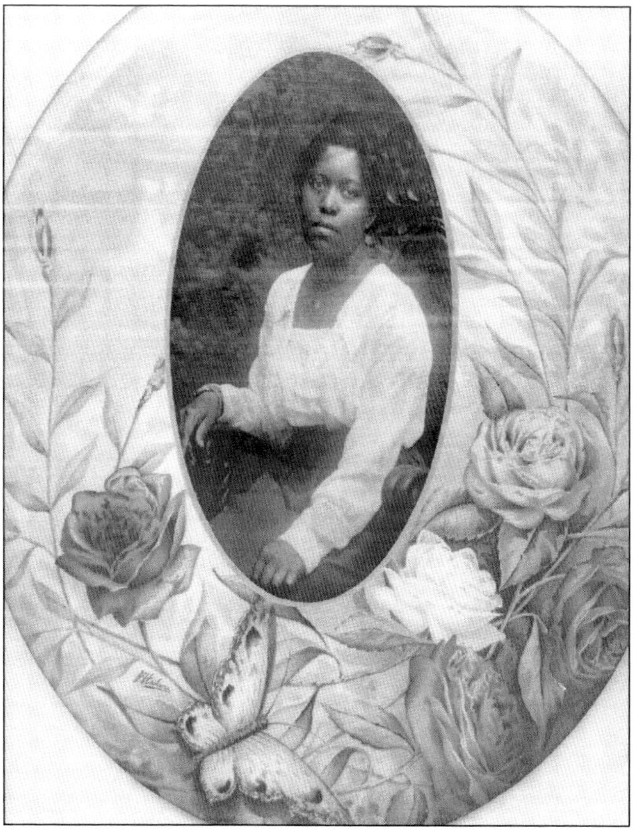

Pictured here is Mary Elizabeth "Lizzie" Brown DePriest, who was born in Seven Pines in 1896. She was a wife to Oscar Depriest and mother of 10 children. Every Sunday morning, DePriest could be found in Seven Pines Baptist Church, serving as clerk and reading announcements. (Burnette D. W. Burgess.)

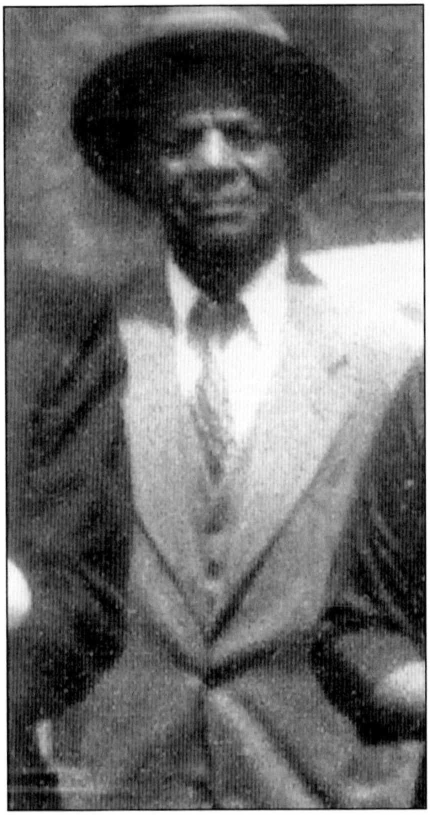

This picture is of Oscar DePriest, who was born in Boar Swamp in 1891. DePriest fought in World War II, and after an honorable discharge, he worked for the Chesapeake and Ohio Railway for 33 years. He and his wife, Elizabeth, had five daughters (Virginia, Elizabeth, Isabell, Willieann, and Burnette) and five sons (Jesse, Herman, Ellwood, Willie, and Earl), who helped farm their land. The youngest daughter, Burnette Burgess, still lives on the family land. (B. D. W. Burgess.)

This good-looking couple is the Manuels. Merlis Manuel was born in 1910 in King William County and moved to Boar Swamp. In 1928, he met and married Roberta Marrow (born in 1914), and the couple had 19 children. Manuel supported his family by holding several jobs. His main work was for the Chesapeake and Ohio Railway, but he also formed the Manuel Construction and Logging Company. In addition, he worked as a cement finisher laying concrete for Interstate 64, which flows through Henrico County. (Rachel M. Rogers.)

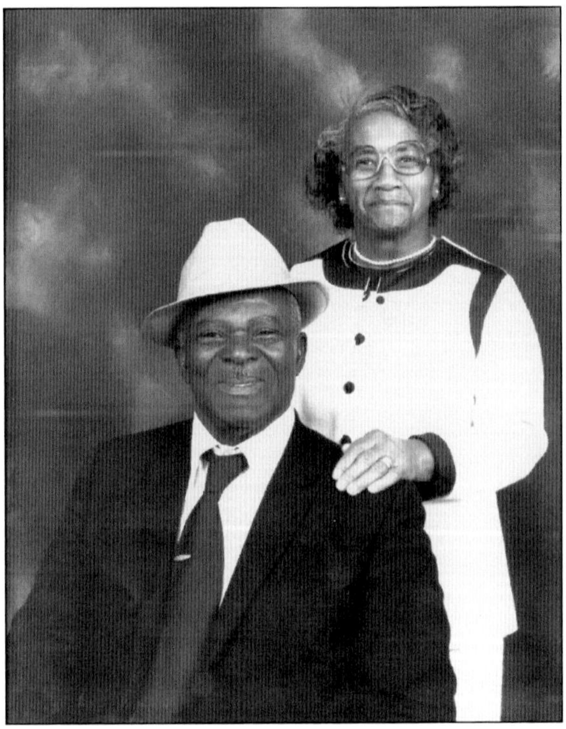

Other Boar Swamp neighbors included the Allen family. This well-dressed gentleman is Elijah Allen at age 18. He had a farm where he raised chickens, pigs, mules, horses, and cows. He and his wife, Pearl Johnson Allen, had 10 children. (Mary A. Johnson.)

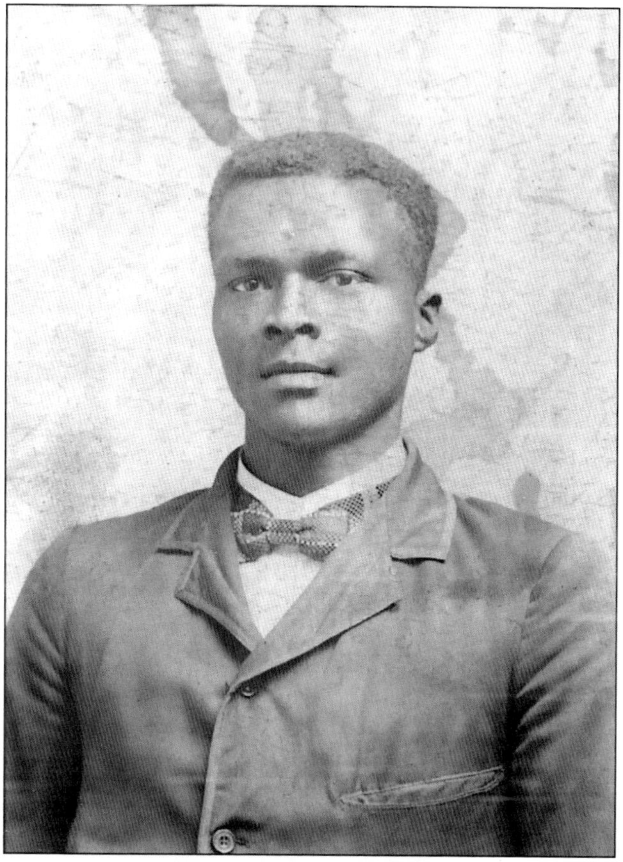

Shown here is Luther S. Allen Sr., a son of Elijah and Pearl Allen. He married Mary Elizabeth White and worked for Brooks Delivery Truck Company and an Oscar Mayer meat packing plant. (Mary A. Johnson.)

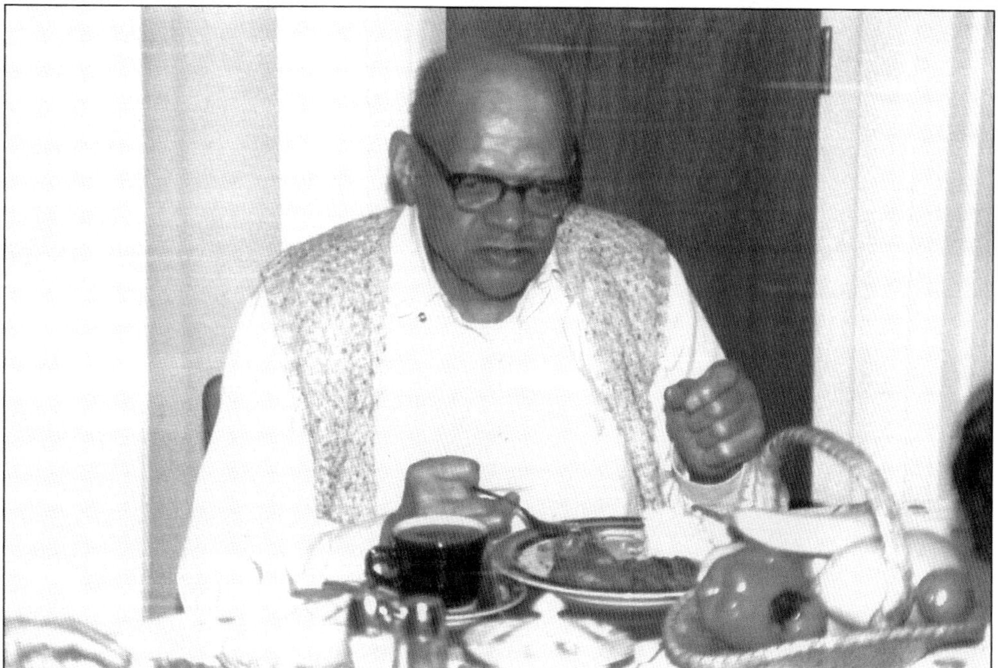

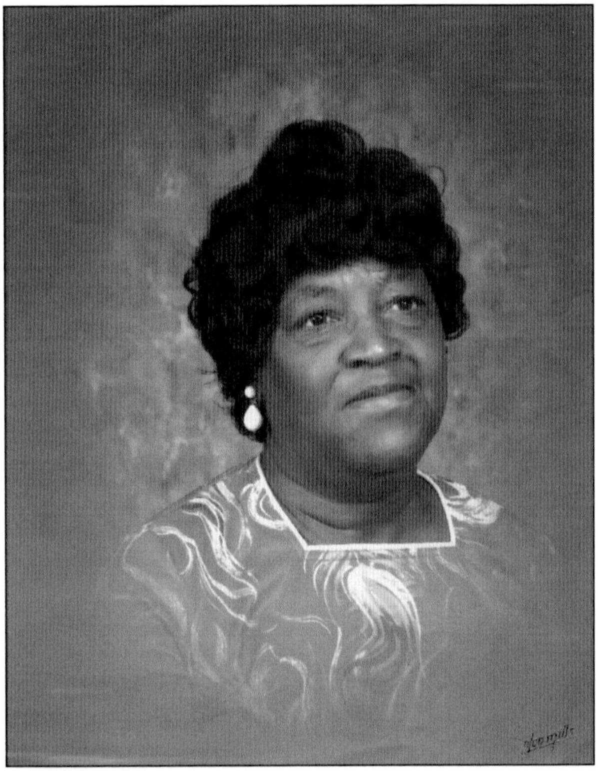

At left is Mary Elizabeth White Allen, who was born in 1914 to Emily and Robert White in Poplar Springs, another small community in Henrico County. To earn a living, she worked as a domestic laborer, as many African American women did. She was married to Luther S. Allen Sr., and they had 13 children. (Mary A. Johnson.)

Pictured below is the home of the Nash family, located on Whiteside Road. They owned Nash Family Trucking, operated by Floyd Sr., his wife, Joanna Annie Harris, who was the bookkeeper, and two children, Floyd Jr. and Mary Magdalene. They had a sizeable farm and sold their merchandise in the city of Richmond. Floyd Sr. also owned a tavern called Shady Grove Inn. (Mary M. Nash.)

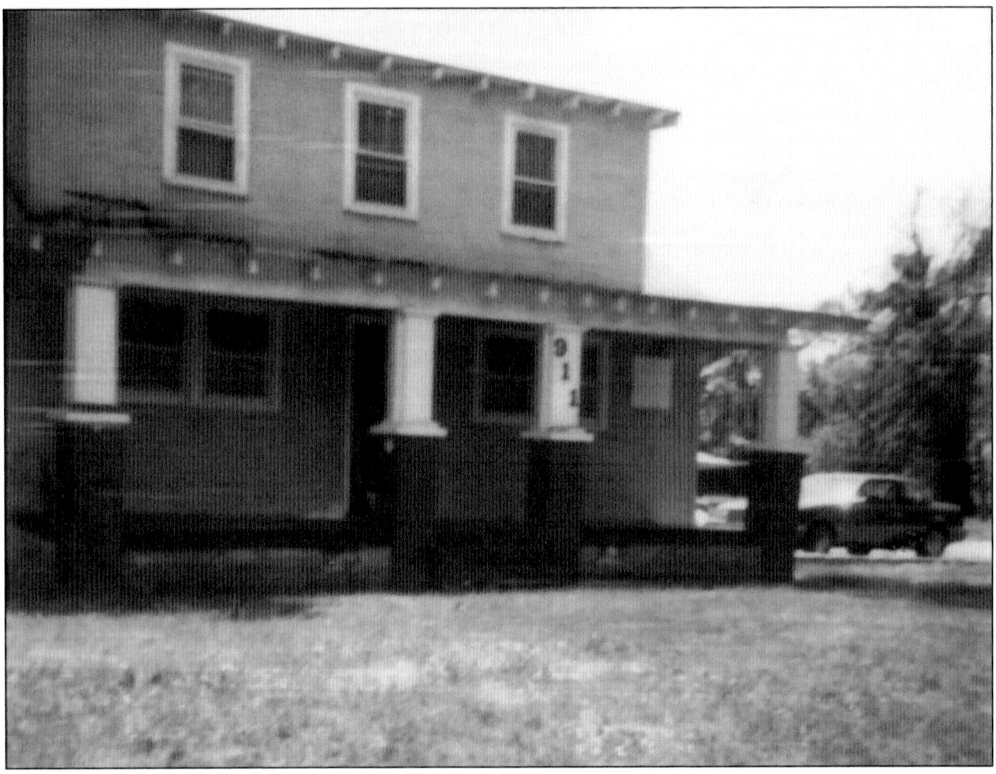

Floyd Nash Sr. is pictured sitting on his tractor. (Mary M. Nash.)

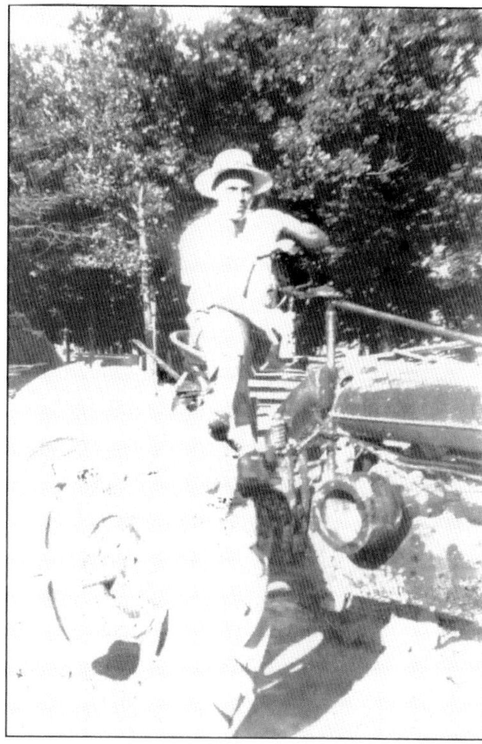

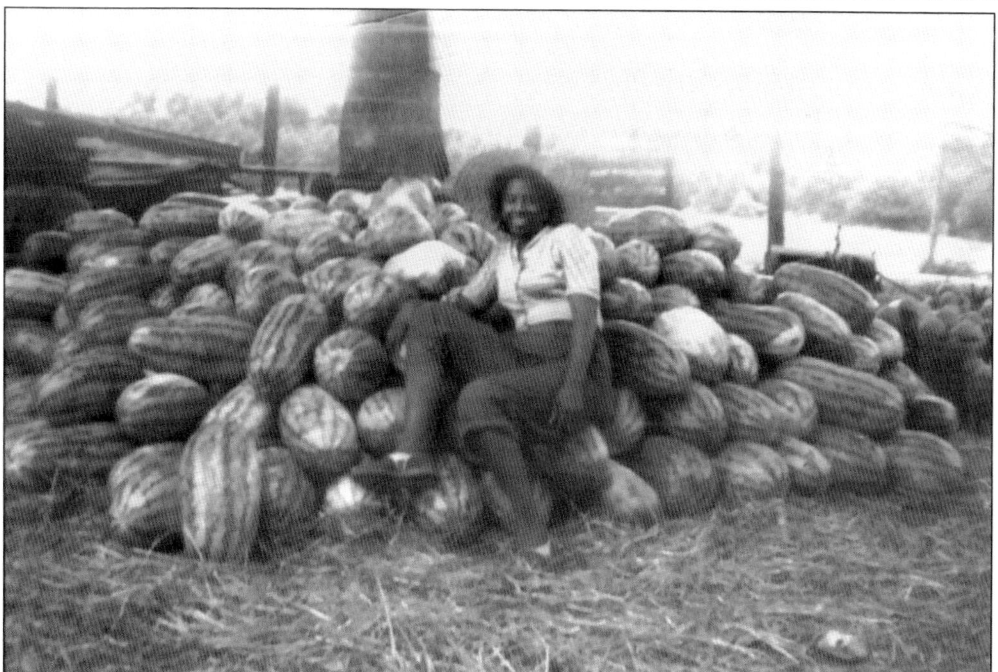

In addition to the trucking business, the Nash family was also known for their ample farm. They planted sweet and white potatoes, greens, squash, and other vegetables. Here is Joanna sitting on 100 watermelons. The Nash family sold their large amounts of produce at the Sixth Street Marketplace in downtown Richmond. (Mary M. Nash.)

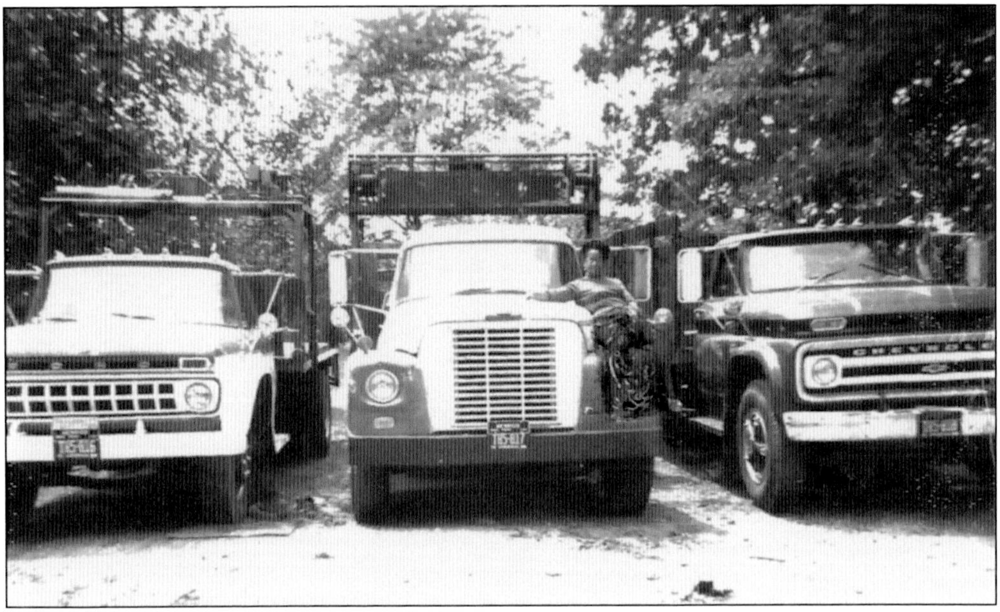

Nash Family Trucking hauled bricks for the Redford Brick Company and Southside Brick Company. After raising animals, growing vegetables, and marketing them, Floyd Sr. also hauled bricks and sold wood in the Fulton and Churchill areas of Richmond. (Mary M. Nash.)

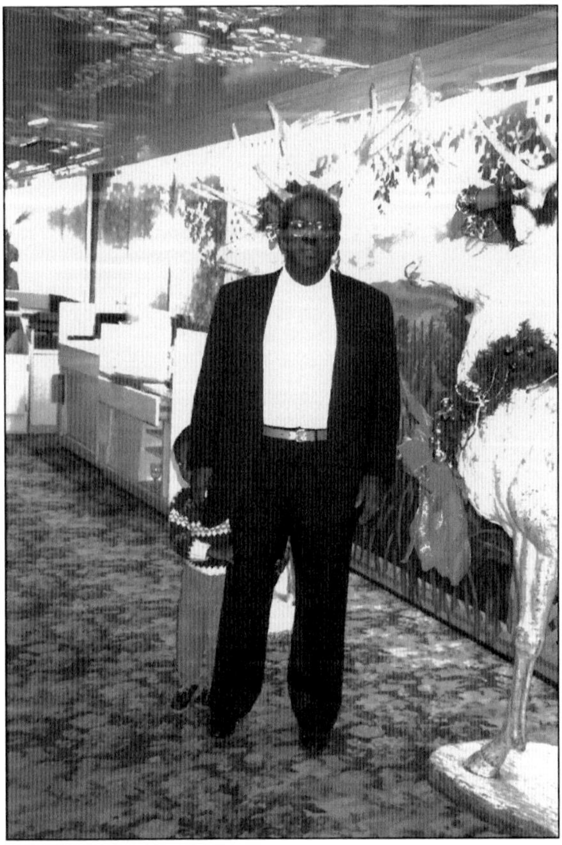

In addition to the entrepreneurial spirit that these communities inspired, they also created educated persons. This is Ernest Davis, born in the Whiteside community on Nash Road. He was proud to be one of 10 children born to Walter Davis Sr. and Lizzie Harris Davis. He graduated from Virginia Union University in the city of Richmond and earned a bachelor's degree in elementary education and a master's of education in social work from Rutgers University in New Brunswick, New Jersey. His career spanned the areas of health and education. (Ernest Davis.)

Three

VARINA

The Varina district is located in the eastern part of Henrico County. It is an old battleground area with a rich history. The town of Varina was named for Varina Farms, a former plantation on the James River owned by John Rolfe. Four historical neighborhoods that became home to African Americans in Varina are Gravel Hill (formerly known as Gravelly Hill), Bethel, Antioch, and St. James. There was also the adjacent Fulton community, named after landowners. Originally there were both First and Second Bethel neighborhoods, but mostly the church exists in Second Bethel, named Second Bethel Baptist Church. Each community fashioned a school to educate its children—Gravel Hill, Bethel, and St. James Schools. Family names in Gravel Hill include Atkins, Bigger, Brown, Harris, Johnson, Lewis, Pleasants, Price, Rooks, Truman, and Young. Gravel Hill dates back to 1777, according to the Henrico County Historical Society.

The Battle of New Market Heights was fought in September 1864 during the Civil War. The Medal of Honor was given to 14 African American as a result of their actions during this battle. In his will, a Quaker named John Pleasants freed some of his slaves. John Pleasants's will was contested by relatives who did not want to honor his last wishes. Two attorneys, John Wordman and John Marshall (who would become the first chief justice of the United States Supreme Court), won the case for his son Robert Pleasants. Robert followed in his footsteps, freeing his 78 slaves in 1782 and giving them 350 acres of Pleasant Plantation for their use. This community would become known as Gravel Hill. In 1801, Robert Pleasant established Gravelly Hill School (later Gravel Hill School), and the Gravel Hill Baptist Church was founded in 1866, after the end of the Civil War. More families of freedmen settled in Varina on various plots of land that were once portions of plantations. Those 350 acres and other plots of land would expand into admirable and resilient communities and families for generations.

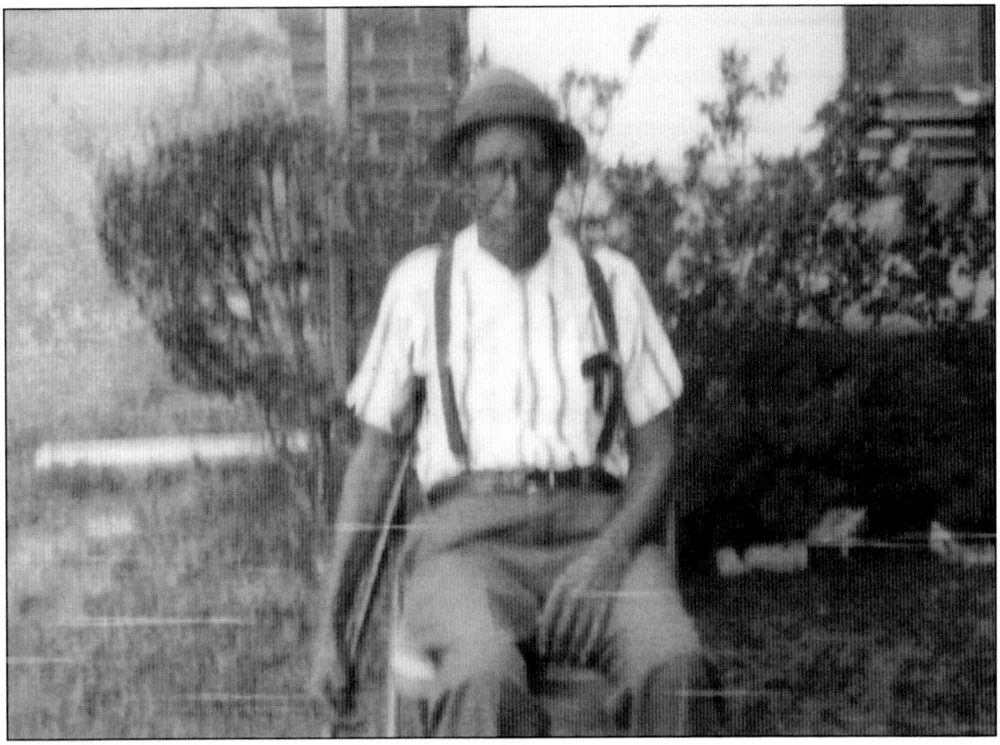

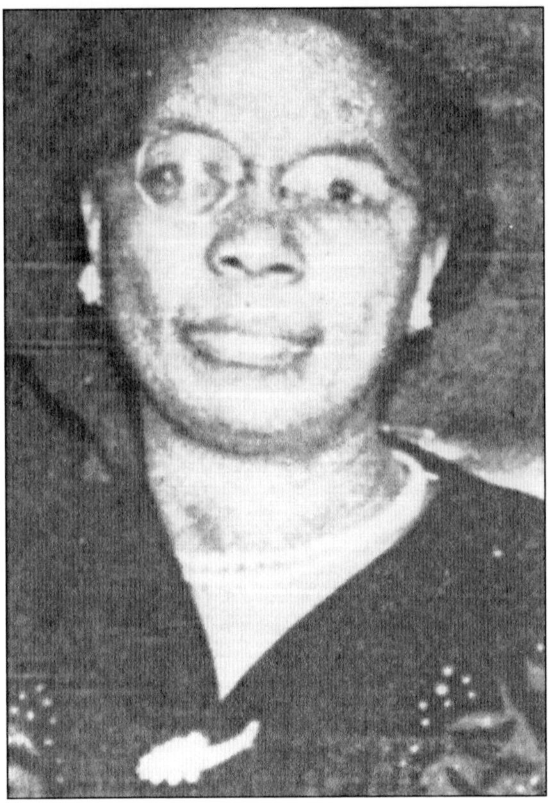

Shown above is Phillip U. Price (1891–1980). He worked for the Chesapeake and Ohio Railway for 33 years and lived in the Gravel Hill community. (Cornelius and Doris Price.)

At left is Ida Jones Price, a homemaker born in 1895. (Cornelius and Doris Price.)

This is a picture of the early structure of Gravel Hill Baptist Church, founded by formerly enslaved persons in 1866. The church is located on Longbridge Road off Darbytown Road near the New Kent County line. Enslaved persons worshipped with their masters at Four Mile Creek Baptist Church. (Dr. Ray McKenzie.)

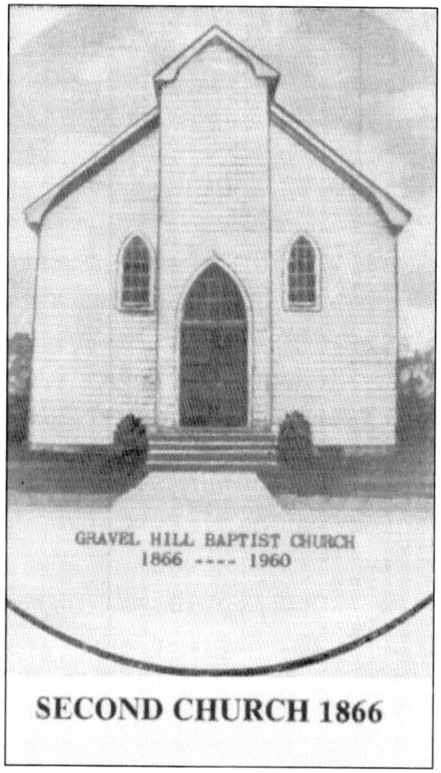

Pictured below around 1963 from Fair Oaks Elementary School are the following, from left to right: (seated) Pearl Reid, Zenobia Scott, Dr. Lloyd Jackson (principal), Nathaniel Edwards, and Sarah Walton; (standing) Ethel Easter, Mamie Kenney, Eleanor Boyd, Hilda Cosby, ? Grey, and Emma Jones. (Hilda Cosby.)

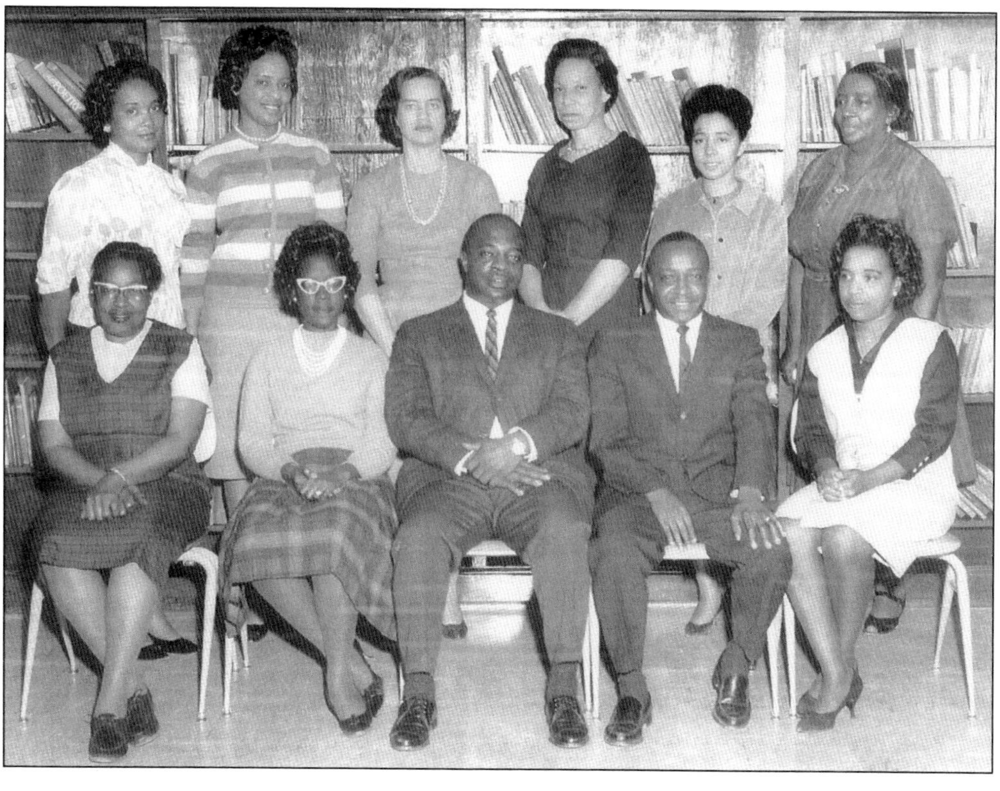

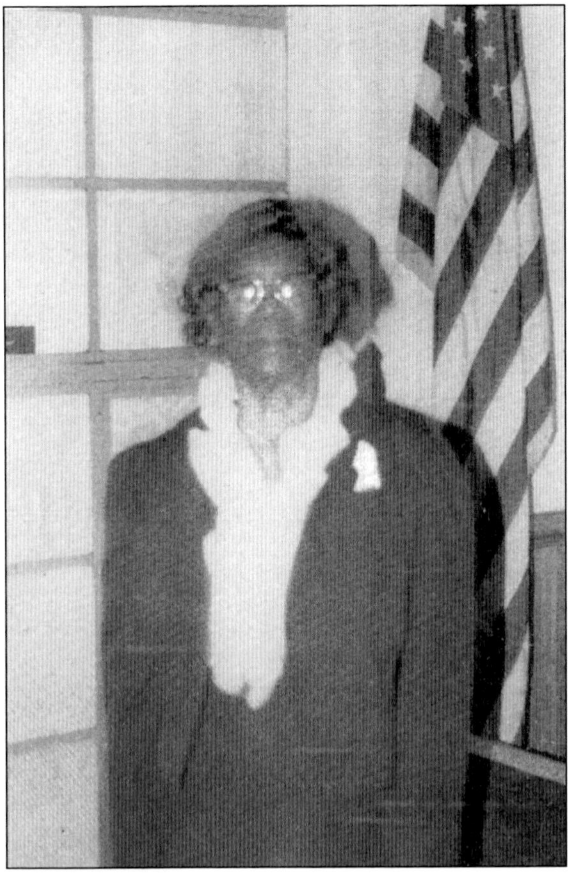

Pearl Johnson, born in 1900, is the subject of the photograph at left. In 1913, she joined Gravel Hill Baptist Church and became one of its early organists and choir directors. (Dr. Ray McKenzie.)

Below is the St. James School. The neighborhood surrounded the school and the church. Children educated at this school later matriculated to Virginia Randolph. (Brenda Nichols.)

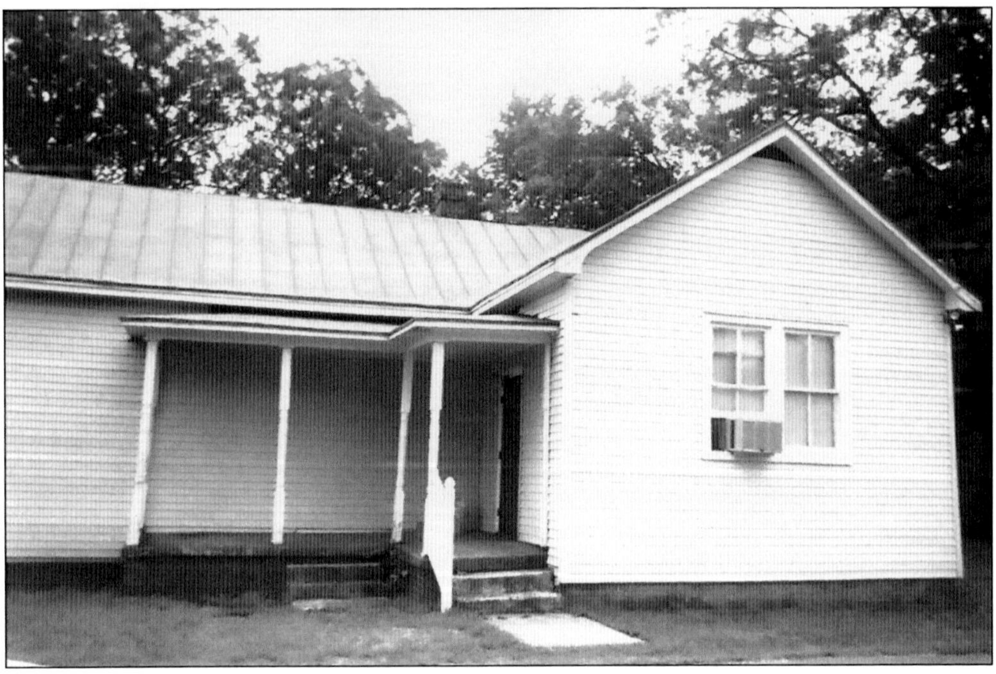

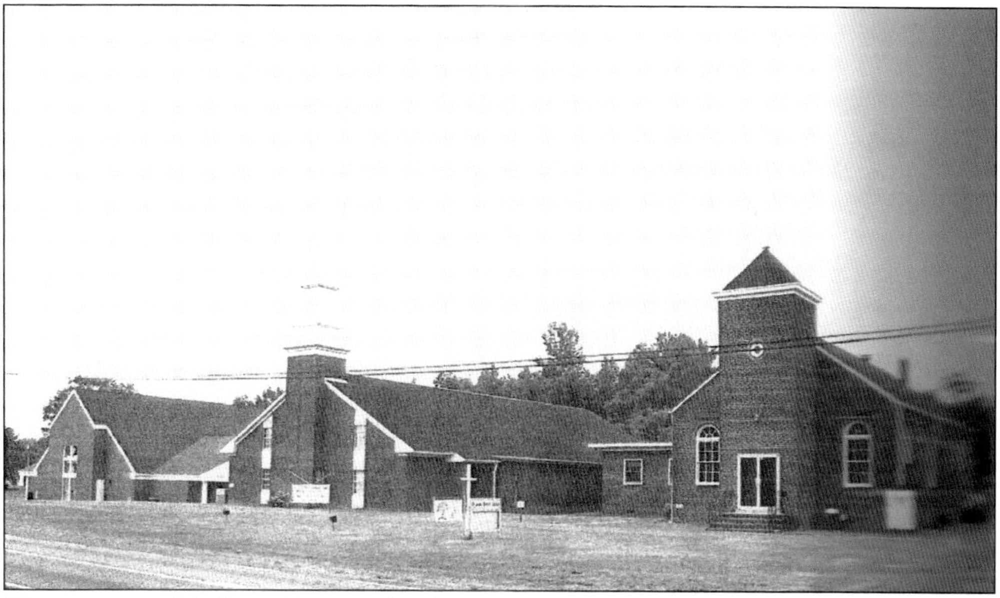

This picture is of St. James Baptist Church, which had its beginnings in 1871, six years after the Civil War ended. Congregants met in the old St. James Hall in Varina and purchased a tract of land known as Varina Grove for $50. Some of the family names associated with the church are Coleman, Frooks, James, Johnathan, and Logan. In April 1945, the church was destroyed by fire. Only the cornerstone and the church bell were salvaged, but the church persevered. (Mable K. Fields.)

Newlyweds Cornelius (born in 1921 in Gravel Hill) and Doris Price (of the St. James community) are pictured here. Their wedding and reception was held at the Williams Lodge Elks Home. Price worked for Brook Transportation Trucking Company, Richmond Ford, and the U.S. Post Office. He also served for 22 years (1952–1974) as church clerk at Gravel Hill Baptist Church. (Cornelius and Doris Price.)

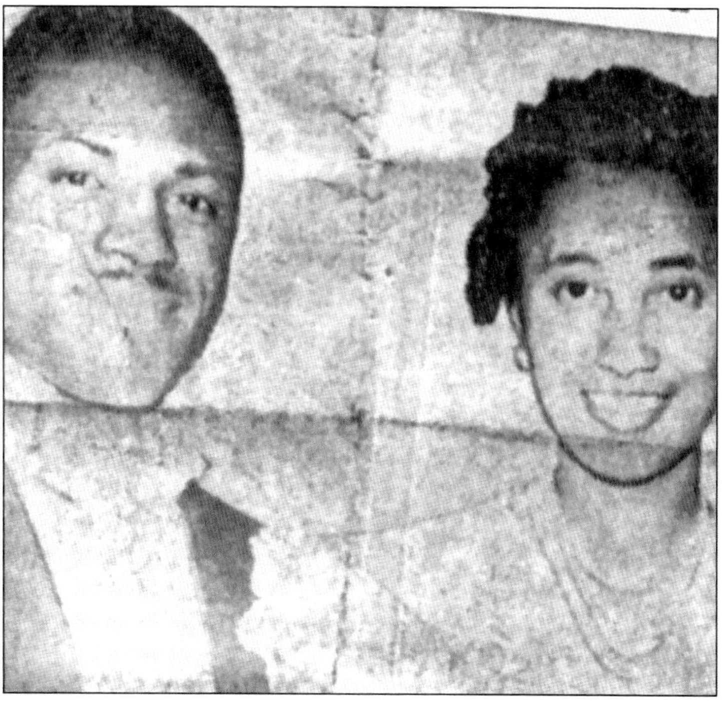

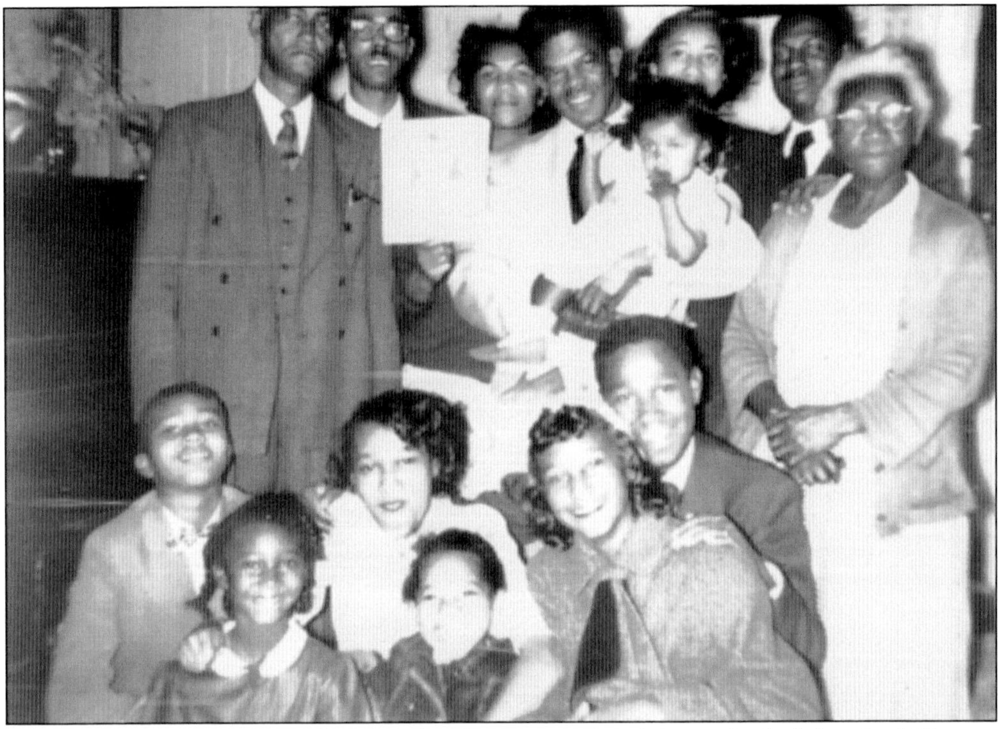

This portrait was taken at a Johnathan family reunion. Standing on the far left is Carl Christie Johnathan (1891–1963). His wife Blanche Baugh Johnathan (1903–1990) is third from the left (holding a picture). Carl owned a store on New Market Road and worked for the Lucky Strike Tobacco Company for 22 years. Blanche grew and marketed flowers for the Southern Railroad Company on Seventeenth Street. (Doris J. Price.)

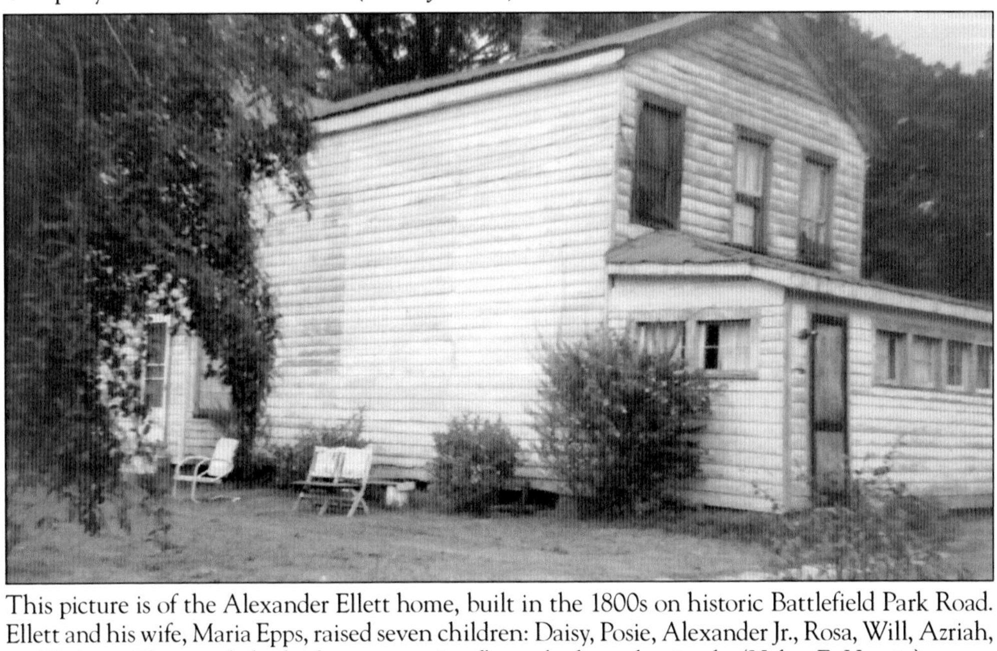

This picture is of the Alexander Ellett home, built in the 1800s on historic Battlefield Park Road. Ellett and his wife, Maria Epps, raised seven children: Daisy, Posie, Alexander Jr., Rosa, Will, Azriah, and Robert. The couple had a farm, attractive flower beds, and animals. (Helen E. Harris.)

Pictured here are Epps siblings Maria Epps Ellett (left), Azriah Epps, and Martha Epps Rogers (right). (Helen E. Harris.)

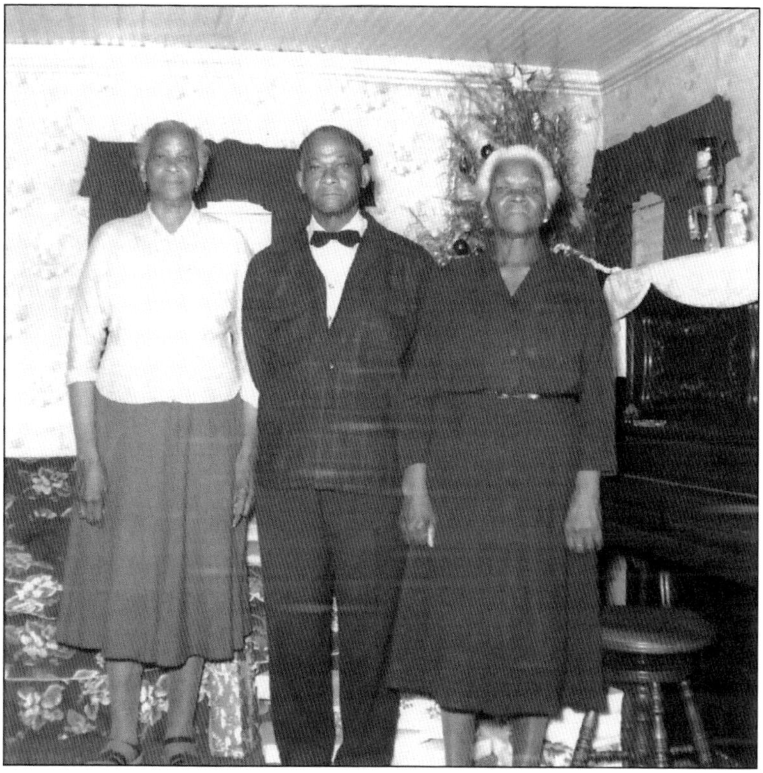

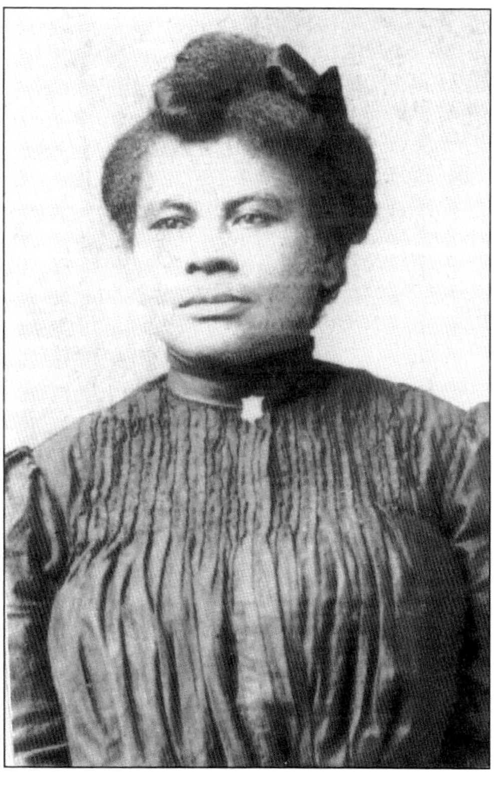

This is a picture of Henrietta Washington Morgan (1865–1949), wife of Alpheus Morgan and mother of Alice Morgan Holmes. She was one of the longest-serving Sunday school teachers at St. James Baptist Church and taught catechism classes to new members. (Veora H. Waller.)

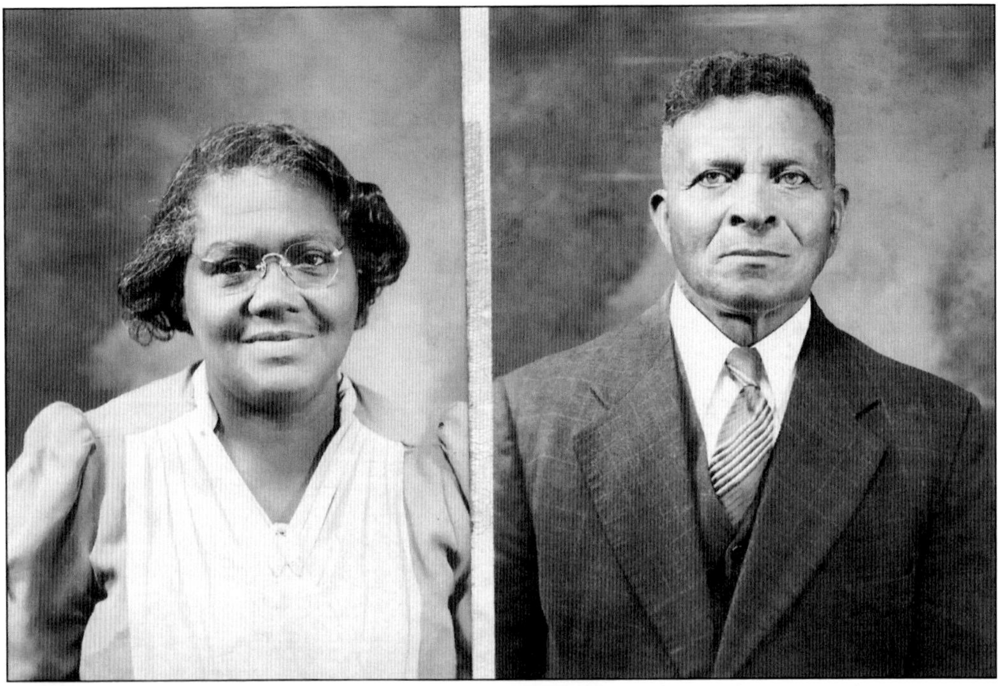

Shown above are Alice Morgan and Thomas Holmes, who were married on December 5, 1905, in Henrico County. They had 14 children, and all helped with the farm. (Veora H. Waller.)

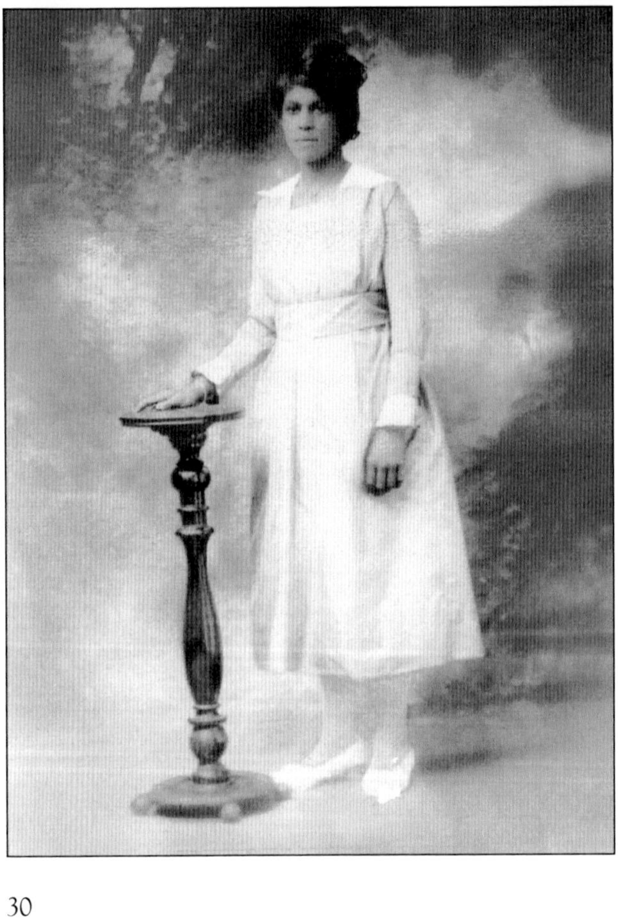

Henrietta Morgan raised her relative, Irene Frances Morgan Johnson (pictured here), as her own daughter. Irene was born on February 26, 1902, and died on November 25, 1941. She was the second organist at St. James Baptist Church for 15 years. (Lucille J. Hall.)

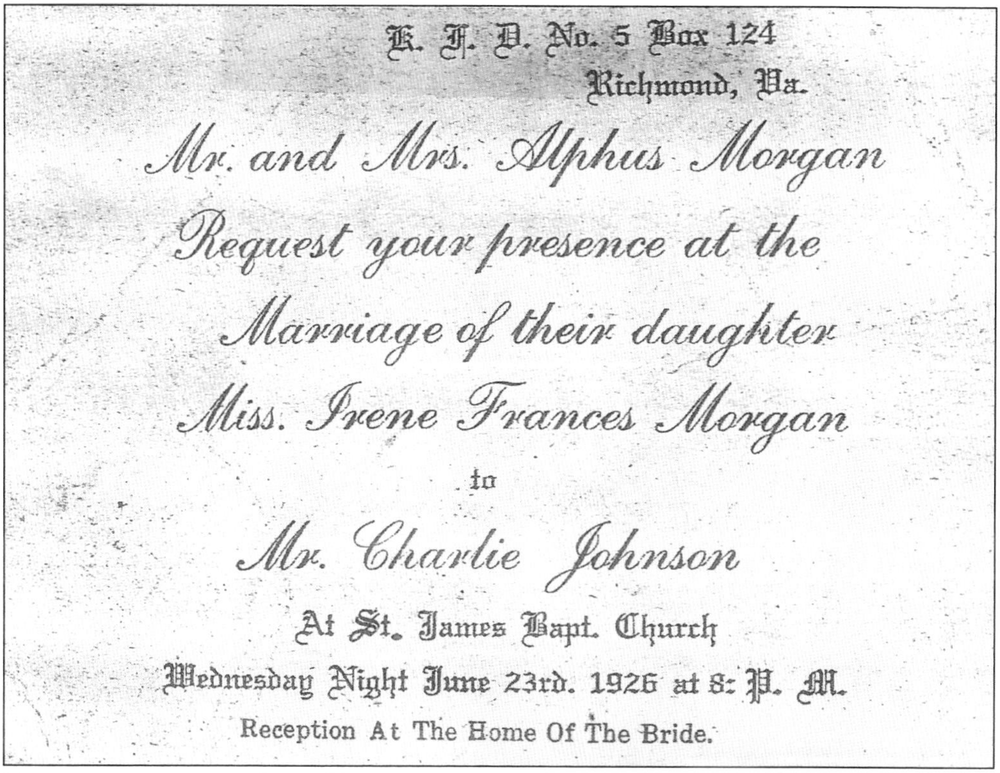

R. F. D. No. 5 Box 124
Richmond, Va.

Mr. and Mrs. Alphus Morgan
Request your presence at the
Marriage of their daughter
Miss. Irene Frances Morgan
to
Mr. Charlie Johnson
At St. James Bapt. Church
Wednesday Night June 23rd. 1926 at 8: P. M.
Reception At The Home Of The Bride.

This is an invitation to the wedding of Irene Frances Morgan to Charlie Johnson. They were married on June 23, 1926, at 8:00 p.m., and their union produced six children. Printed wedding invitations were rare butt symbolic of progress and advancement. (Lucille J. Hall.)

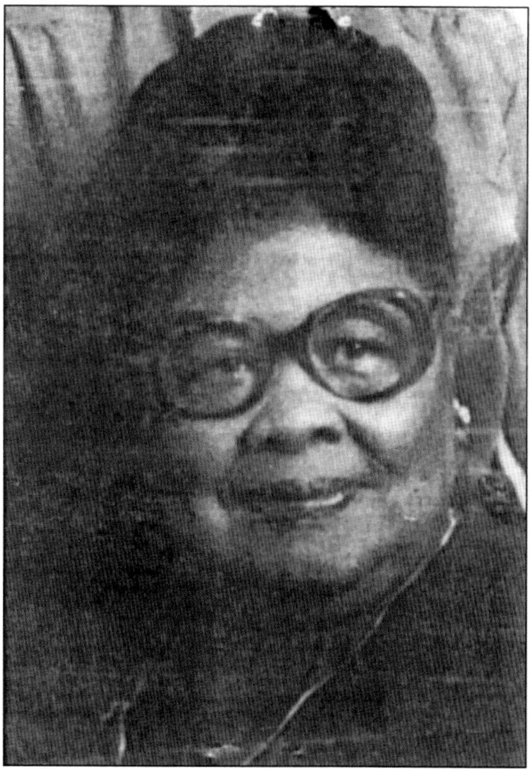

Deaconess Harriet Beatrice Holmes Miles (1908–1992) is pictured here. For 24 years, Miles was director of music at St. James Baptist Church and also served as president of the Star of the East Association, a religious organization. She held a bachelor's of science degree from Virginia State College (later Virginia State University) and taught in Henrico County for 40 years. (Veora H. Waller.)

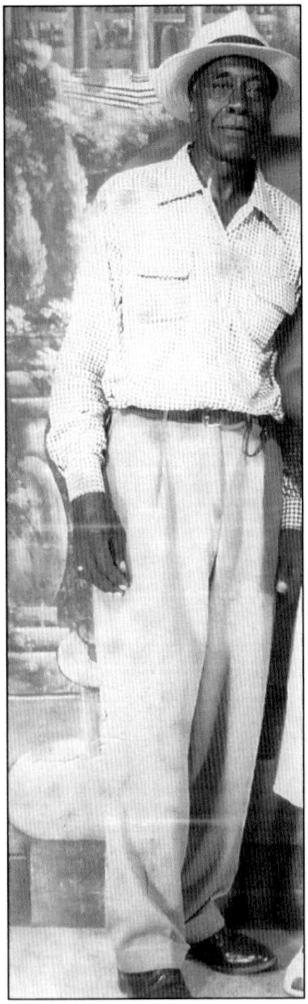

Pictured here is John Henry Coles (1886–1975), son of Emmanuel (Westwood community) and Sallie Washington Coles (St. James community). He had three sisters, Mandy, Mary, and Mattie. His wife was named Hester, and they had one daughter, Dorothy. He was employed at Continental Canning Company in Richmond and upon his retirement was hired by the company as a security guard. Coles slept with a gun under his pillow. (Doris Coles Jones.)

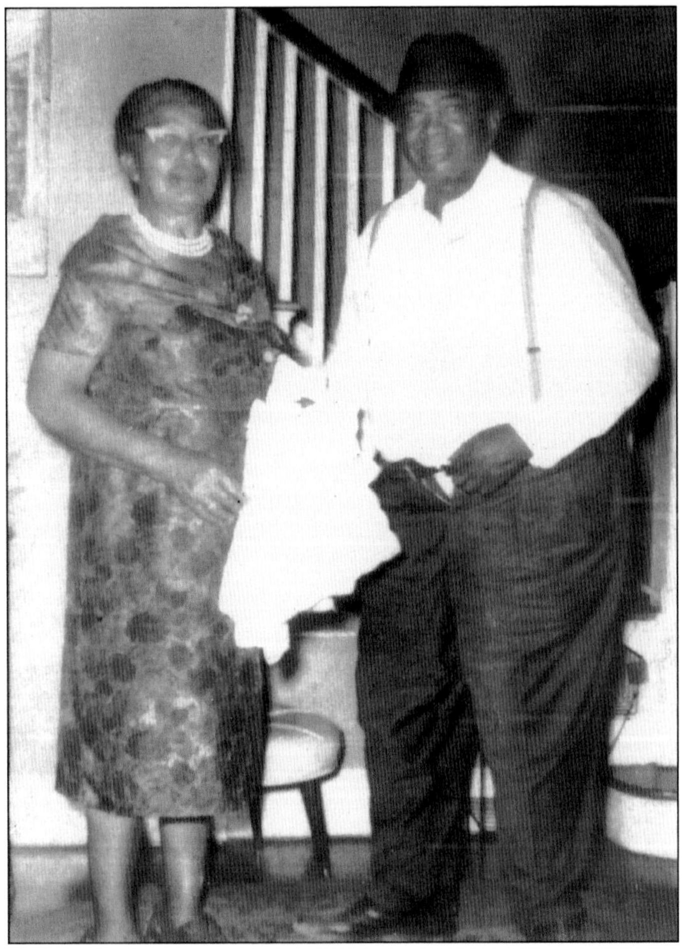

Here are Thomas Jeter (1886–1966) and his wife, Rebecca Hampton Jeter (1896–1989). Thomas, born in Varina, was a brakeman on the Chesapeake and Ohio Railway for 40 years. Rebecca, from Charles City, Virginia, was a homemaker to their 10 children and a sexton at St. James Church for 30 years. The Jeters owned 15 acres in Varina. (Annie J. Lewis.)

This picture is of Annie Jeter Lewis and her husband, Martin, on the occasion of her sister Louise's wedding. Martin worked for the American Tobacco Company for 32 years. (Annie J. Lewis.)

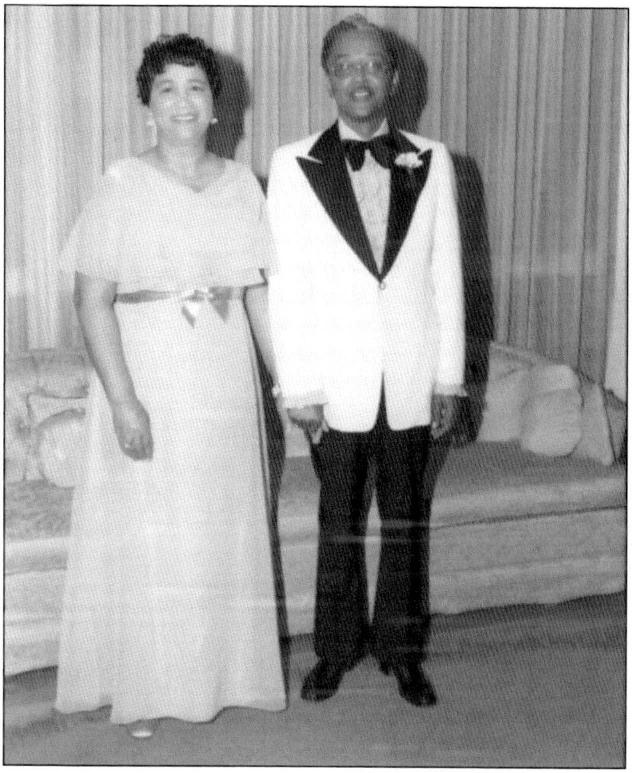

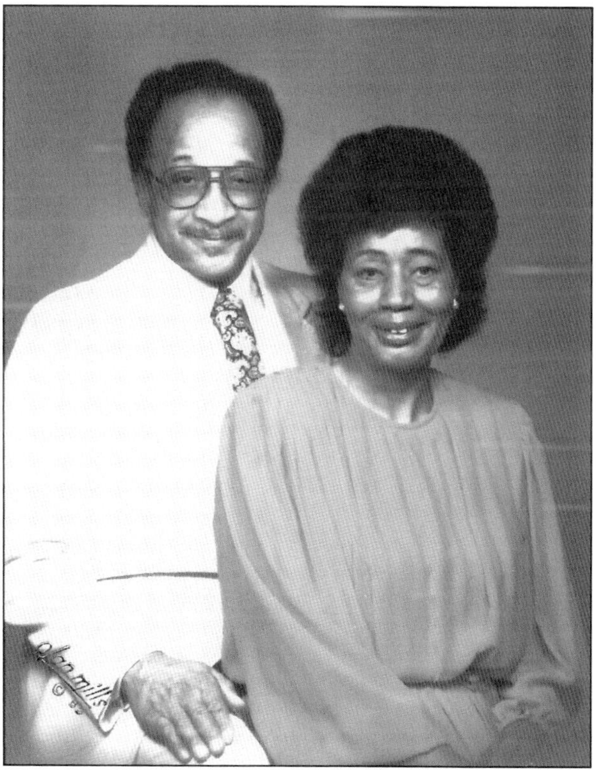

This is Louise Jeter Lee and her husband, Rudolph. Louise worked as a secretary at Fairfield Middle School in Henrico, and Rudolph worked for Smithfield Ham Company as a long-distance truck driver for 30 years. (Louise J. Lee.)

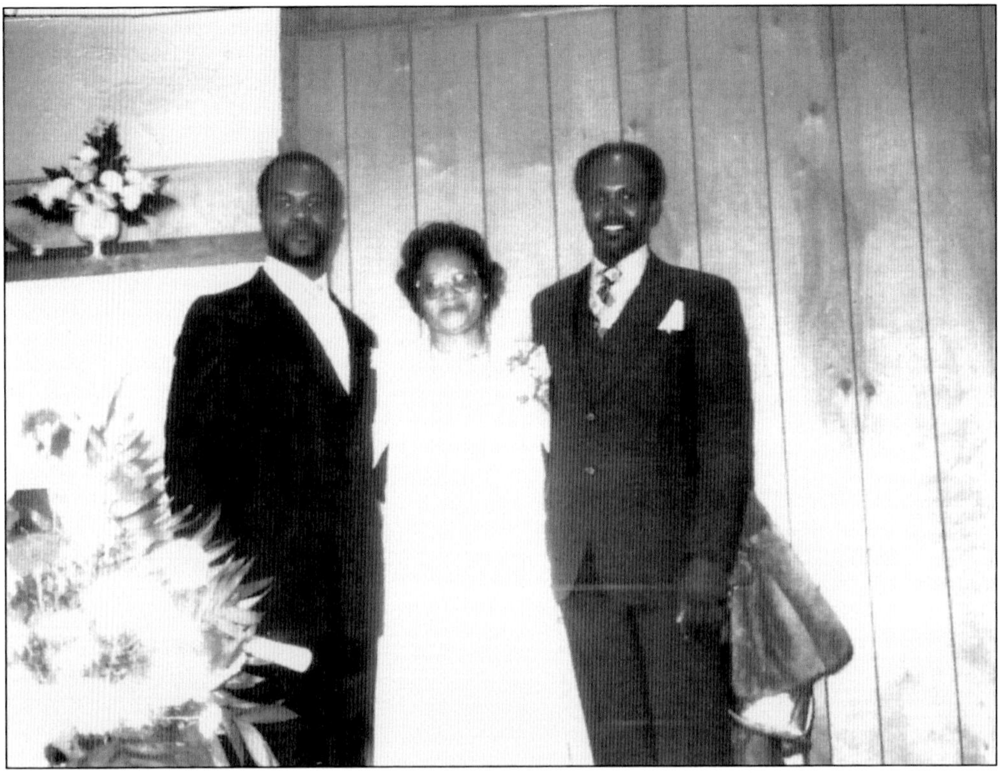

Lucille Johnson Hall was born in 1928 to a family of lifelong residents of the St. James community. She and her husband, Earl Hall Sr., had two sons, Charles (left) and Earl Jr. (right), with whom she is pictured. Lucille was an organist at St. James Baptist Church for 25 years, retiring in 1973. She also served as organist for St. John Baptist Church in neighboring Charles City for 33 years. (Lucille J. Hall.)

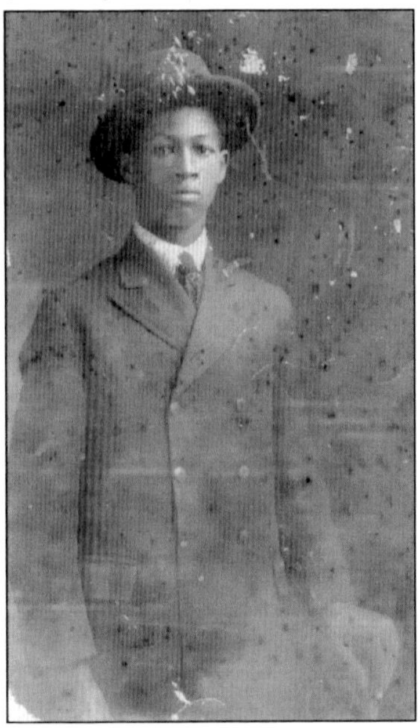

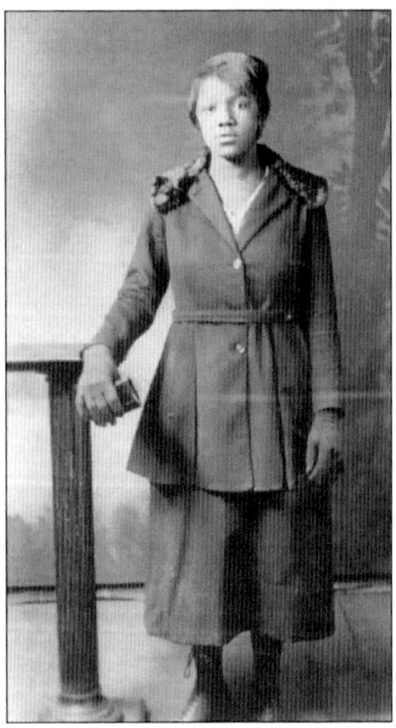

Pictured here are Horace A. Fields Sr. (1901–1963) and his wife, Rachel Johnson Fields (1903–1981), whom he married in 1922 in Chesterfield County. They had five children: Horace Jr., twins Lewis and Leon, Bernard, and Rachel. Rachel Fields taught school in Chesterfield and Henrico Counties. The Fields were upstanding citizens in the community and faithful members of St. James Baptist Church. (Mable K. Fields.)

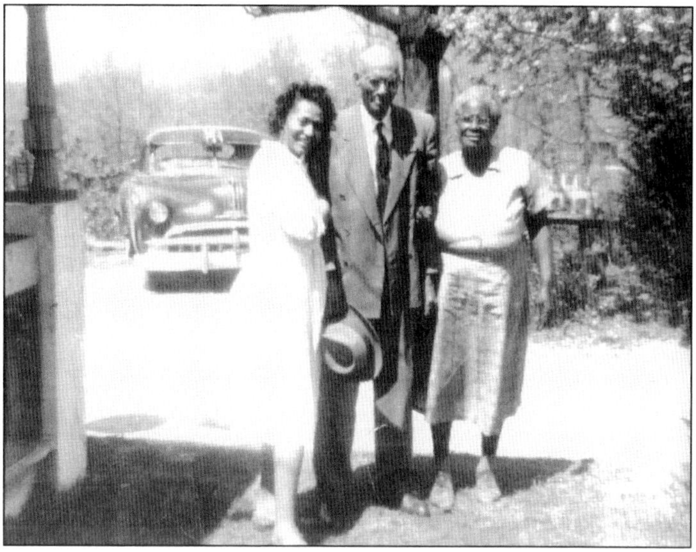

Albert Fields Sr. (1894–1971) poses happily in front of the family car with his wife, Alberta Staves Fields (1894–1979), and one of their 13 children. Albert farmed for a living, and his wife, a homemaker, reared their eight girls and five boys. The Fields owned land in the Fort Harrison Battlefield Park historic area. (Mable K. Fields.)

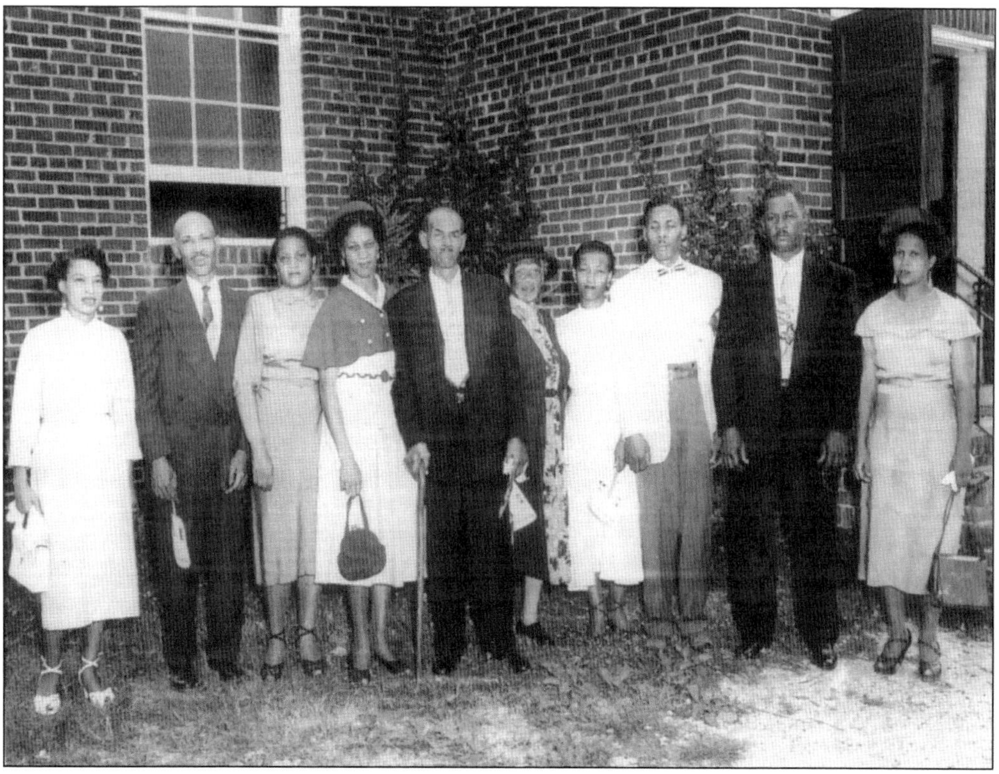

This picture was taken at a gathering of the family of Elijah Fields Sr. (1877–1882), older brother of Horace Fields Sr. Elijah was married to Minnie E. Fields, who died in 1967. Members of this handsome family include, from left to right, Mary Fields Johnson, George W. Fields, Blanche Lena Fields Johnson, Minnette Fields, Elijah Sr., Minnie Fields, Martha Fields Johnson, Elijah Fields Jr., and Horace Fields Sr., and Marjorie Fields Walker. (Mable K. Fields.)

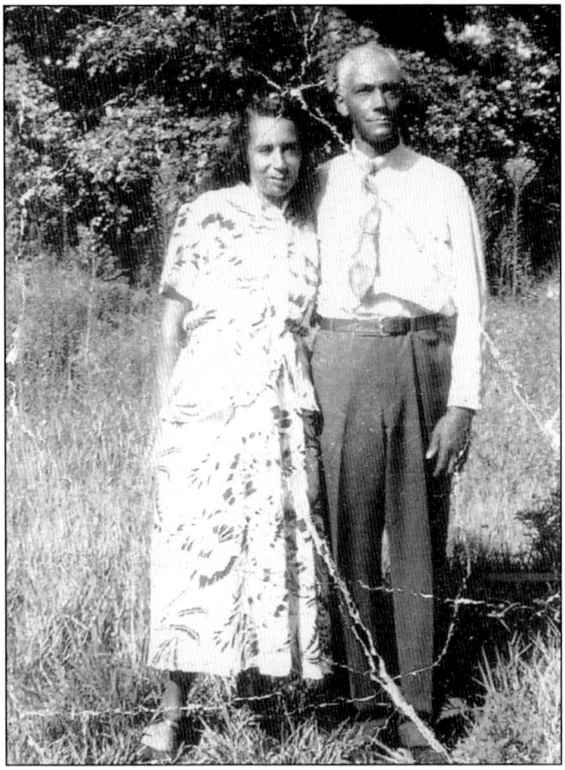

Pictured here are George Robert Knight (born in 1887 in Lunenburg County, Virginia) and Mary Branic Bullock Knight (born in 1895 in Winston-Salem, North Carolina). Mary (a widow and mother of four) and Robert (a widower and father of two) were married in 1925. Together they reared 14 children and celebrated 53 years of marriage. During the early years of their marriage, they lived in the city of Richmond (Churchill). They moved to Varina (First Bethel community) in the mid-1930s and later moved to the St. James community. He died in 1978, she in 1986. (Mable K. Fields.)

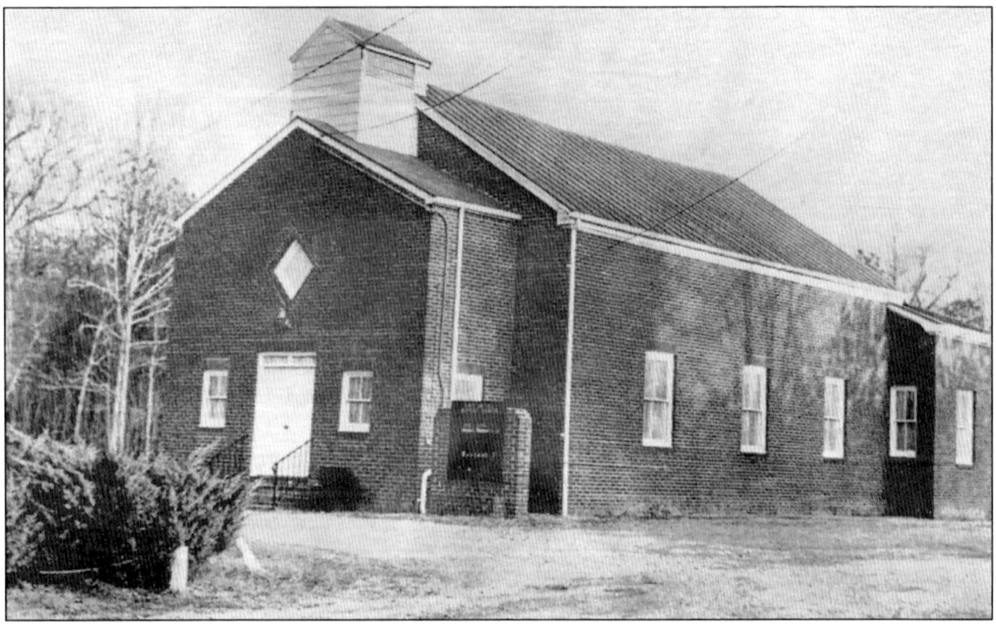

Pictured here is First Bethel Baptist Church on Kingsland Road. First Bethel Church, in the First Bethel community, has survived since 1874, whereas the Second Bethel community has become almost extinct. First Bethel's boundaries are New Market Road, Strath Road, Kingsland Road, and Buffin Road. Families in the community include the Adkins, Dandridge, Dye, Gibbs, Knight, Temple, and Tyler families. (Shirley Carter.)

The Second Bethel Baptist Church, built in 1876 on Charles City Road in Henrico, is shown in this picture in the early 1900s. Reverend Cobbs was its first pastor. Active families in this church included the Allen, Boatwright, Brown, Burrell, Harris, Henry, Johnson, Taylor, Watkins, and Williams families. (Shirley Carter.)

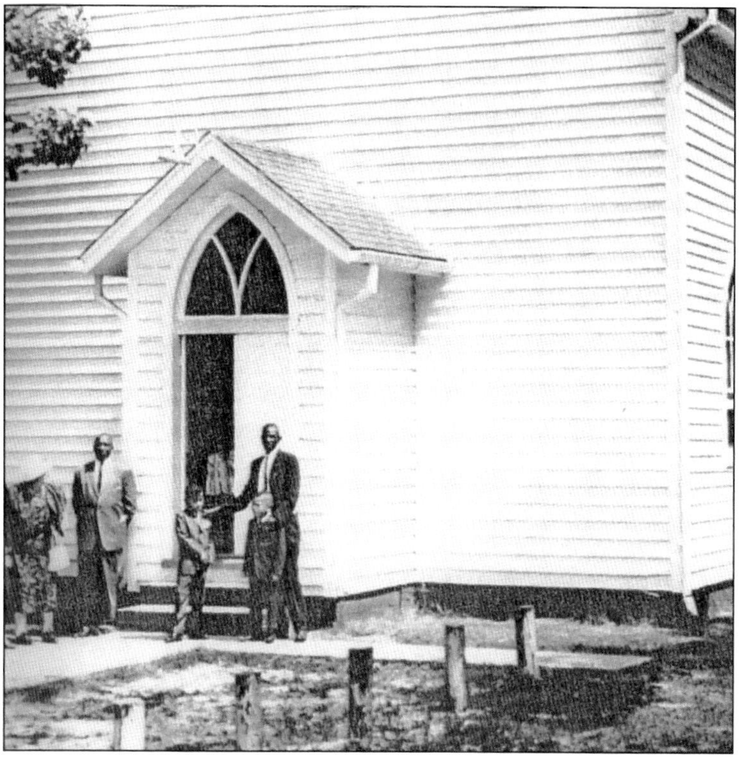

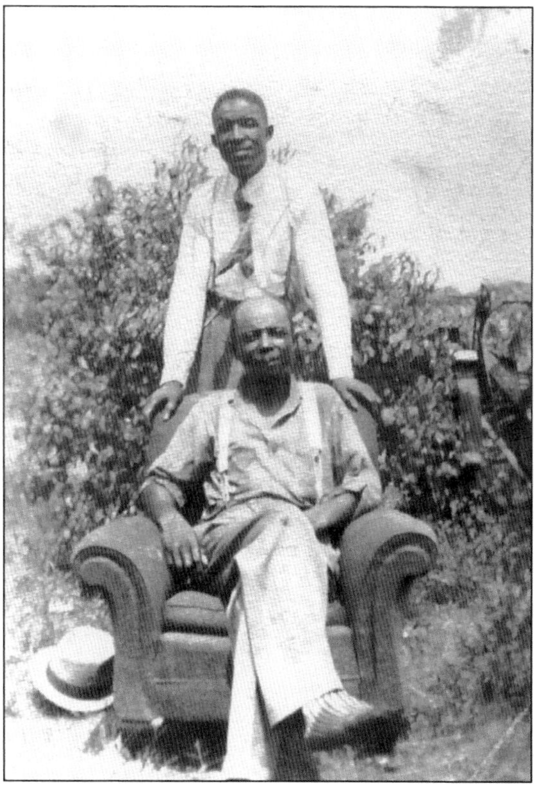

Pictured here is William James Tyler (1891–1941) with his son William Henry Tyler (standing). The elder Tyler worked many jobs as a carpenter and farmer and was also employed by Stem Tobacco Factory. In 1922, he was licensed and ordained at First Bethel. (Mildred T. Temple.)

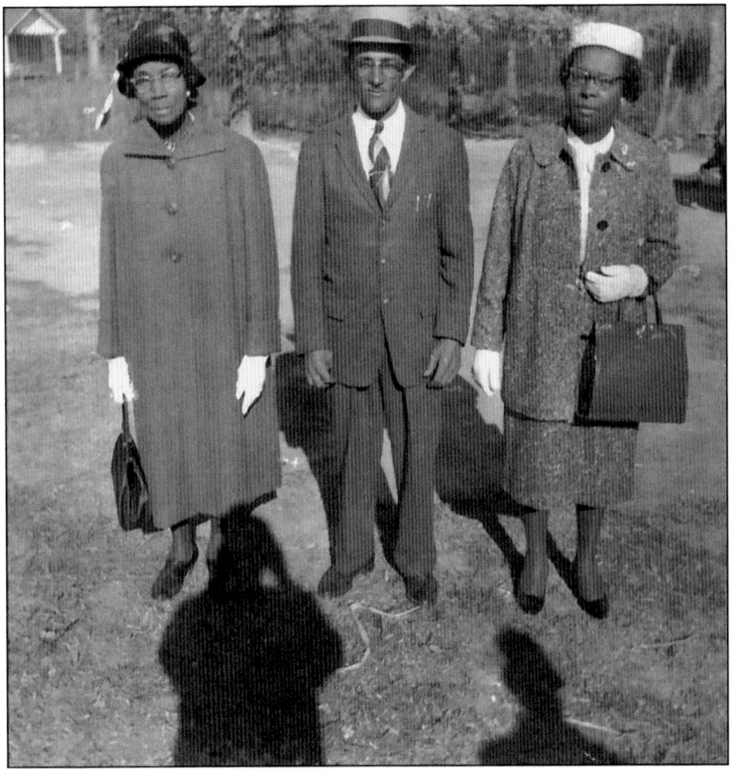

Alice Patsy Ann Dandridge Tyler (1894–1979) was born in Henrico County to Prince and Alice Hayes Dandridge. She was the wife of William James Tyler, with whom she had eight children. She is pictured on the left with her son-in-law, Rev. Hilliard Temple, and daughter Mildred. (Mildred T. Temple.)

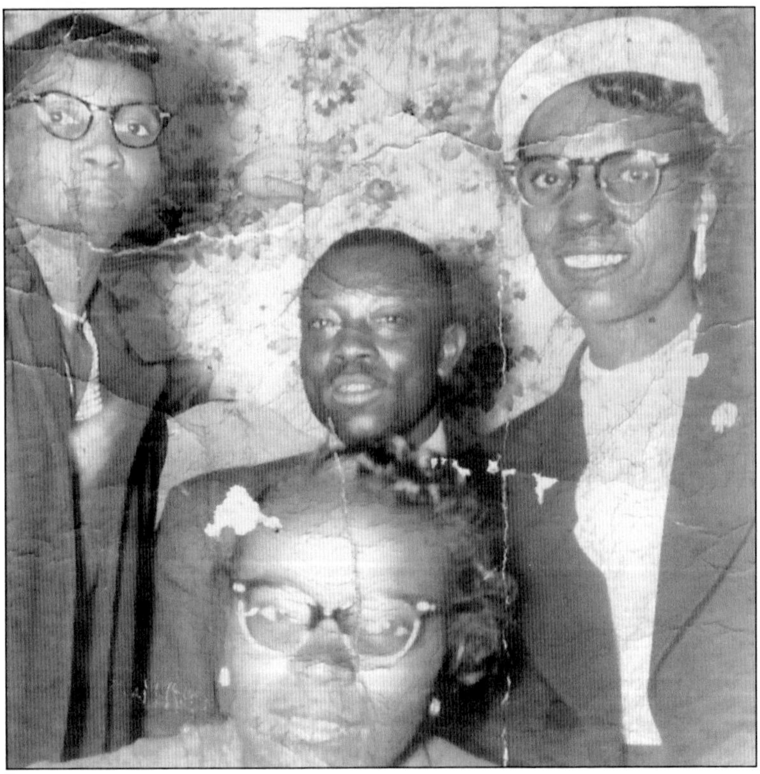

Pictured from left to right are the Bethlehem Gospel Singers—Rosa Tyler Smith (sister), William Johnson (pianist), Elizabeth Tyler (sister-in-law), and Emily Tyler Corbin (sister). They were broadcasting at radio station WANT on Main Street in the early 1950s. (Emily T. Corbin.)

This is Joseph Dandridge Sr., brother of Alice Dandridge Tyler, husband to Carolina Johnson, and father of six. The Dandridges lived on Kingsland Road near First Bethel Baptist Church. Dandridge worked for Henrico County as a machinist for almost 30 years and was an active deacon at First Bethel Church. (Rebecca Hewlett Dandridge.)

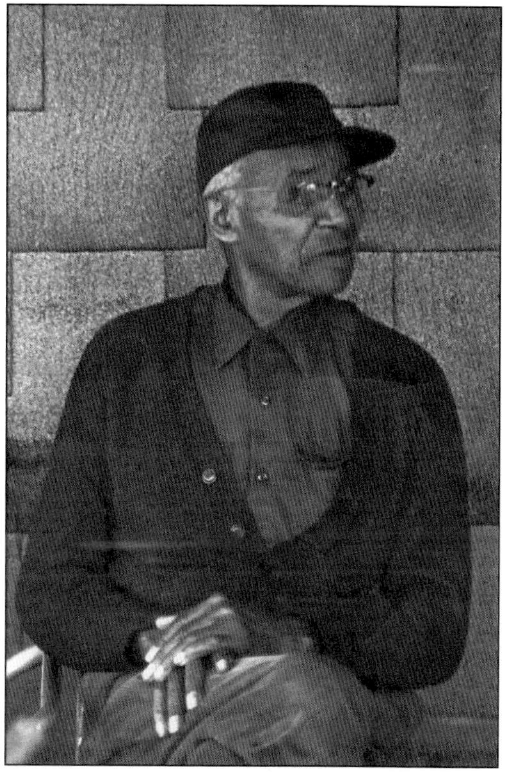

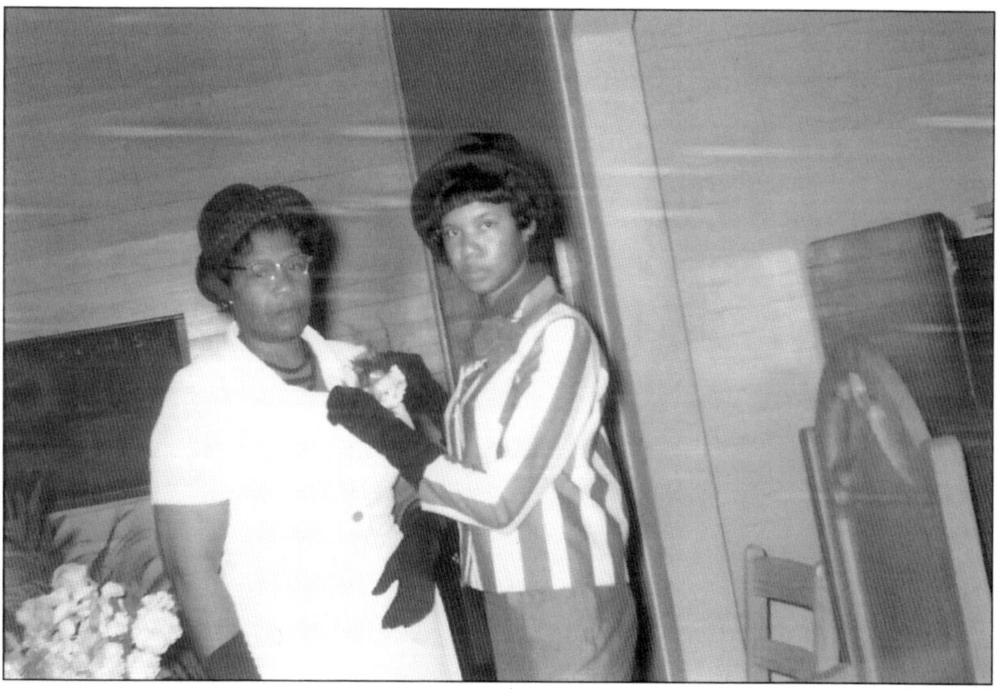

In this photograph, Carolina Johnson Dandridge is being honored as mother of the year at First Bethel Baptist Church. Her daughter, Helen Dandridge, is pinning her corsage. Note the black gloves and hats worn by both ladies. (Rebecca H. Dandridge.)

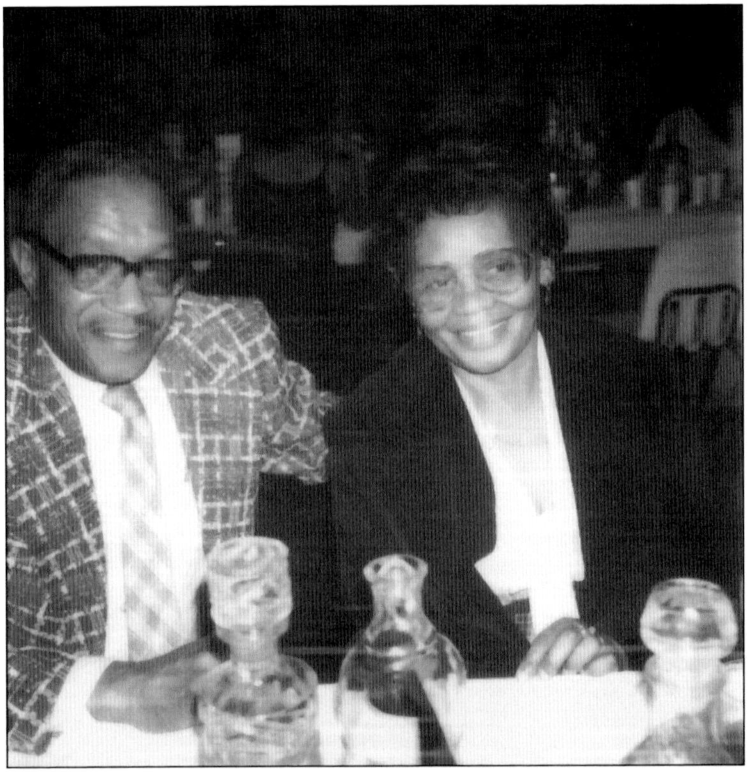

Rebecca Hewlett Dandridge and her husband, Joseph Jr., enjoy an evening out in this photograph. Joseph Jr., a son of Carolina and Joseph Dandridge Sr., worked for the U.S. Postal Service as a driving instructor for 36 years. He was also a deacon and a member of H. L. Harris Masonic Lodge as a 33rd-degree Mason for 40 years. Rebecca worked for American Tobacco for eight years. (Rebecca H. Dandridge.)

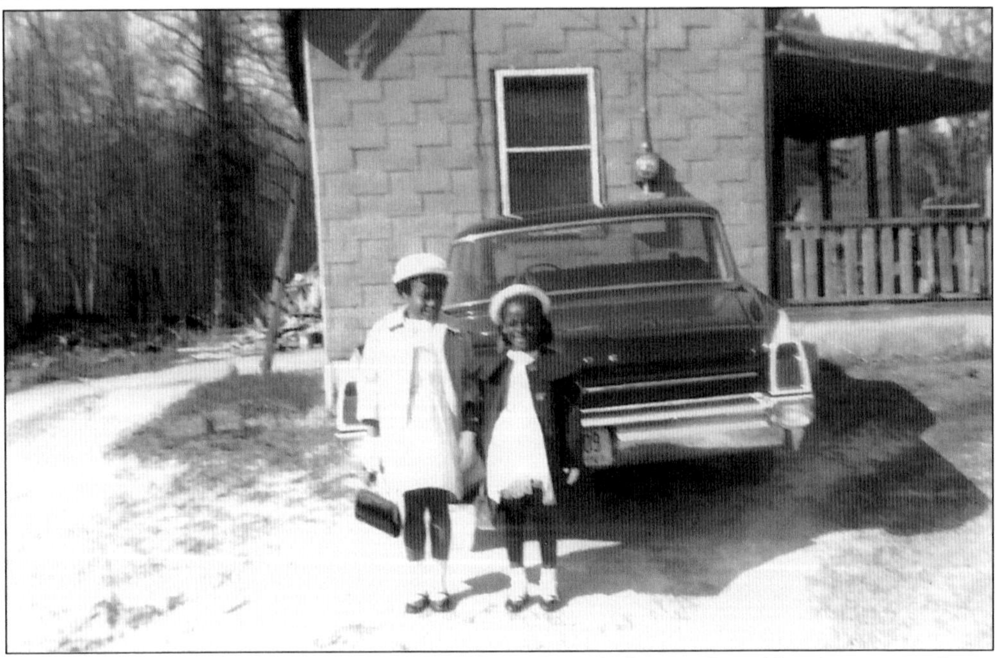

Featured above in this 1964 photograph are LaVerne Dandridge, age 7, and her first cousin, Joyce Adkins, age 5, dressed in style for church with pretty bonnet dresses, shoes, and purses. These grandchildren of Joseph Dandridge Sr. are standing outside of his Kingsland Road residence. (Rebecca H. Dandridge.)

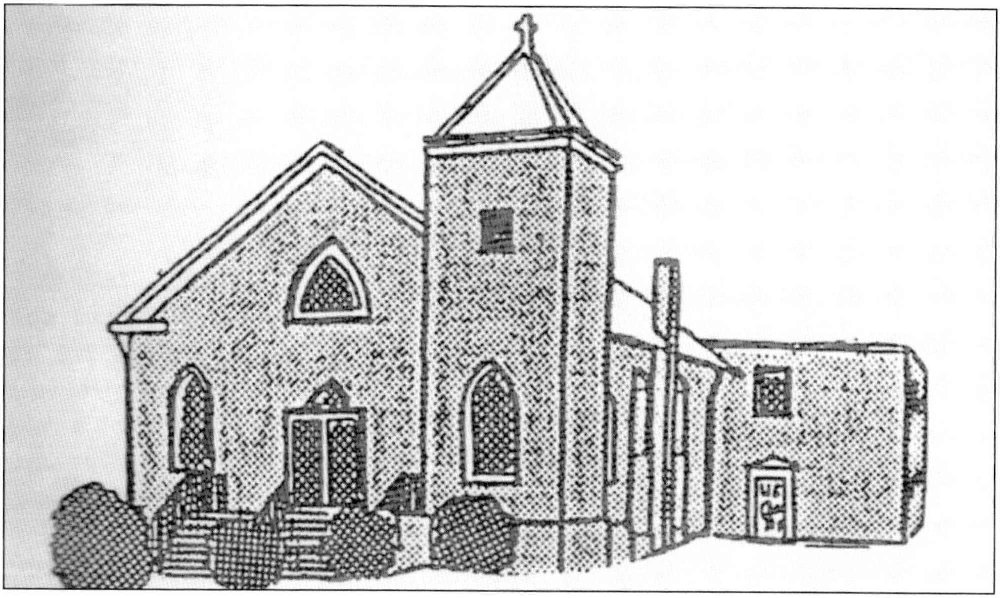

Pictured here is Antioch Baptist Church, organized in 1925 at the home of Lawson Goode on Route 5. The church school began in 1908, in an old hall owned by a benevolent society called the Grand Order of Rising Sons and Daughters of the Star of Bethlehem, No. 6. The hall also served as a church and a mortuary. Families associated with the church were the Goodes, Jacksons, Jeters, Logans, Mileses, Moodys, Skippers, Smiths, Wallaces, and Washingtons. (Shirley Carter.)

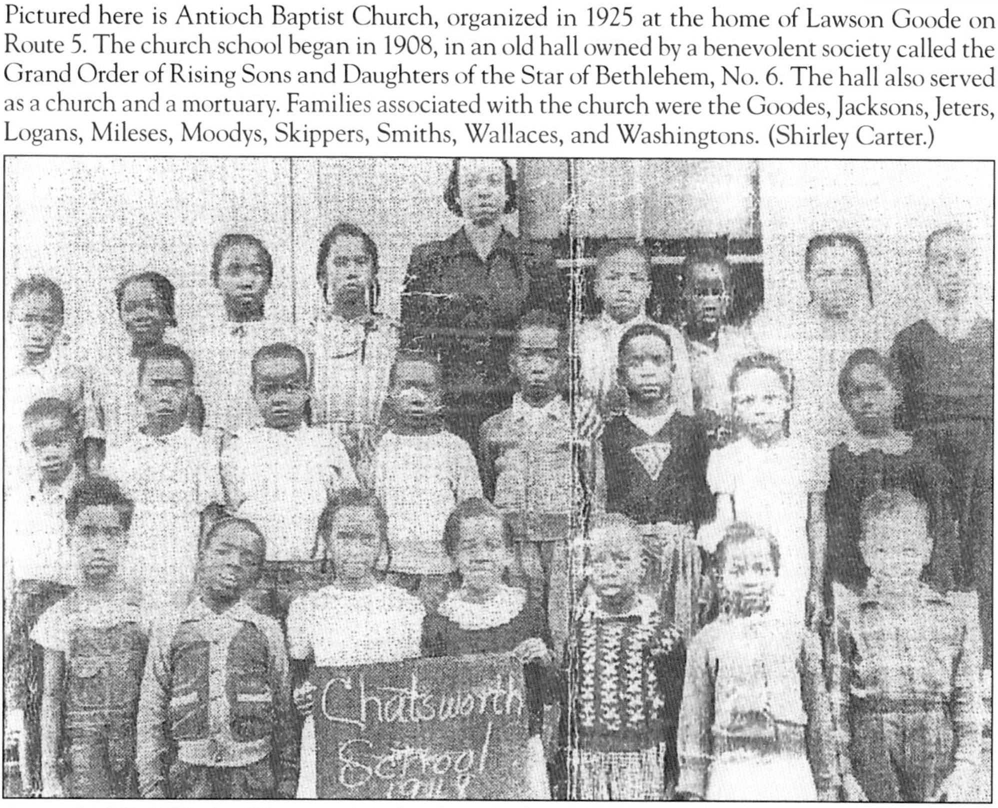

Around 1910–1920, the Chatsworth School was built on Chatsworth Road to serve this segregated community. It was one of 32 schools for African American children throughout Henrico. Chatsworth School was a Rosenwald School, which meant it received funds from the educational philanthropist Julius Rosenwald. St. James School was the nearest school. Students from Antioch, St. Paul, and Drinker Towns, the area around Messer Road, attended the Chatsworth School. (Shirley Carter.)

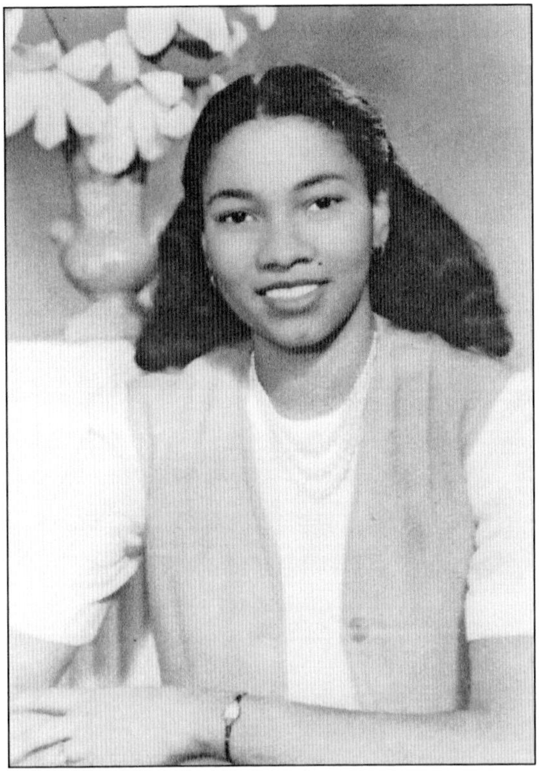

This beautiful young lady is Christina Johnathan Jackson, sister to Doris J. Price and siblings. She was the secretary at Virginia Randolph High School for many years. (C. Manning and Doris J. Price.)

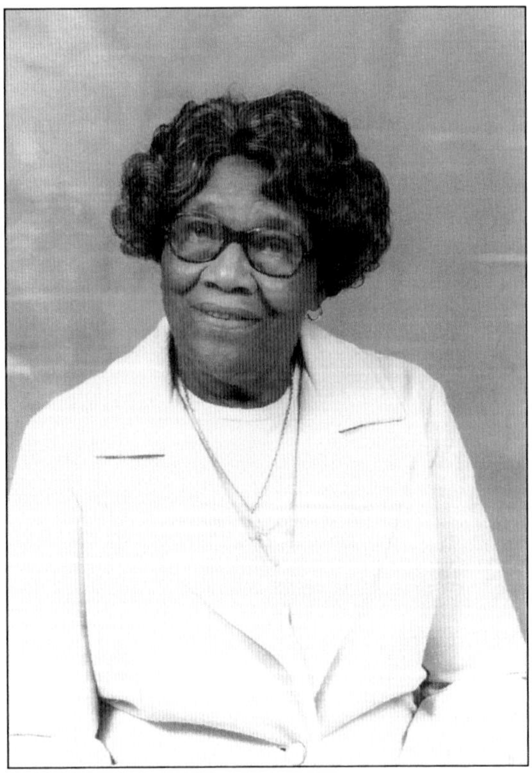

This is Eliza Bigger Wallace (1903–1985) from Gravel Hill. She married James G. Wallace of Charles City. They moved to the Antioch community with a set of twins and later had seven more children. James worked for the Virginia Department of Transportation. Eliza was a homemaker and was known as a stern disciplinarian. (Irene W. Lester.)

This 1957 photograph shows Eugene and Irene E. Lester at the annual Phillip Morris Employee Banquet at the Landmark Theater in Richmond (formerly known as the Mosque). Irene, a daughter of James and Eliza Wallace, is a graduate of Virginia State College and retired from Henrico County Schools, where she worked for 36 years as a librarian. She also served concurrently as Antioch Baptist Church clerk and treasurer for 30 years. Eugene was employed at Phillip Morris Tobacco Company for 33 years as a machinist. (Irene W. Lester.)

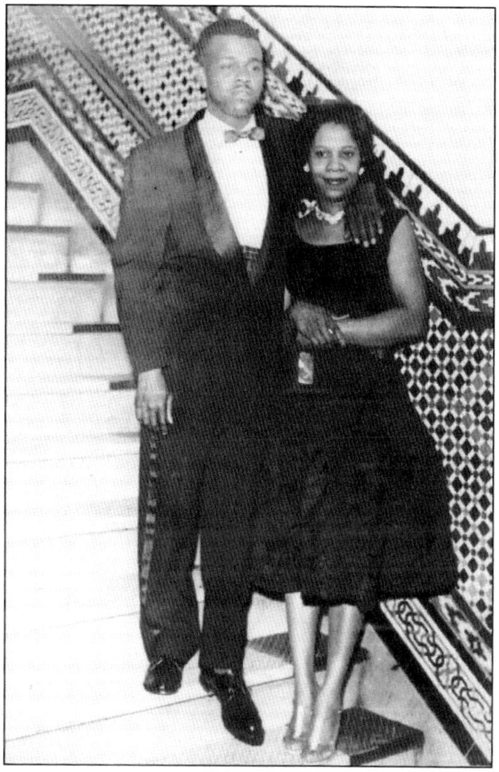

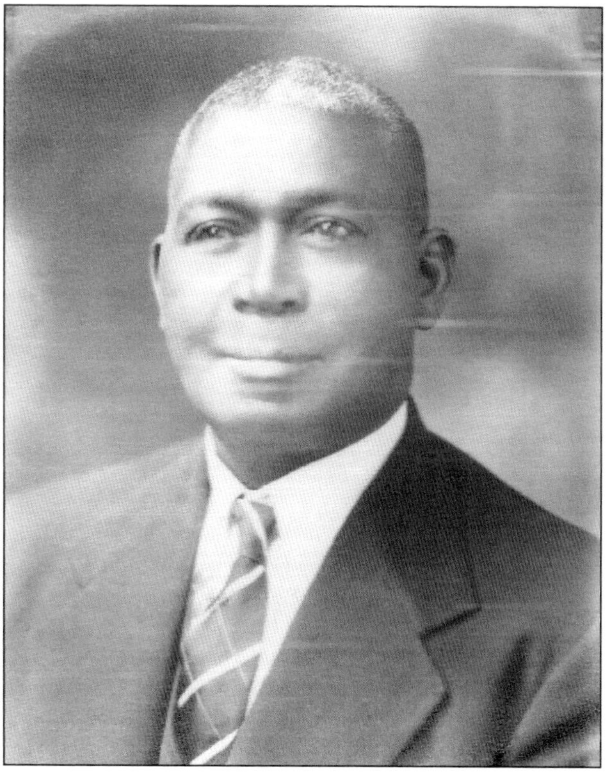

The Logan family was one of the most successful families that lived in Antioch. Pictured here is James Edward "Eddie" Logan, who was a deacon and trustee at St. James Church. Logan was a businessman, farmer, well digger, and fuel supplier. In his later years, he helped form Antioch Church. He and his wife, Addie, had one son, James Harold Logan. (Jean L. Jackson.)

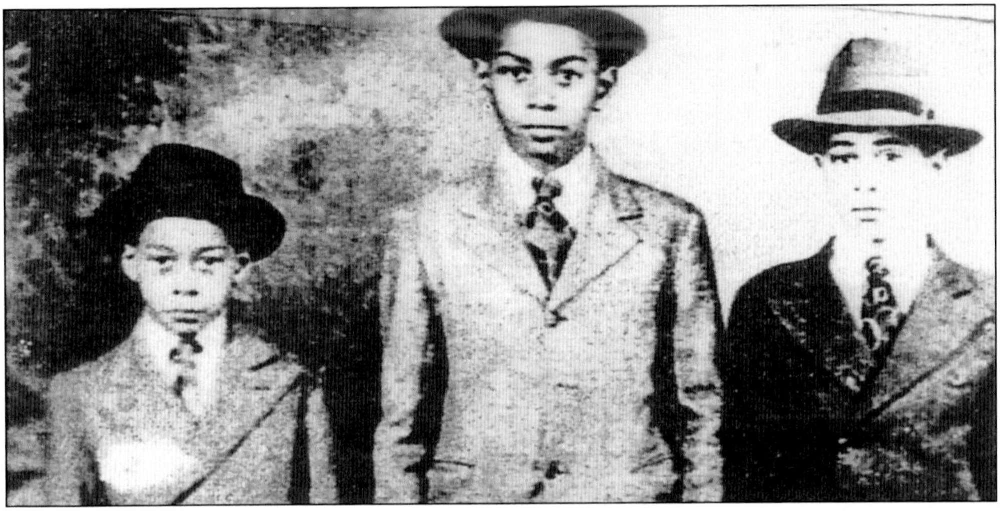

Pictured from left to right are James Harold Logan Jr., Robert Edward Logan, and Stewart Leroy Logan, who are the sons of Pearl Crawley and James Harold Logan Sr. Pearl graduated from the historic Hartshorn College. She taught Sunday school and was well known for her cooking. James Sr. worked for the Chesapeake and Ohio Railway for over 30 years and built his home on family property. They were members of St. James Baptist Church. (Jean L. Jackson.)

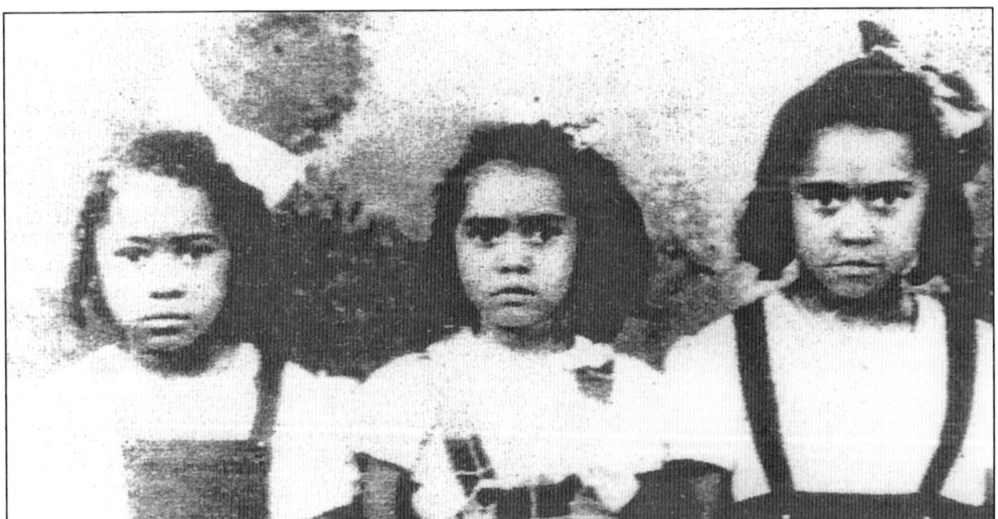

Pictured from left to right are cute little sisters Edith Logan Trent, Jean Logan Jackson, and Norma Logan Davis. They are the daughters of Pearl and James H. Logan Sr. and the granddaughters of James E. and Addie Logan. (Jean L. Jackson.)

Four

Providence Park

The earliest formation of the Providence Park Baptist Church was in 1875. Members met at various homes for prayer, such as Brother Richard Jones's home near Ladies Mile and Meadowbridge Roads. Gatherings were also held in the homes of Brothers Louis Cooper, William Edwards, and Wesley Jones near Brookland Park Boulevard. Henrico County Courthouse records show that on May 27, 1876, three trustees—Richard Jones, Enoch Braxton, and Peter Markins—purchased one half-acre of land for $45 from H. P. Taylor and his wife. In 1879, the first meeting place was established for the church in a chapel known as Dick Jones Meeting House, and in 1885, the Sunday school was organized. The present-day church sits on the original site. Providence Park Baptist has had many distinguished pastors; Rev. Ben Gentry was the first, and Rev. John J. Woodson was the next, serving from 1903 to 1957. Rev. Dr. Miles J. Jones succeeded Woodson, serving 30 years from 1958 to 1988. Jones was also a citywide civic leader, serving as chairman of the Richmond City School Board and a professor at the Virginia Union University School of Theology.

Some who made significant contributions to the Providence Park Baptist Church were the Braxton, Cluff, Cooper, Dance, Davis, Edwards, Evans, Garner, Hocker, Jones, Lankford, Morton, Randolph, Taylor, Turner, Waddy, and Winston families. By the beginning of the 20th century, a part of Ladies Mile Road was the heart of a black Providence Park community. The southern part of this property was in the city limits, and the northern portion was in Henrico County. William Prince Hocker married Harriet Early and built a house at 450 Ladies Mile Road. In 1906, his son Andrew J. Hocker, the fifth of seven children, was born. Andrew worked with his brothers, father, and uncle Joseph to farm the land they rented on Strawberry Hill, a large tract of land in the Fairfield district of eastern Henrico County. In the 1900s, long before anything else, Strawberry Hill was used for farming, but it was later developed into the Atlantic Rural Expedition, home of the Virginia State Fair. The land is now the Richmond International Raceway, home to NASCAR racing events, which brings $467 million annually into Henrico County. The City of Richmond later annexed a portion of Providence Park. The front portion of the church is in the city. The rear section of the church and the parking lot are in the county.

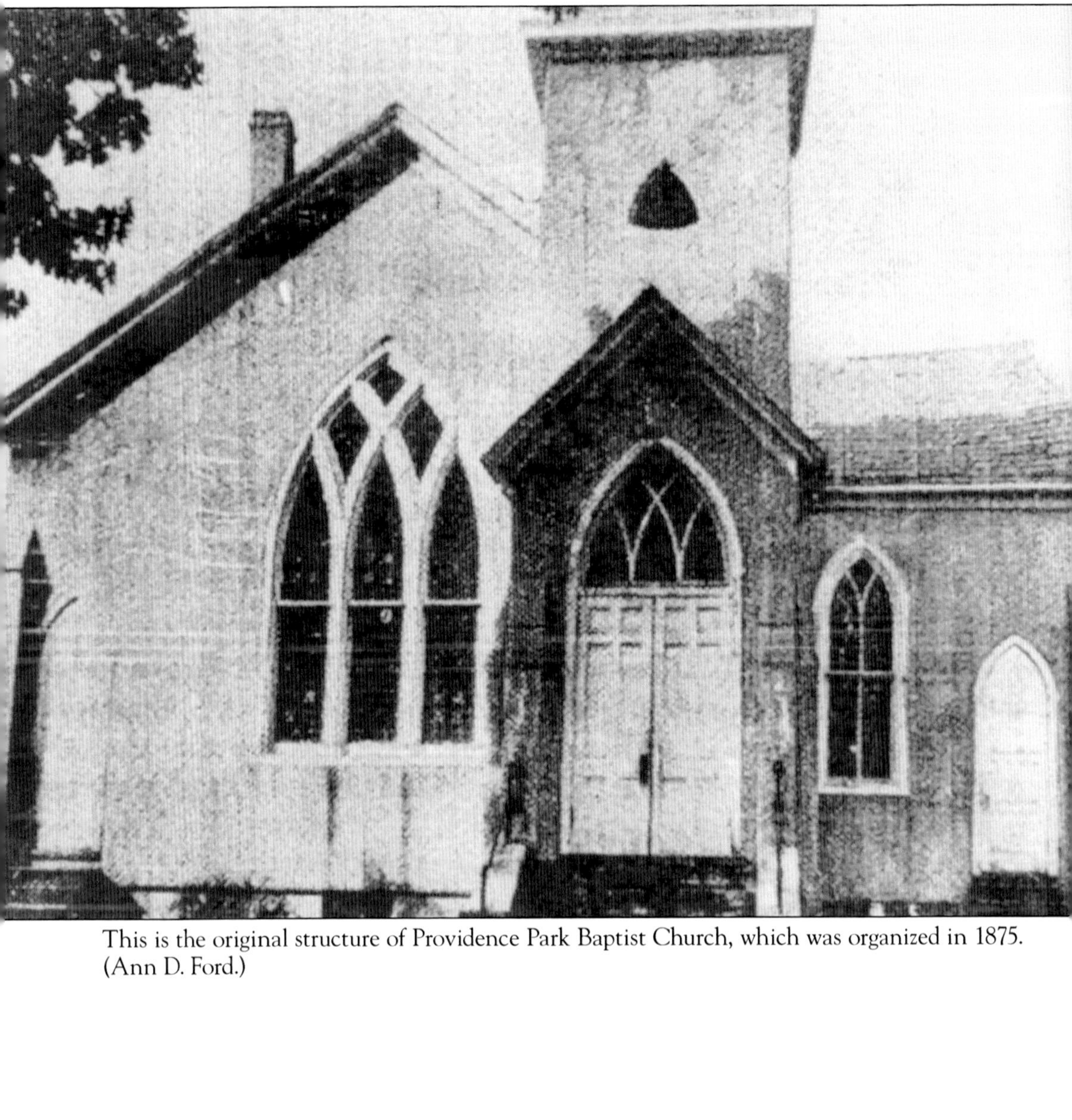
This is the original structure of Providence Park Baptist Church, which was organized in 1875. (Ann D. Ford.)

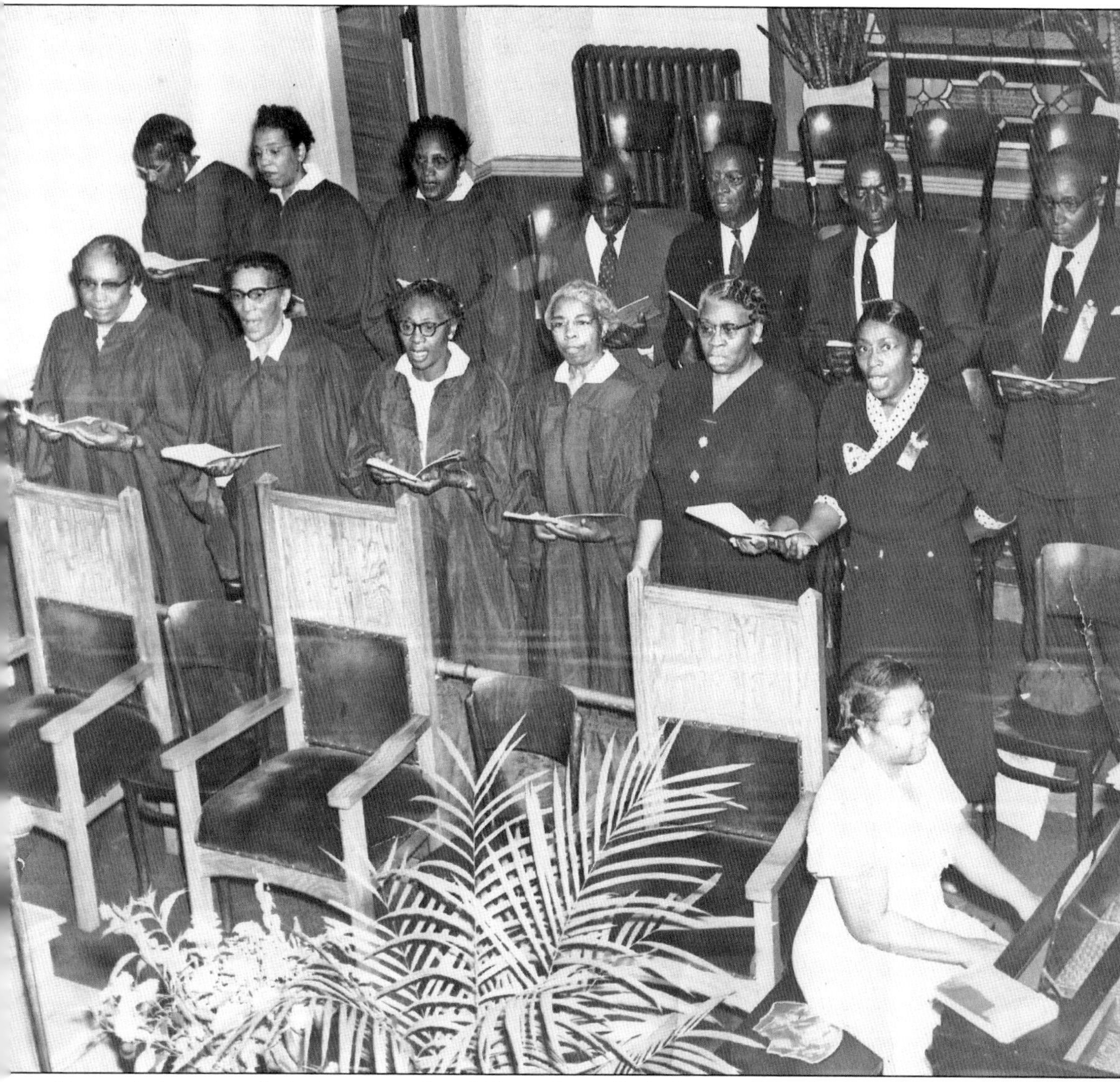

Pictured above is a choir singing in the old Providence Park Baptist Church. The chairs were of dark wood, and the choir wore dark robes. (Ann D. Ford).

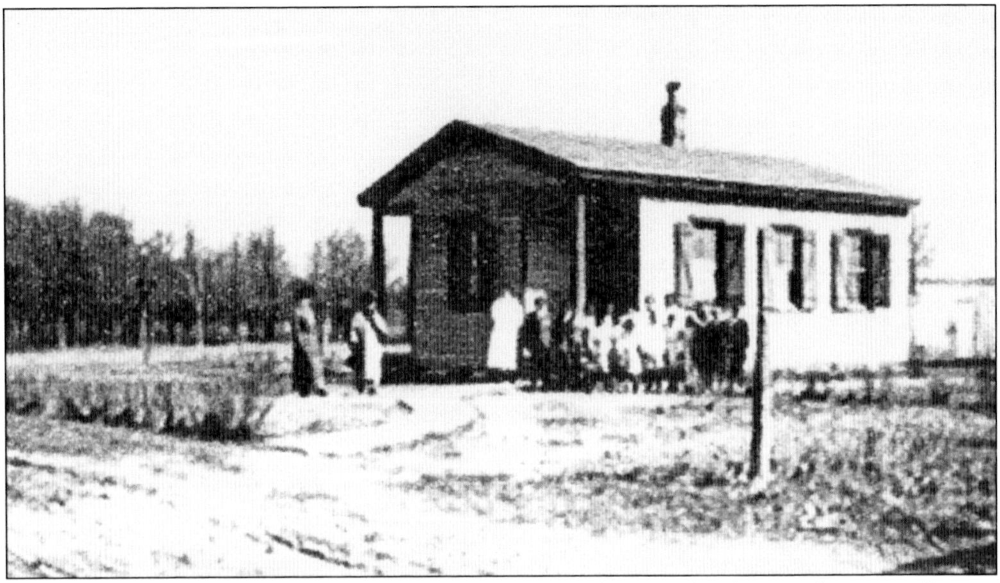

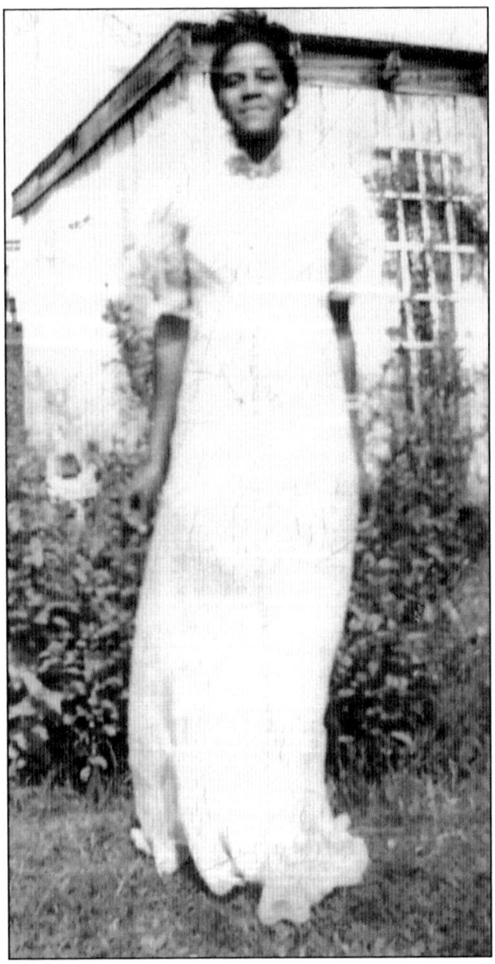

The old Jeter School on Taylor Street (later Delmont Street) is pictured here. The wooden-frame structure had two rooms. The children of Providence Park attended this school during segregation, walking from far away, as this was the only school in their proximity. It was torn down in 2001, with the original slate blackboards still on the walls. (Jackson Davis Collection, University of Virginia Special Collections Library.)

Alma Lucille Early stands in her wedding gown on the day of her 1931 marriage to Andrew Hocker. The pair started from humble beginnings and during the Great Depression raised three daughters, Winifred, Marlene, and Martha Annette. (Martha H. Bradley.)

Andrew Hocker is shown working on a house. Hocker, a natural carpenter, calculated all construction plans, specific cuts of lumber, and other materials in his head. In 1938, he built a house on Winston Road, which still stands 250 yards southwest of the main entrance to the Richmond International Raceway. This house was within the jurisdiction of the Henrico County portion of Providence Park. (Martha H. Bradley.)

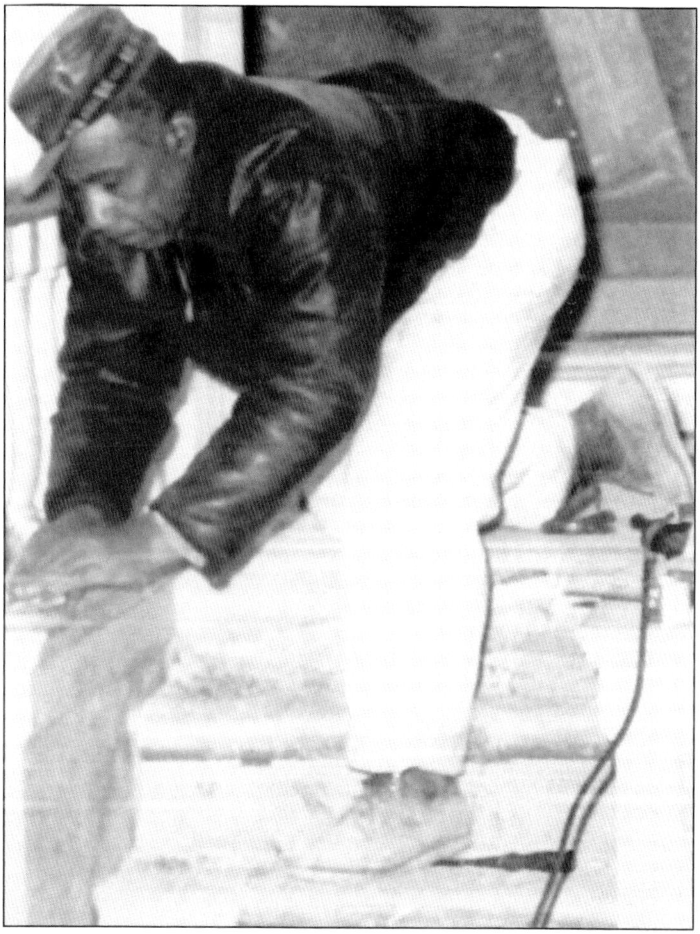

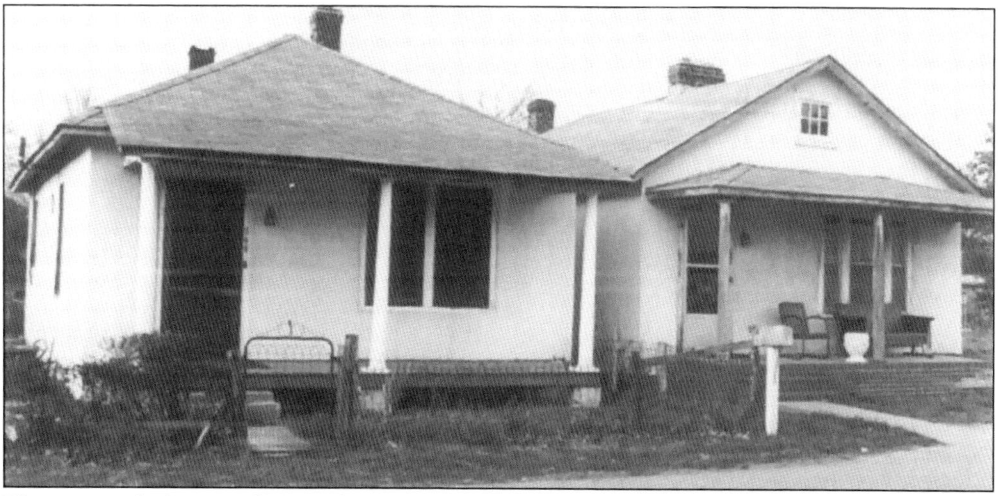

These were the homes of Mr. and Mrs. Benjamin Curtis (left) and Mr. and Mrs. Robert Lankford (right), both built by Andrew Hocker and owned by the Curtises. Each house typically had a porch and a small mailbox. In the early days of mail, the letters were not taken to individual homes. (Martha H. Bradley.)

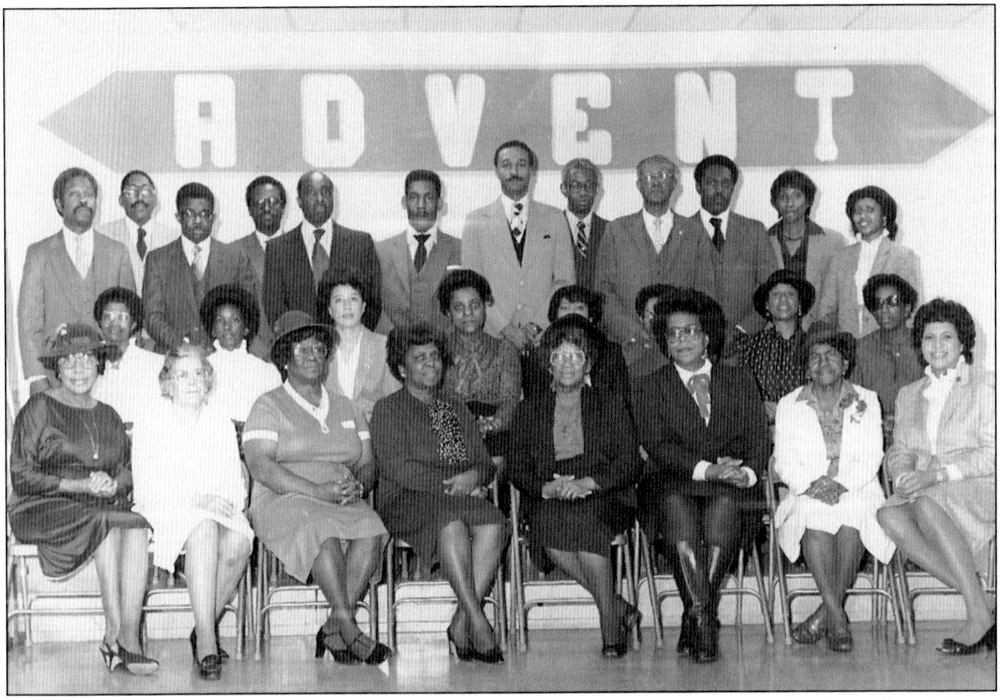

Members of the Providence Park Baptist Church Sunday School pose around 1959 in this Advent celebration picture. (Billy Randolph.)

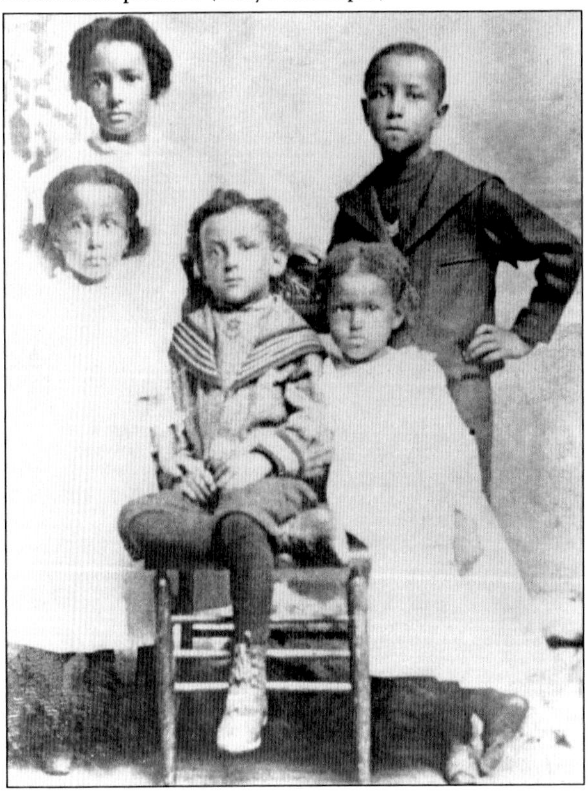

Pictured here are five of William and Mary Quarles Randolph's seven children. Henrietta (wife of Norman Strauss) and James are standing. Seated, from left to right, are Maude (wife of Bill Gibbons), Ulysses (husband of Melissa Roberts), and Lillian (wife of Rev. Robert Pervall). Daughters Gertrude (wife of William Davenport) and Marian (wife of William Settle) are not pictured in this photograph. (Billy Randolph.)

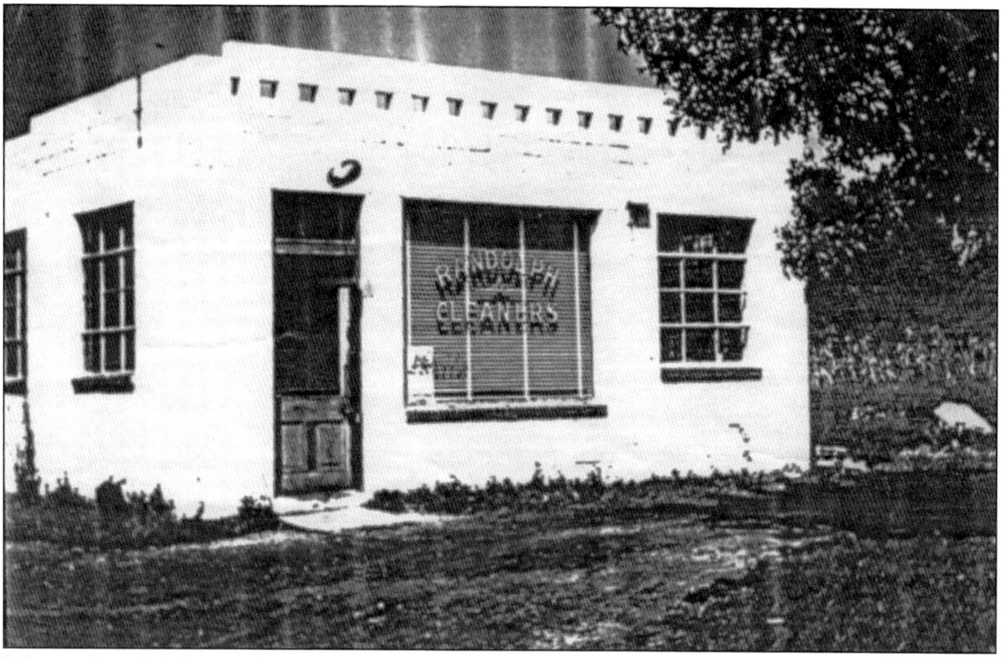

Ulysses Randolph was the owner of the thriving Randolph Cleaners, located at 3808 Taylor Street (later Delmont Street). According to his son William (Billy), Andrew Hocker and Ulysses constructed this building in 1948. The business delivered and picked up on Saturdays, going out west to black communities such as Westwood, Zion Town, Quioccasin, Washington Park, and downtown. Randolph Cleaners closed in 1974. (Billy Randolph.)

Pictured at right are Ulysses and Melissa Randolph and their children. They are as follows, from left to right: (first row) LaVerne, Melissa, Ulysses, and Constance; (second row) Phyllis, Norman, and Billy. In 1928, Ulysses moved with his wife, Melissa, into his parents' home. Randolph Cleaners originated in the backyard. (Billy Randolph.)

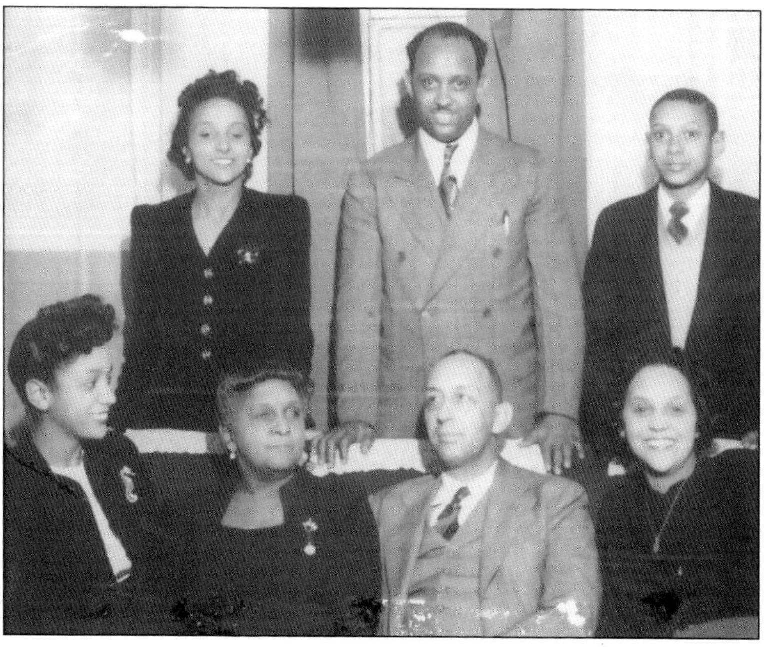

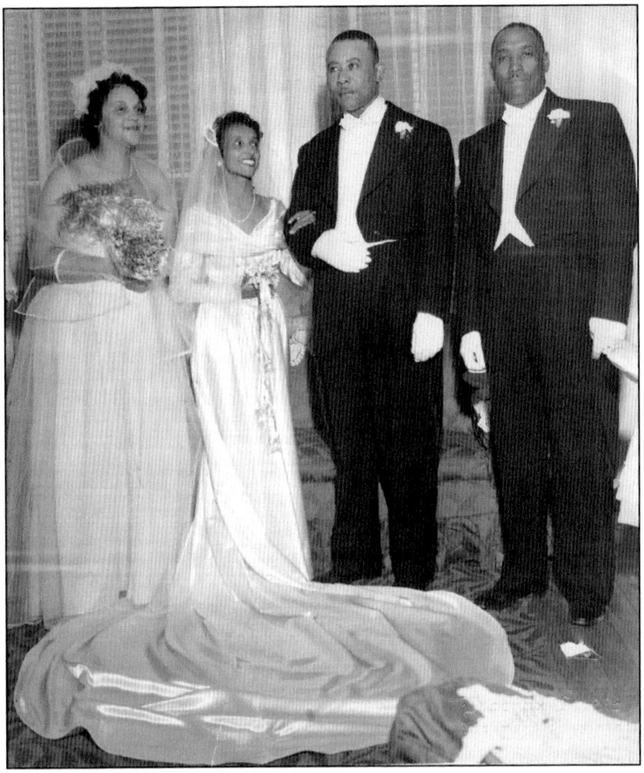

This picture is from the 1950 wedding of Phyllis L. Randolph (born in 1922 to Ulysses and Melissa Randolph) to Wilbert V. Dance (born in 1911) at Providence Park Baptist Church. The maid of honor was Constance R. Gettis, sister of the bride, and the best man was Irving Jackson. Rev. John J. Woodson officiated. (Billy Randolph.)

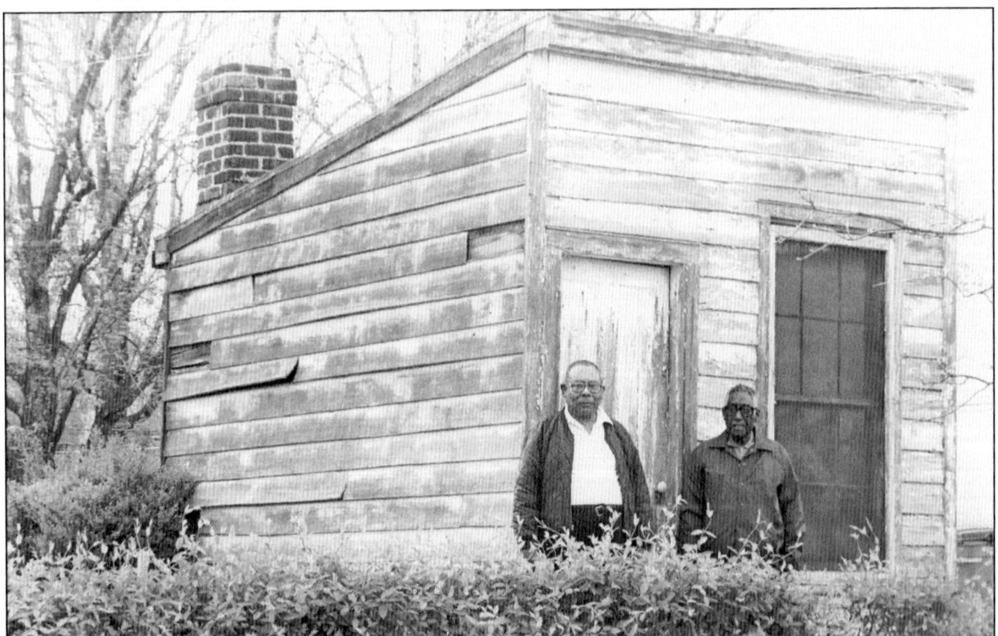

This picture shows Wilbert Dance (left) and Irving Jackson at Evans Barber Shop, which was generally open on Friday and Saturday evenings. After work, the neighborhood men would crowd into the shop, full of conversation from the week. Owner Robert J. Evans was also the night caretaker at Evergreen Cemetery. (Ann D. Ford.)

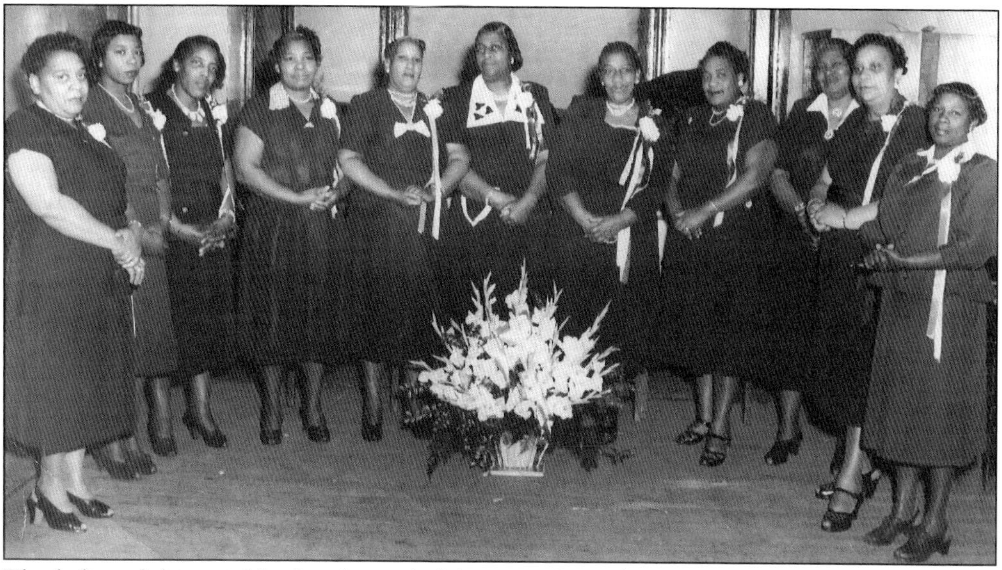

The ladies of this neighborhood social club met at Providence Church. Pictured from left to right are Elnora Parham Cain, Rosa Knight, Mary Robinson, Viola Crawford, Florence Woolfolk, Dolly Winston, Florence Jones, Dollice B. Coleman, ? Franklin, Norma D. Lewis, and Christine B. Quirley. (Billy Randolph.)

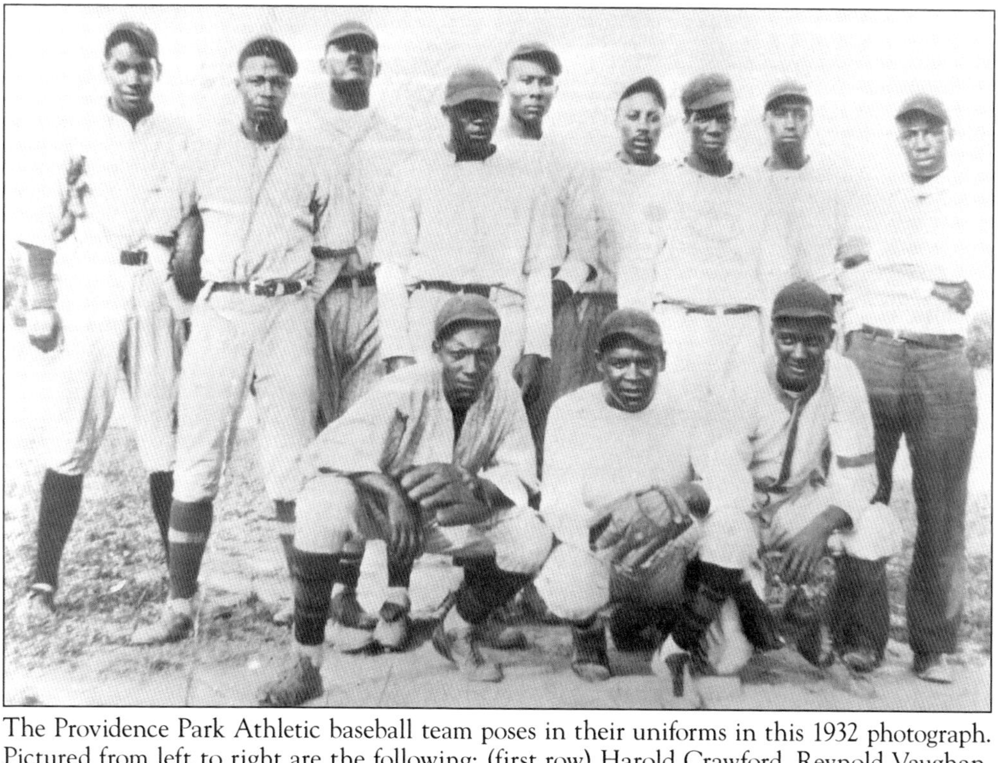

The Providence Park Athletic baseball team poses in their uniforms in this 1932 photograph. Pictured from left to right are the following: (first row) Harold Crawford, Reynold Vaughan, and Lee Crawford; (second row) Melvin Jackson, Joseph Woolfolk, Robert Thompson, Samuel Collins, Wilbert Dance, Eddie Jackson, Grayson Claiborne, William Irving Jackson, and Randolph Woolfolk. (Billy Randolph.)

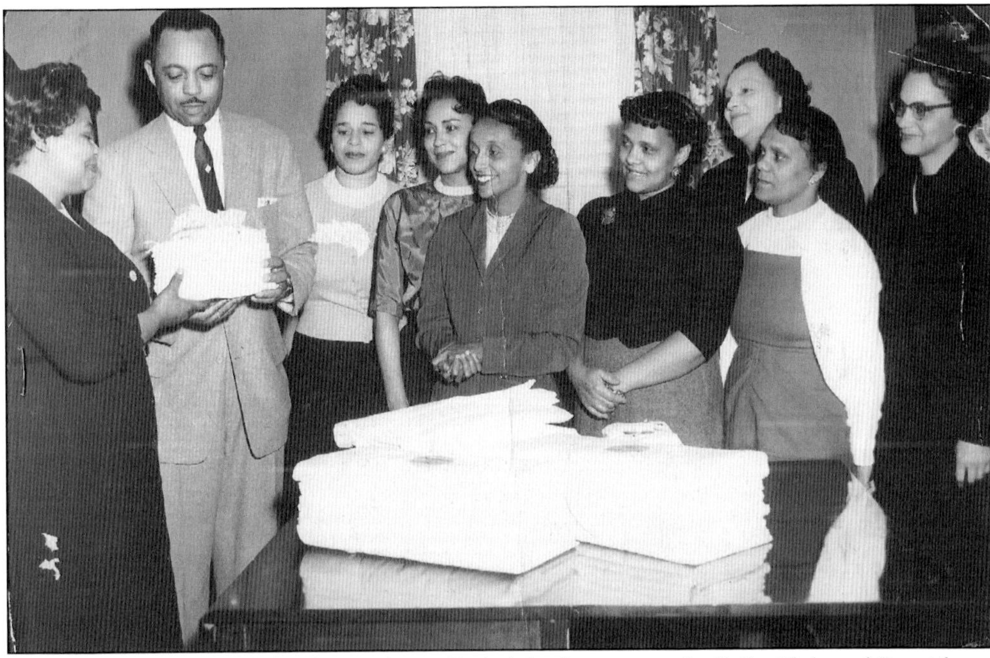

The Young Women's Club of Providence Park (also known as the Jolly Club and Providence Dramatic Club) began in 1930. In this photograph, club members donate linens to Old Richmond Community Hospital, the area's black hospital during segregation. Pictured from left to right, Rose Gillison (club president) gives linens to John Mapp (head of the hospital), while club members Florence Jones Dabney, Ruth Major, Phyllis Dance, Marie Norris, Helen Davis, LaVerne Grady, and Vernell Myers look on. (Billy Randolph.)

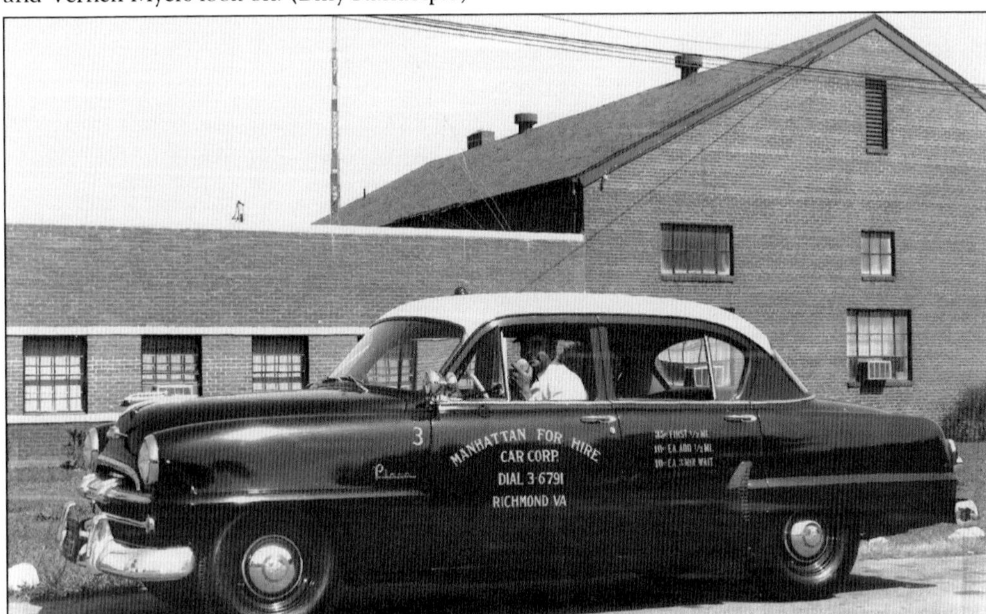

Clinton Whittle is pictured in his Manhattan Cab Company taxicab on a walkie-talkie. Manhattan Cab Company was a black-owned and -operated business located on Brook Road with a reputation for being dependable and polite. Whittle retired from the U.S. Postal Service. (Billy Randolph.)

Ella Logan Curtis (1892–1997) is pictured in her later years. Ella was the daughter of William and Ida Robinson Logan and a native of Louisa County, Virginia. She married Benjamin Curtis of Raleigh, North Carolina, and had one daughter, Elsie Curtis. She worked until she was 90 years of age and was an active member of Moore Street Baptist Church. In later years, she joined Providence Park Church. (Jean L. Fountain.)

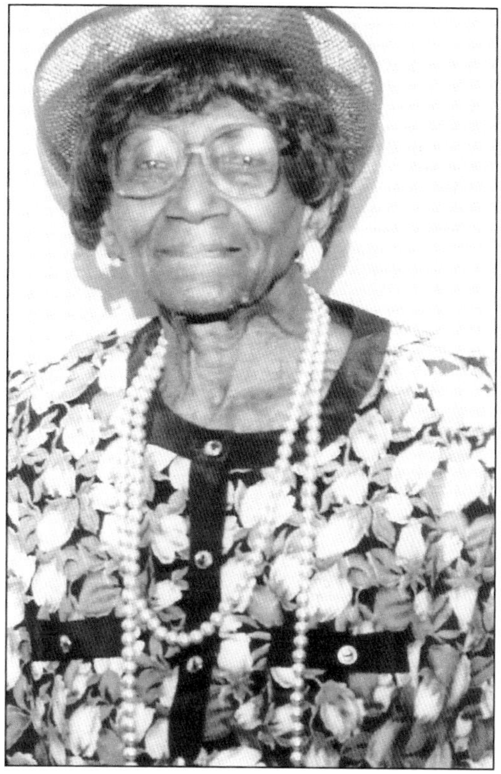

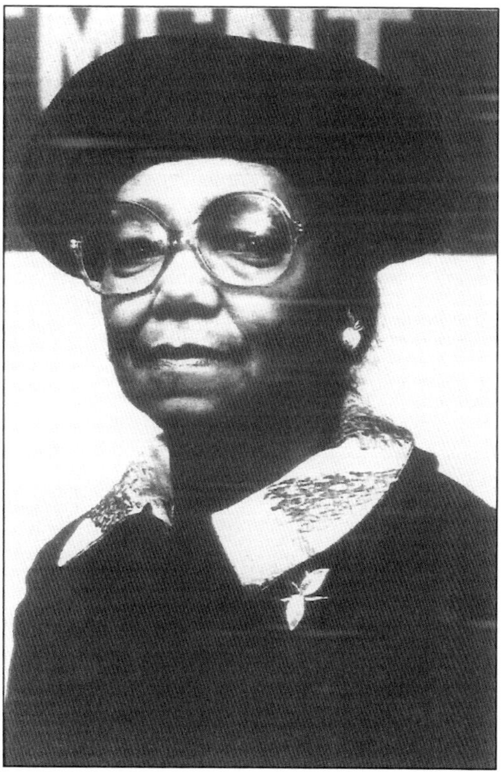

This is Elsie Curtis Lankford, daughter of Ella Curtis. Elsie, born in 1912, was a graduate of Armstrong High School and the Van de Vyver School of Business. Van de Vyver exclusively trained African Americans in business education. She was a homemaker and a seamstress with many clients. In 1933, she married Robert Lankford (1910–1969) of Louisburg, North Carolina. He worked faithfully for Chesapeake and Ohio Railway. Their five children were all college graduates. (Jean L. Fountain.)

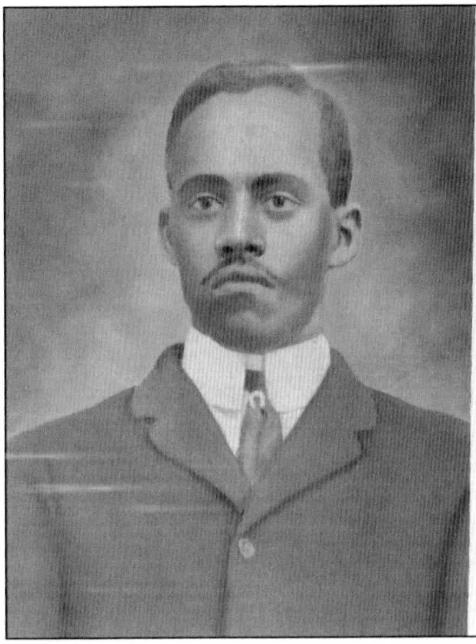
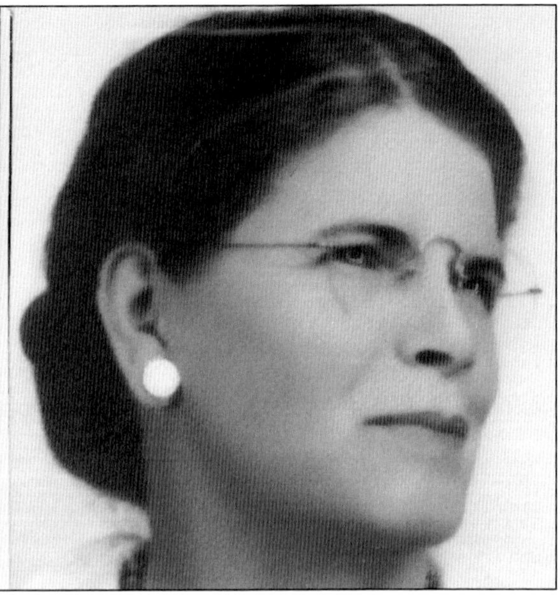

Deacon Thornton Frederick Davis (1881–1947) married Adelaide Turner (1888–1951), and they lived across from the lumber company where he was employed. In 1914, the couple moved to Providence Park. Davis was a fast learner in the lumber business, and in Providence Park, he founded the Davis Construction Company, which has since grown into an established family business. Davis Construction built the present edifice of Providence Baptist Church. The couple had nine children: William, James, Howard, Leonard, Melvin, Myron, Calton, Edith, and Vernelle. (Vernelle D. Myers Nelson.)

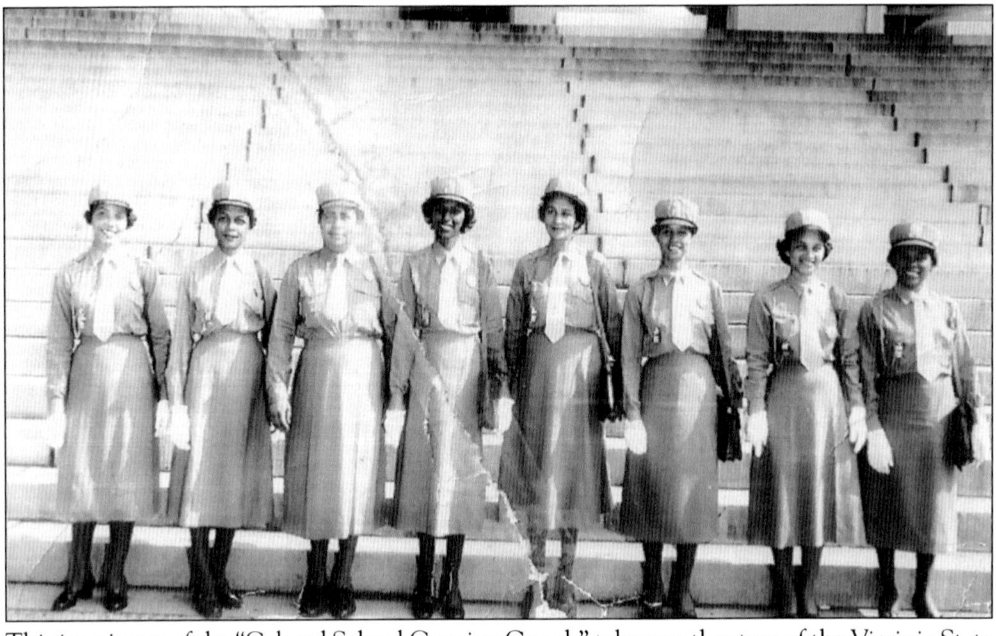

This is a picture of the "Colored School Crossing Guards" taken on the steps of the Virginia State Capitol. These eight ladies look so charming in their full dress, gloves, ties, and smiles. Vernelle D. Myers, second from right, was appointed as a special police officer of the City of Richmond in 1951 to preserve the peace, safety, and good order of the community. (Vernelle D. Myers Nelson.)

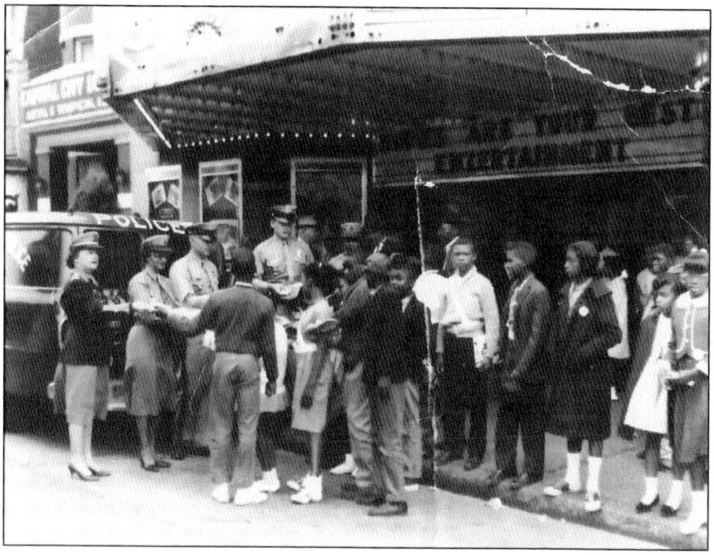

This picture shows the police department and school guards distributing items to black schoolchildren (some of whom were crossing guards) in front of Richmond's historic Hippodrome Theatre in Jackson Ward. Vernelle D. Myers is shown second from the left passing out literature to the children. Note that the children are neatly dressed. (Vernelle D. Myers Nelson.)

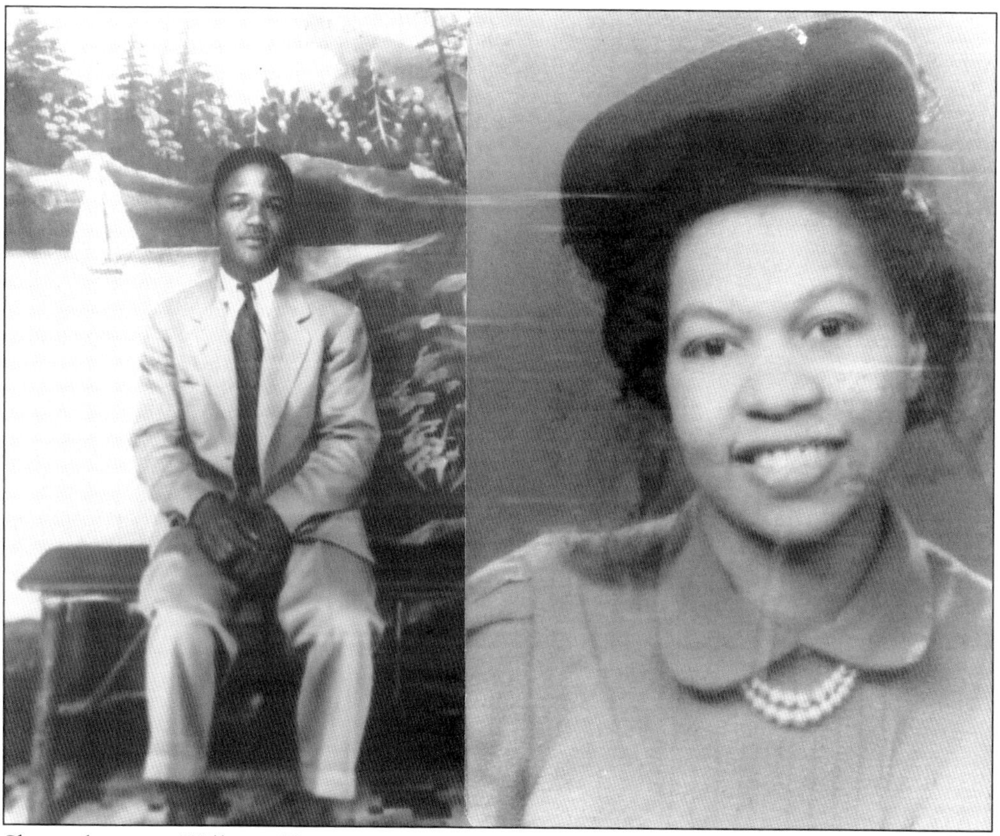

Shown here are William Claire Turner Sr. (1918–1994) and his wife Ruth, Randolph Turner (1921–). The couple married in 1944 and raised nine children in their home at 58 Taylor Road (which later became 3807 Delmont Street). William Sr. attended Virginia Union University and worked for the Seaboard Railroad Company for 25 years. Ruth majored in history at Virginia Union University and taught in Hanover County public schools. (Wilhelmina Turner.)

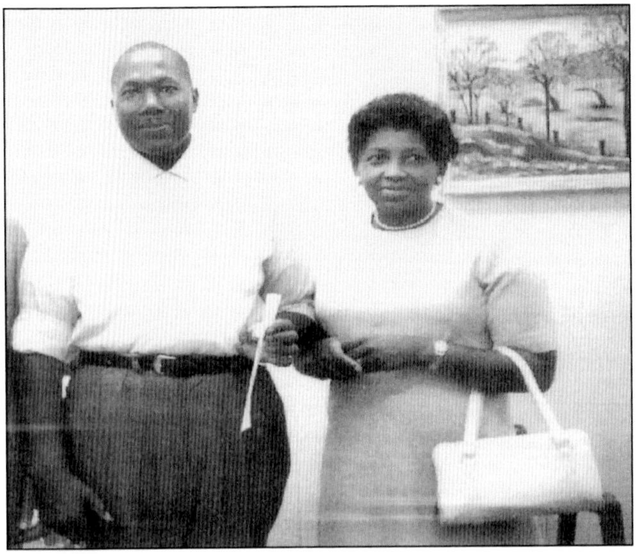

Freddie White Sr. is pictured here with his wife, Lula. The couple moved with their four daughters to East Ladies Mile Road in Providence Park in 1947. Later two sons were born. White, born in the Westwood community of Henrico, worked for the Internal Revenue Service. (Lula B. White.)

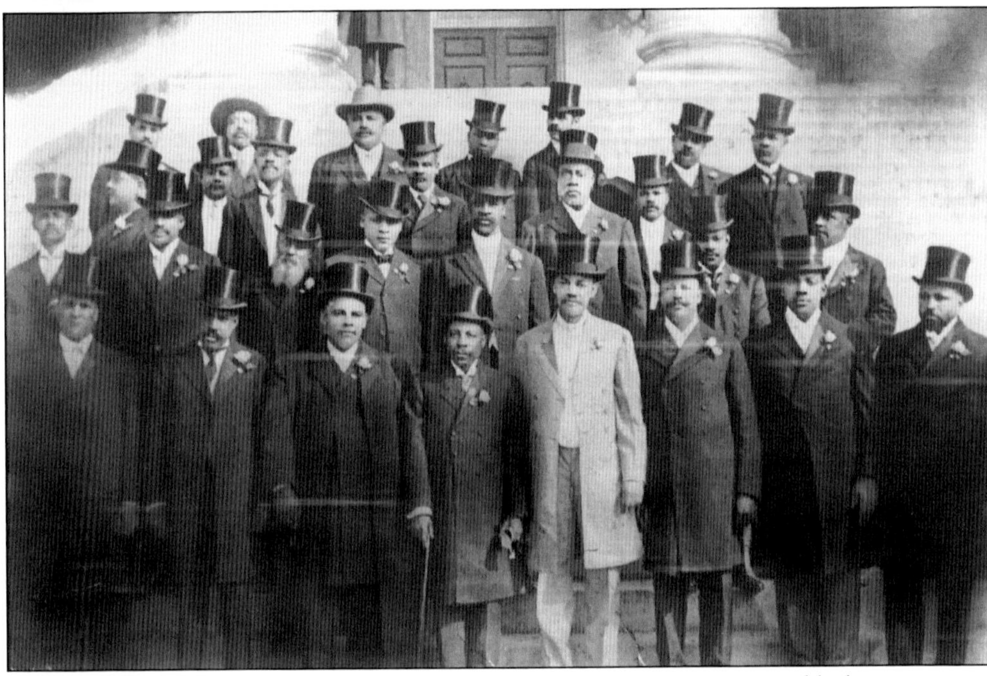

In 1909, this delegation of business, civic, and professional leaders representing black communities in Henrico County and Richmond met with Pres. William Taft. Pictured on the steps of the Virginia State Capitol in silk hats and Prince Albert coats are the following, from left to right: (first row) John F. Taylor, Henry Mallory, Rev. W. L. Taylor, George St. Julian Stephens, John Mitchell Jr. (editor), Thomas M. Crump, Thomas H. Wyatt, and W. B. Burrell; (second row) Edwin A. Randolph, E. W. Brown, William W. T. Forrester, Joseph R. Pollard (attorney), Rev. William T. Johnson, Dr. Barrington Bowser, and William Isaac Johnson; (third row) Alfred D. Price, R. J. Hill, Emmett C. Burke, Rev. J. E. Jones, Rev. Evans Payne, Edward F. Johnson, and Beverly F. Turner; (fourth row) William H. Hughes, Giles B. Jackson, Rev. Zeke D. Lewis, and three unidentified. Not included in the picture was delegation member Rev. D. Webster Davis. (Billy Randolph.)

Five

Washington Park

Washington Park, originally known as Oak Park, is a black community dating back to the early 1870s. It is located in Henrico County in the Brookland district, approximately 3.5 miles from the city of Richmond. In March 1877, special commissioner W. H. Beveridge sold Asa W. Shields the 60.75 acres of land that make up the core of Washington Park. Upon his death, his widow sold the acreage to Annie Purvis, who sold it to John C. Cheatwood in 1906. That same month, Cheatwood sold the land to the Washington Land Corporation.

Washington Park had two churches. Lewis Ginter, a wealthy white businessman, donated land on the east side of Brook Road to St. John Baptist Church, organized in 1870. The land was deeded to three trustees of St. John Baptist Church: Edmond Carter, Robert Carter, and Henry Crawford. In 1893, Ginter gave funds necessary to remodel the church. In 1921, Rev. Archie M. Kent left St. John Church with his family, several deacons, and their families and started a new church, Kent's Temple Baptist. The church was originally located on Second Avenue near Piney Road and in 1925 relocated to Cheatwood Avenue under the new name of First Baptist Church, Washington Park.

Washington Park had a five-room schoolhouse named Washington Park School. It had grades one through seven, with an outdoor toilet and a pump for water. It was located on Maggie Walker Avenue at the corner of Moss Side Avenue. Teachers at this school were Naomi Banks, C. L. Beverly, Carrie Brown, Gladys Vaughan, G. C. Saunders, and principal Emma Randolph Washington. Washington Park School closed in the 1920s and was purchased by the Richmond City School Board in 1942. The community was later annexed by the City of Richmond.

From 1921 to 1925, the U.S. Postal Service delivered all mail to the Brook Hill Estates. A store owner named Mr. Beard would pick up the local mail and keep it in his store for the residents to retrieve. In 1925, Washington Park got its first postmaster, Christopher Williams. In 1921, Robert Long opened Market Inn at Maggie Walker Avenue and Booker Street as an ice cream stand. It grew to become the site of a thriving entertainment business known all over the country as a top black-owned nightclub. Duke Ellington and Count Basie were among the great performers who appeared there. In 1947, the residents of the park organized a baseball team. In 1975, Market Inn began to diminish in attraction due largely to integrated exposure. Washington Park did not have lights and running water until 1975.

Prior to 1870, there was another very small group of African Americans living in an area called Randolph Town, a few miles north of Washington Park. Randolph Town was located on Wilmer Road at Chamberlayne Avenue, in close proximity to two plantations: Brook Hill and Brookfield. The families living there were the Bassetts, Gardners, Joneses, Saunderses, and Washingtons. Ned and Lucius Randolph and Charlie, Julia, and Mary Saunders were all servants for the wealthy Stewart family, who owned Brook Hill Plantation, consisting of more than 200 acres. Lucius Randolph was also the sexton at the Emmanuel Episcopal Church, where the Stewarts worshipped. The families donated the land that the church was built on. This community no longer exists. Residents moved to other thriving communities nearby such as Pilgrim and Washington Park. These two still remain quiet and prideful communities.

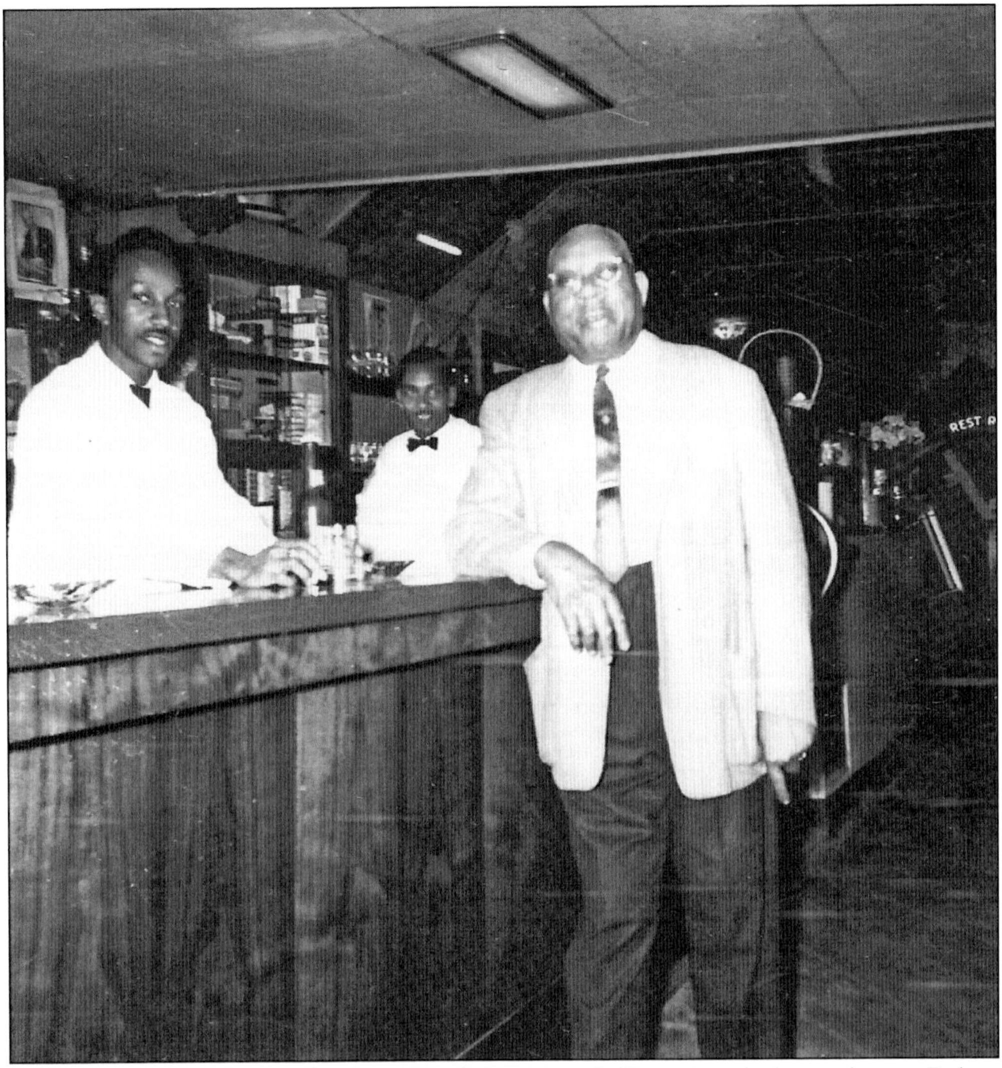

Pictured at Market Inn around 1958 are Winde Lawrence (left), tending the bar, and owner Robert "Bob" Long, posing in his sport jacket. (Winde Lawrence.)

This is a picture of the original structure of St. John Baptist Church, organized in 1893 at 4317 North Avenue. St. John Baptist Church's congregation came out of Ebenezer Baptist Church in the city of Richmond. (St. John Baptist Church.)

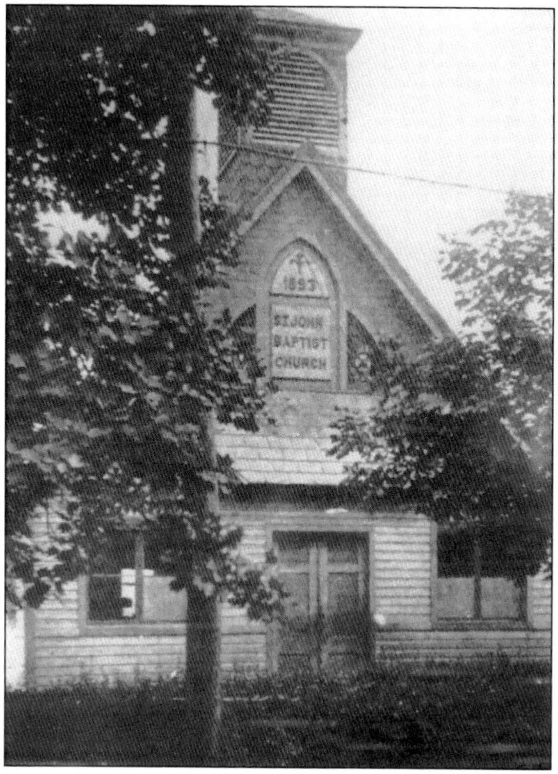

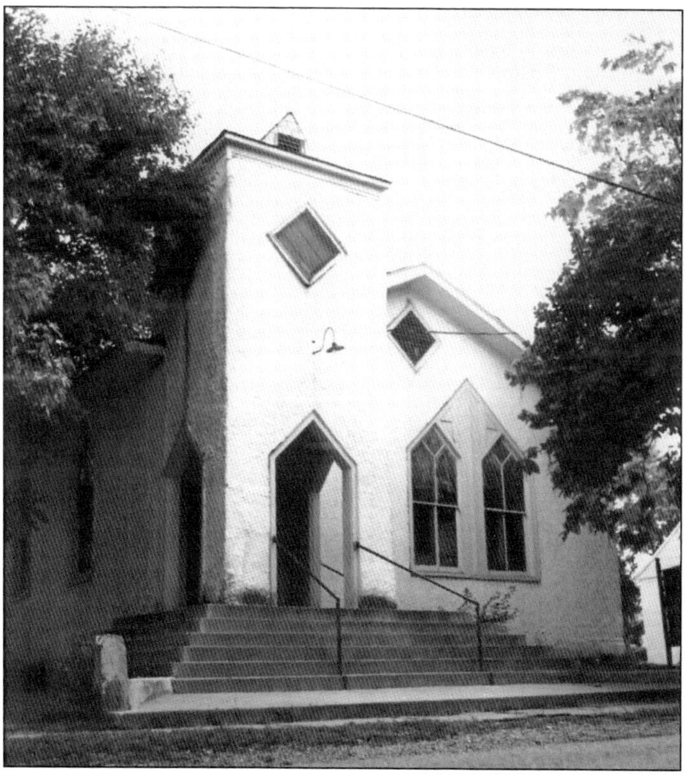

First Baptist Church, Washington Park, pictured here, is located on Cheatwood Avenue. The congregation was originally known as Kent's Temple Baptist Church, and was established when members of St. John Baptist Church broke away to form their own church. (Rev. Arlene Wimbish.)

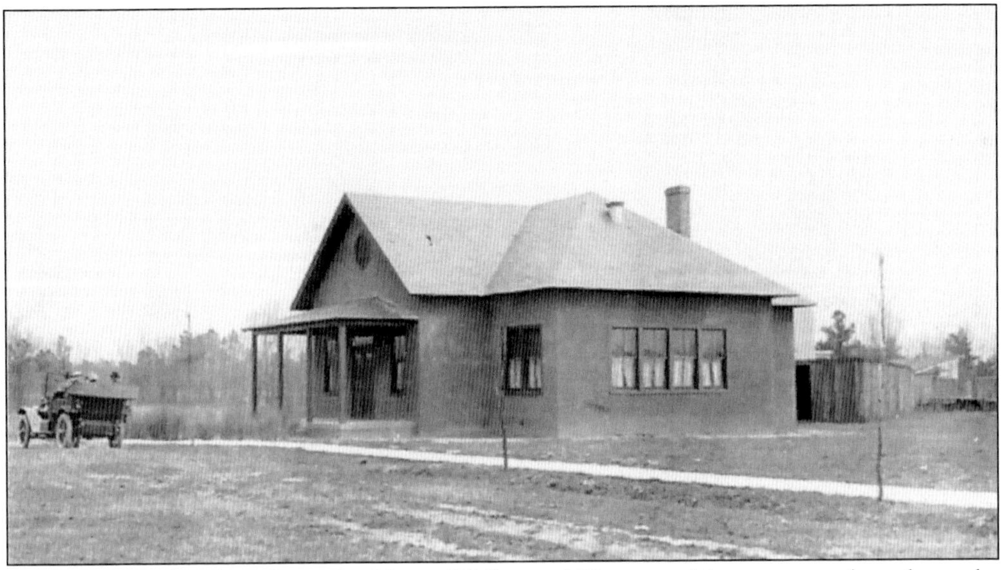

Washington Park School, located at Maggie Walker and Cheatwood Avenues, was the only nearby school for black children to attend. Graduates of the school could continue their education at Virginia Randolph Training School. (Jackson Davis Collection, University of Richmond Special Collections Library.)

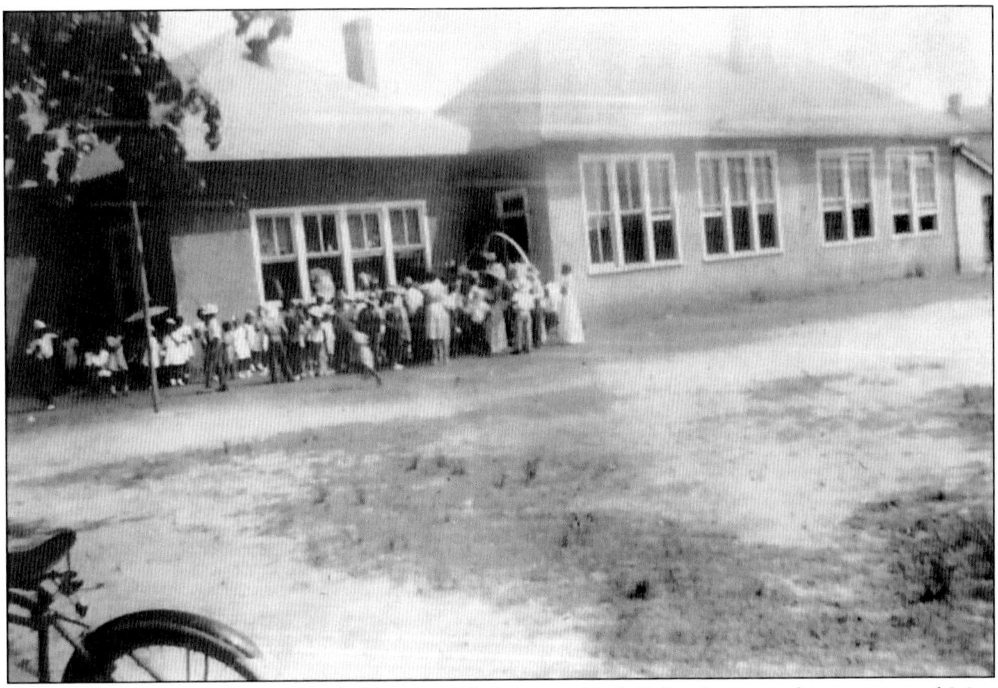

This c. 1920 picture shows the children at Washington Park School engaged in an annual May Day celebration. (Juliette S. Hamilton.)

This early-1940s photograph shows the handsome couple of Florence Jones and Forrest F. Dabney (1918–1999). Forrest was the owner of Dabney Landscaping and Refuse Company, and Florence operated a day nursery in their home at 3912 Moss Side Avenue. (Lavinia and Ernest Dabney.)

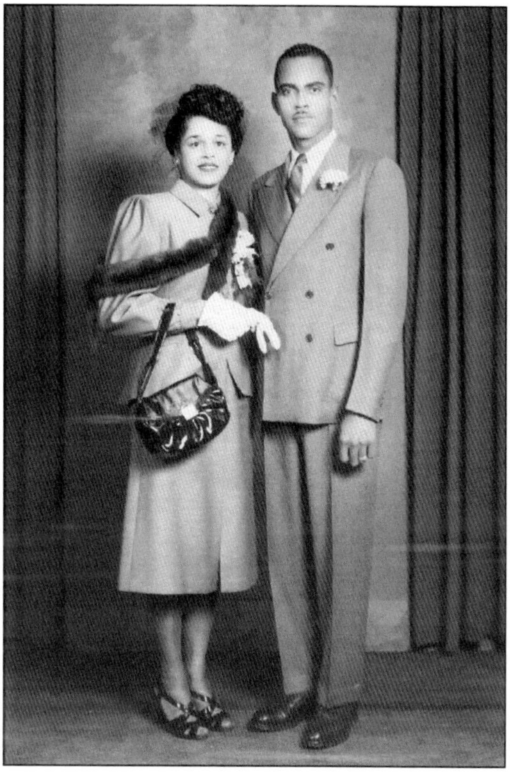

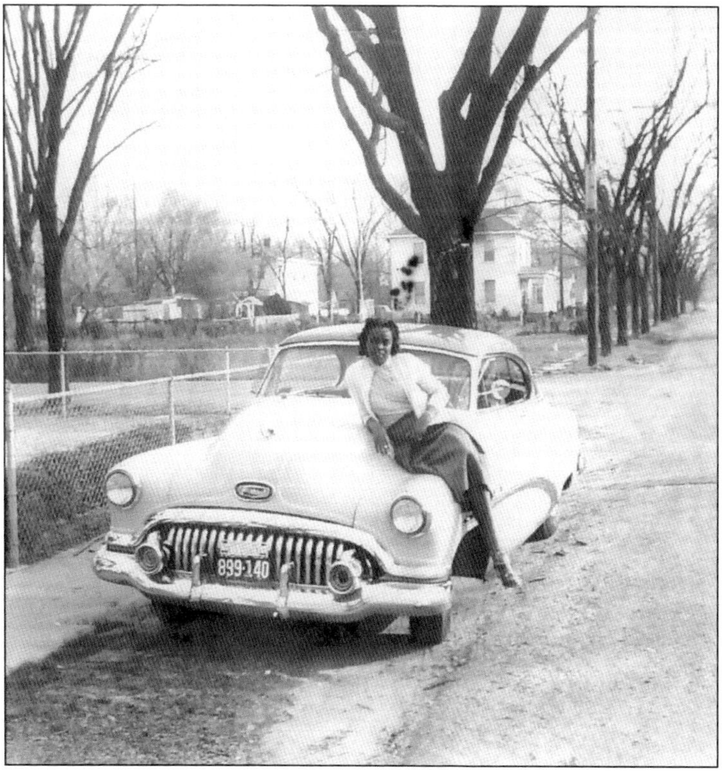

Juliette Stephens Hamilton poses on a 1949 Buick Roadmaster on Moss Side Avenue. (J. Stephens Hamilton.)

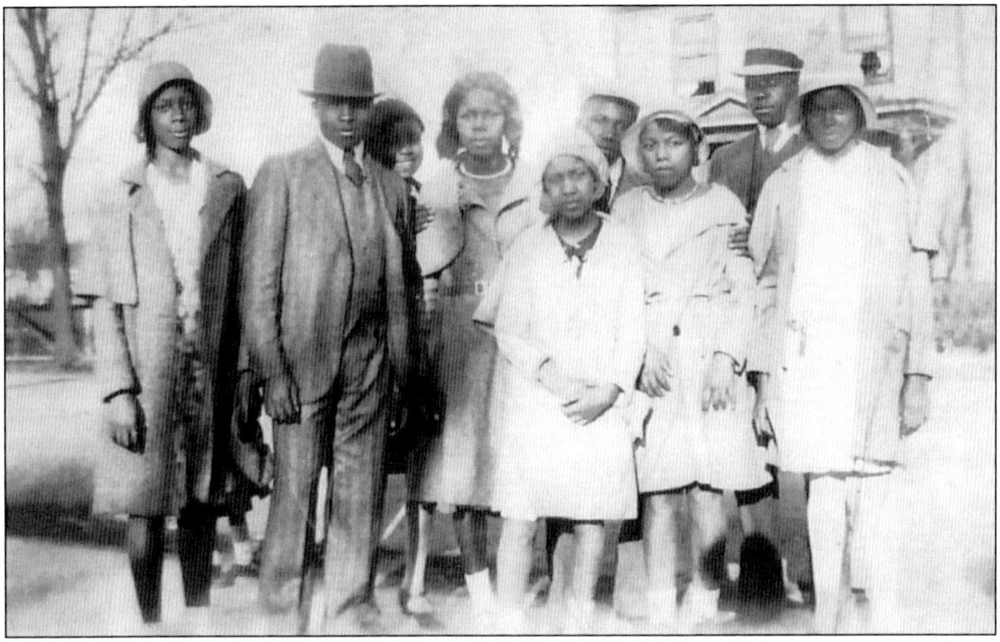

Taken in 1931 in front of the Kemp house, this picture shows a group of Washington Park friends posing for a photograph after church. (J. Stephens Hamilton.)

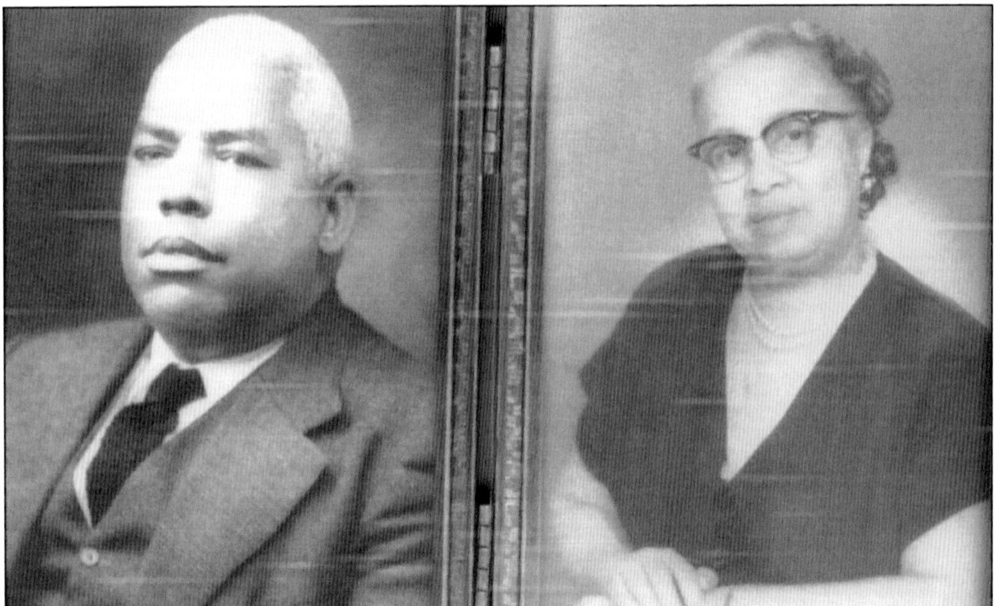

Pictured here are Rev. John William Kemp (1889–1954) and his wife, Hattie Hunter Kemp (1894–1988). They lived on Corbin Street, where they raised four children, Lillian, Berthel, John Jr., and Thomas. After graduating from Wayland Academy at Virginia Union University, Reverend Kemp became pastor of St. John Baptist Church, where he served for 20 years. He also spent time as pastor at Cedar Street Memorial Baptist Church, which was organized by his father, Rev. Robert C. Kemp, who was its first pastor. Robert was married to Nannie Patterson Kemp. (Lillian K. Mapp.)

Pictured here is Blanche Melton West (1906–1993), born in Glen Allen, Virginia, to Ira and Adelaide Melton. She graduated from Virginia Randolph and taught in Hanover County schools. In 1927, she married LeRoy West, with whom she had two sons, Roy and Ira. They moved to Washington Park and joined St. John Church. (Dr. Roy West.)

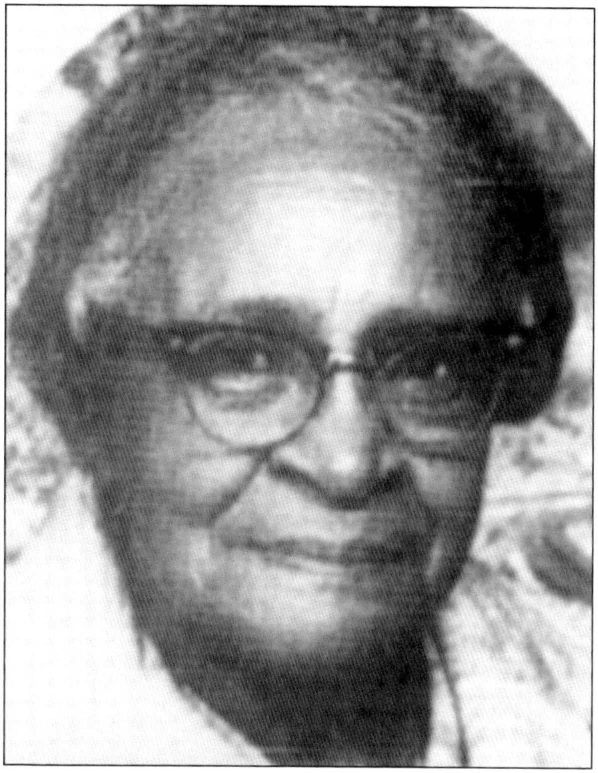

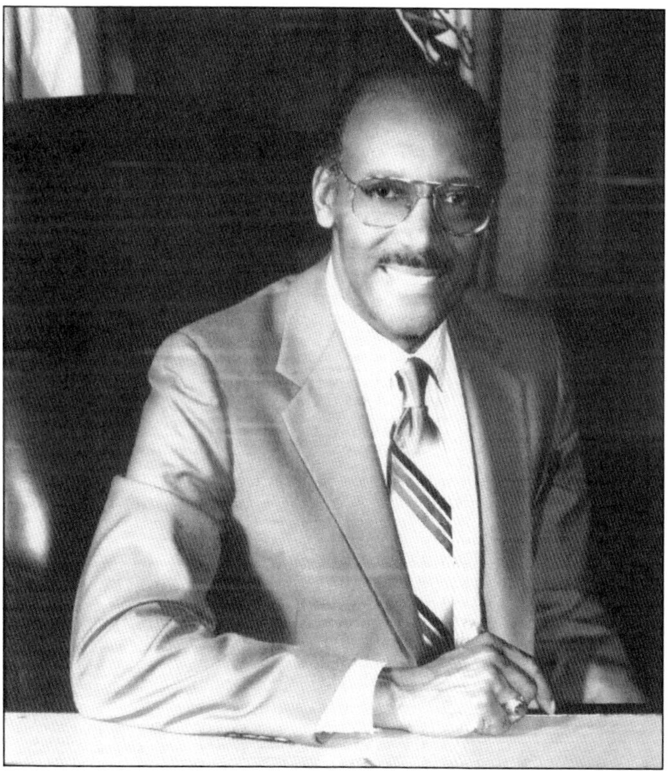

Dr. Roy West, son of LeRoy and Blanche Melton West, was born in 1930 and attended Washington Park Elementary School. He served in the U.S. Army and earned his bachelor's of science degree from Virginia Union University, a master's from New York University, and an doctorate of education from George Washington University. He married Helen Hubbard West and had two children. Dr. West was a teacher in Richmond public schools, principal for 30 years, and Richmond city mayor from 1982 to 1988. (Dr. Roy West.)

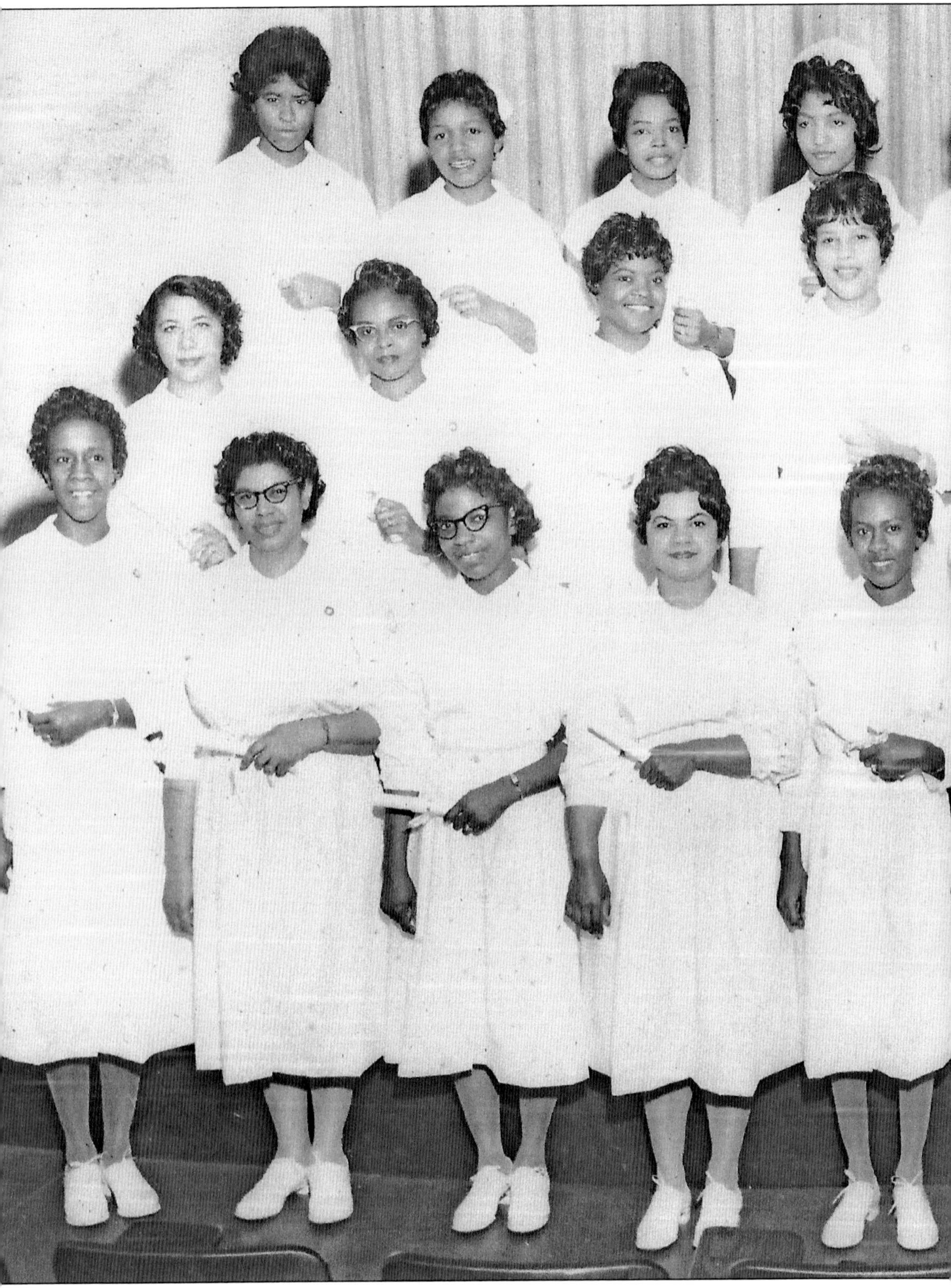

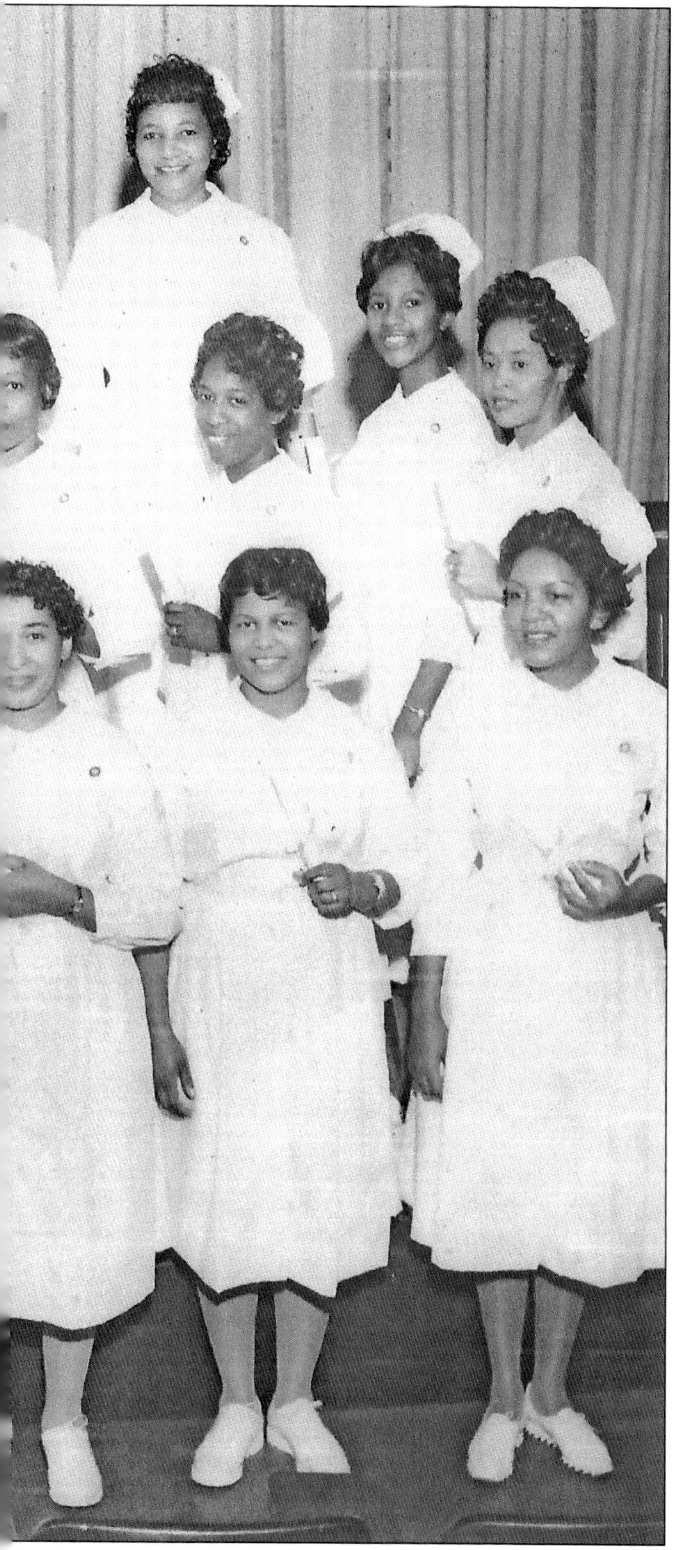

Members of the 1939 graduating class of St. Philip School of Nursing proudly hold their certificates in this photograph. Located in downtown Richmond, St. Philip was one of only two black nursing schools in the state of Virginia during segregation. The graduates are dressed in white nurses' uniforms, caps, and hats. (J. Stephens Hamilton.)

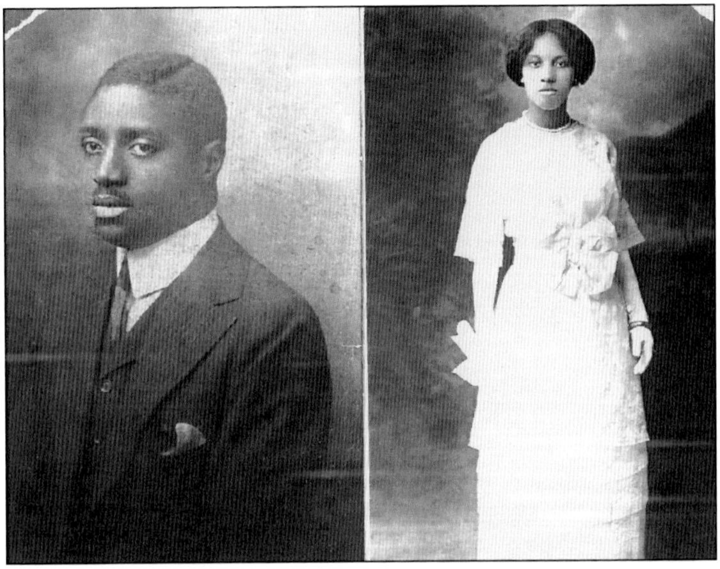

Mary Crafton and Robert Washington Sr., pictured here, lived on Akron Street with their six children, Ophelia, Consuela, Robinette, Anna, Robert Jr., and Claudette. Born in 1896 to Van and Virginia Washington, Robert Sr. worked in the post office and was a milkman for Richmond Dairy. Mary, born in 1894, was a dedicated housewife. (Anna Washington.)

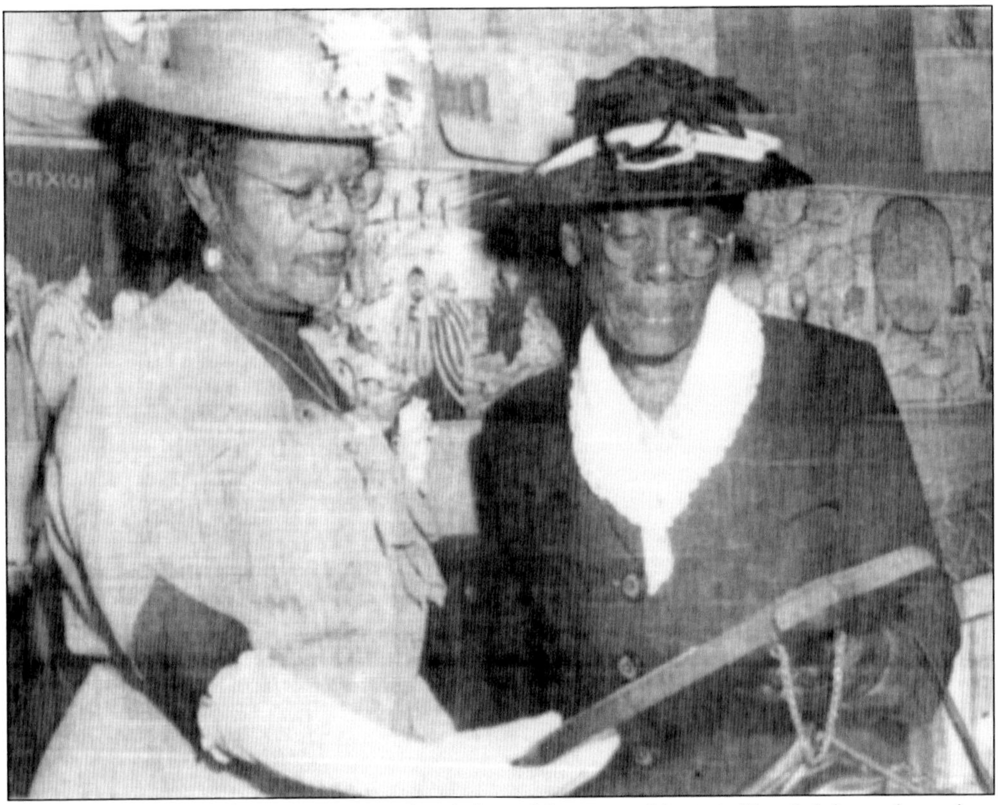

Emma Randolph Washington, pictured at left, and her sister Virginia Randolph are legendary figures in Henrico County. Born to former slaves Sarah Carter and Edward Nelson Randolph, these sisters had a lasting effect on education. Emma was the principal of Washington Park School, and Virginia was the founder of the Virginia Randolph Technical School (later the Virginia Randolph High School). Their sisters were Mary and Sarah Randolph. Emma (1875–1959) married Daniel Washington and had a daughter, Aurelia W. Davis. (Henrietta D. McMickens.)

This is Daniel W. Washington, husband to Emma and brother to Robert Washington. Like his brother, he was a mail carrier for 40 years. Their parents were Van and Virginia Washington. Daniel was a trustee at Sixth Mount Zion Baptist Church, and he helped found the Washington Park Civic League. When he became eligible to vote, he transported his neighbors to the polls so they could vote as well. Washington is regarded as a great civic leader and worker. (Anna Washington.)

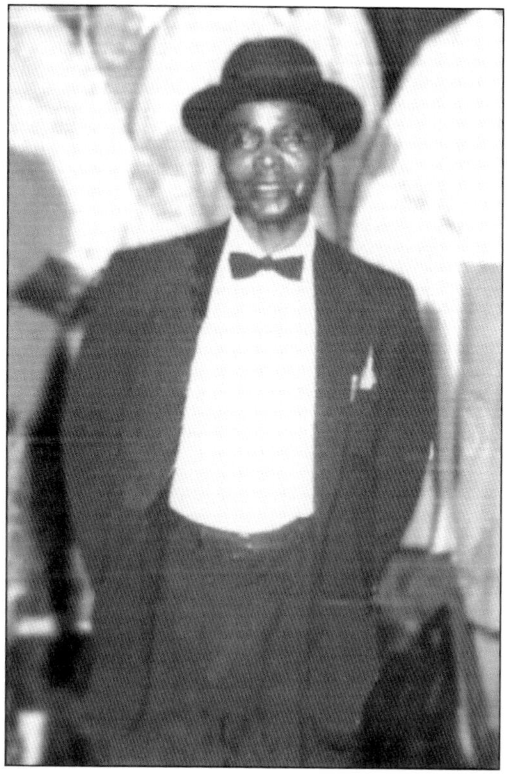

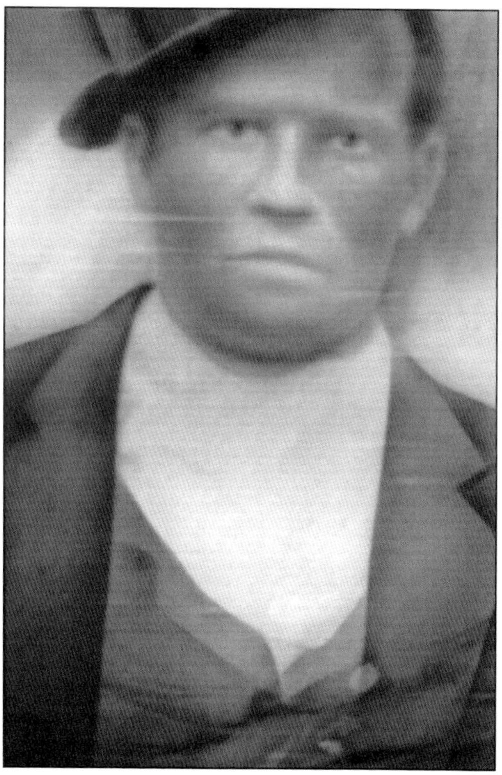

This is Otis Gaines Sr. He and his wife, Louella Bolden Gaines, lived in Washington Park with their two children, Otis Jr. and Mary. (Tonya R. Scott-Hickman.)

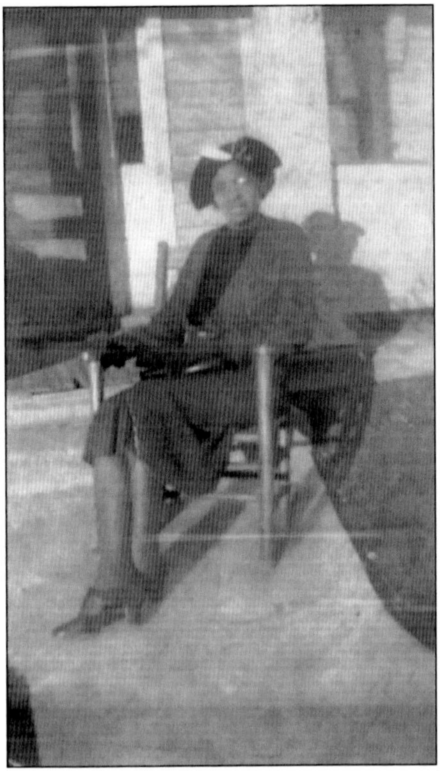

This well-dressed lady is Louella Bolden Gaines, sitting on her porch at 708 Cheatwood Avenue. Louella, a native of Louisa County, Virginia, was first married to Otis Gaines. After his death, she married Rev. J. J. Woodson, noted pastor of Providence Baptist Church for 50 years, becoming stepmother to his three children, James, Floyd, and Beatrice. She died in 1974. (Tonya R. Scott-Hickman.)

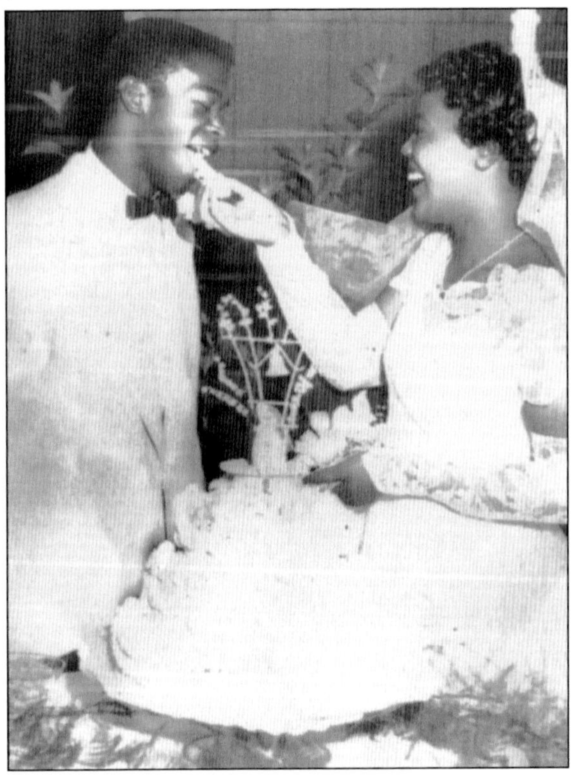

Mary Gaines and Rev. Royal Quarles Sr. celebrate their new lives as husband and wife in this photograph from the early 1950s. Reverend Quarles was pastor of the Union Branch Baptist Church in Prince George County for 29 years. (Tonya R. Scott-Hickman.)

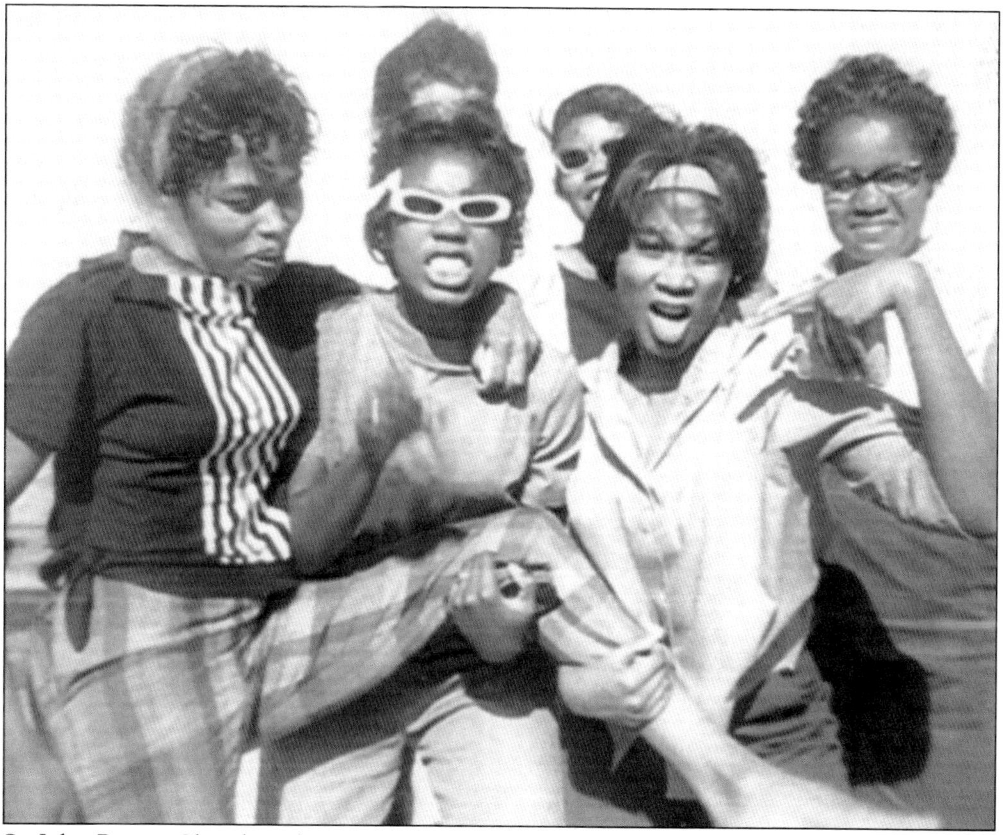

St. John Baptist Church took many Sunday school trips each summer to Buckroe Beach in Hampton, Virginia. This 1962 photograph shows the girls of "The Park" enjoying the beach. Pictured from left to right are the following: (first row) Geraldine Wimbish, Otis Quarles Hayes, and Sarah Quarles Randolph; (second row) Alma Quarles and two unidentified women. Bayshore Beach (and in later years Buckroe Beach) became a popular vacation spot for African Americans during segregation. (Tonya R. Scott-Hickman.)

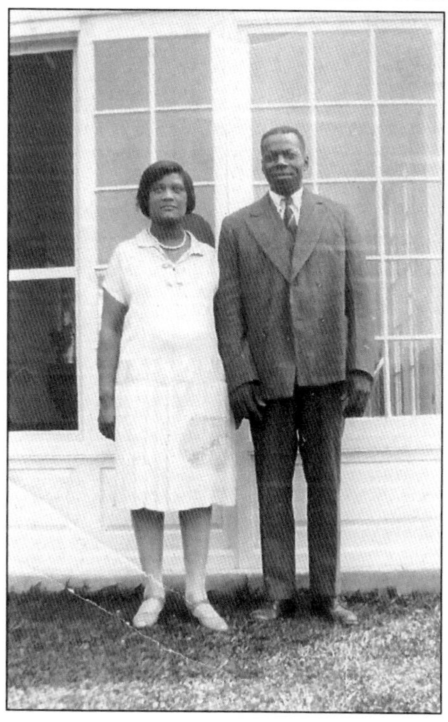

These pioneers were Rosetta Rock and Willie Winston, who came to Washington Park from Powhatan County in 1900. Among their children were Mae, Louise, Ada, and Kate. Kate married John Smith of Hanover County, and the pair raised four children—John, Henry, William, and Valera Ann—in Washington Park. Smith (1898–1990) was a deacon at St. John Baptist Church. Kate Winston Smith died in 1972. (Henry Smith.)

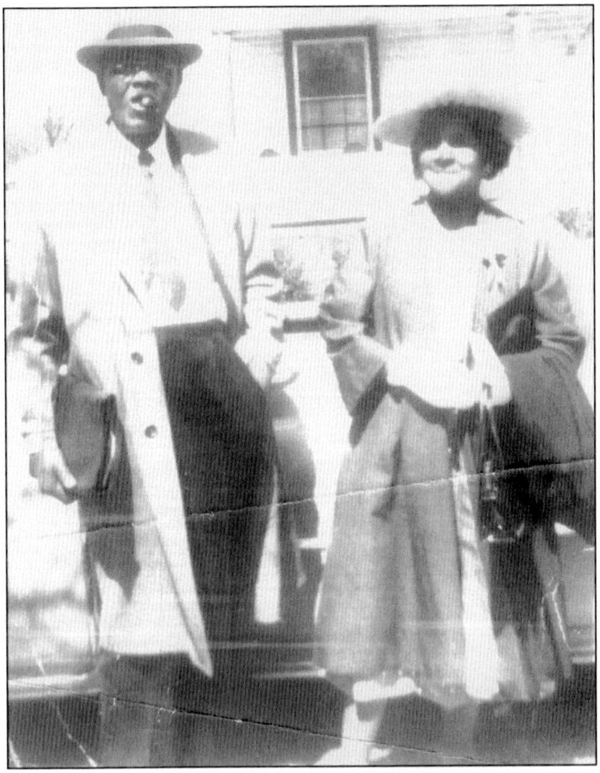

Pictured here are James Robinson Jr., born in 1885 in the Westwood community, and his wife, Mary Smith, born in Dumbarton. They had 11 children. Robinson owned a contracting business and added stucco to the old St. John Baptist Church. He also moved steeples from Mount Carmel on First Street and Hood Temple AME Church on Clay Street. (Mary R. Cooper.)

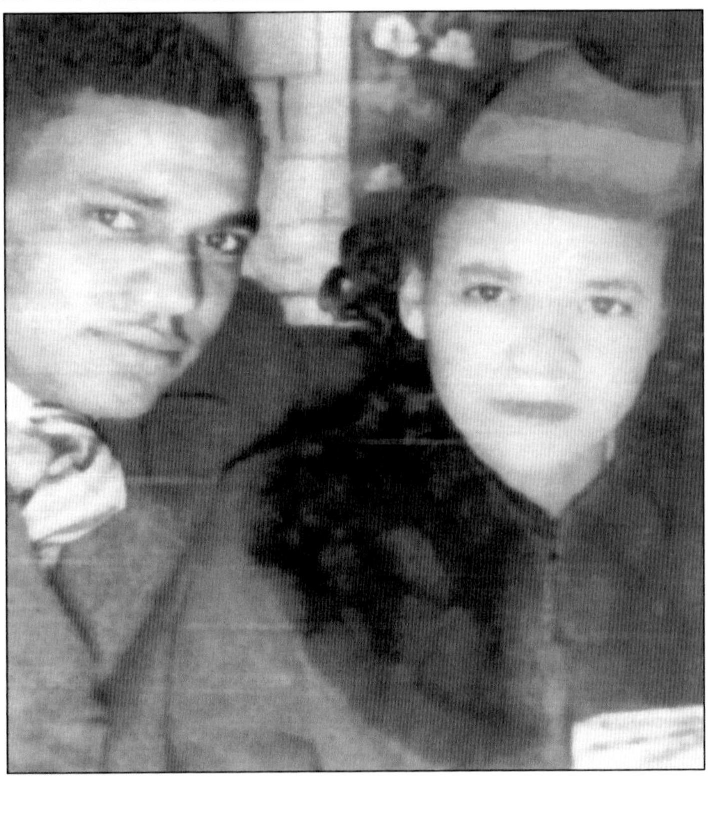

This handsome couple is Willie and Olliebell Jones. Willie "Buck" Jones started Jones Landscaping Company in 1955 while helping to clear land in Washington Park. He employed up to five men on his payroll, and the business lasted until the 1980s. Jones did not have the benefit of formal education, but he made a good living landscaping lawns, laying sidewalks, paving driveways, and building garages. (Olliebell Jones.)

Pictured here is Thomas Henry Robinson (1882–1957), grandfather of Olliebell Jones. Robinson helped to build the famous Market Inn, located on Piney Road. (Olliebell Jones.)

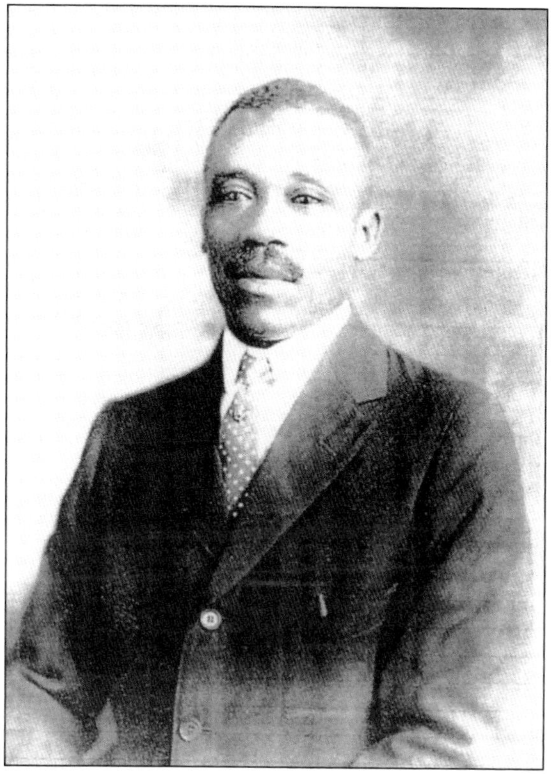

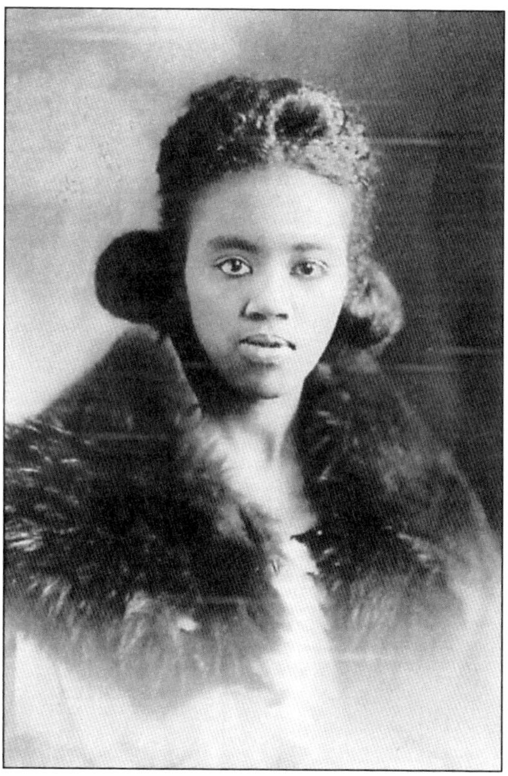

Ethel Braxton Pitts (1899–2003), of Salem, Virginia, was the daughter of Notie Anderson and George W. Braxton. She married Deacon Leonard Pitts and had one daughter and four sons: Hazel, Leonard Jr., Warren, Ethan, and William. A gifted seamstress, she studied at Christiansburg Institute in Christiansburg, Virginia, and Hartshorn Memorial College. She taught sewing for the department of recreation and parks and was an 80-year member of St. John Baptist Church. (Ethan Pitts Sr.)

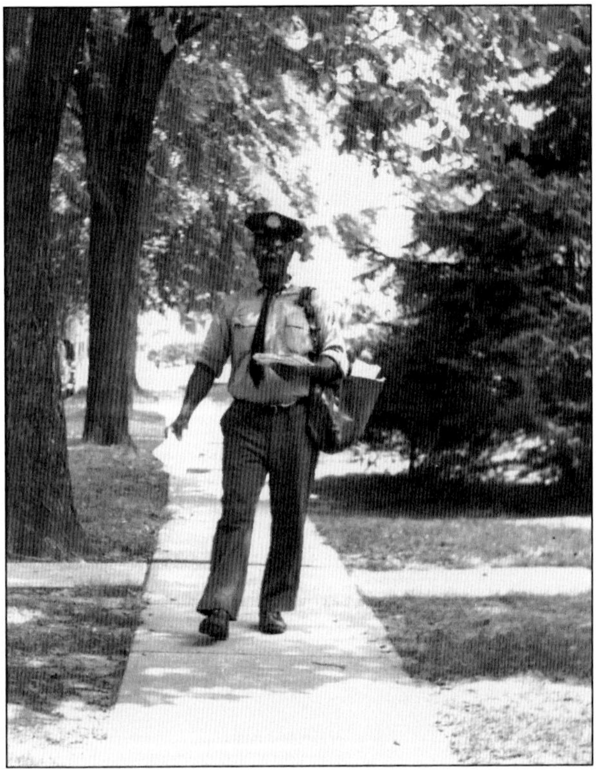

This is Leonard Oneal Pitts Sr. (1890–1971), son of Andrew and Eliza Fleming Pitts of the Westwood community. He married Ethel Braxton in 1920 when he was discharged from the army. He worked for the U.S. Postal Service as a mail carrier for 31 years and retired in 1959. The Pitts celebrated their 50-year wedding anniversary in 1970. Pitts maintained his membership at Westwood Baptist Church, where his funeral was held. (Ethan Pitts Sr.)

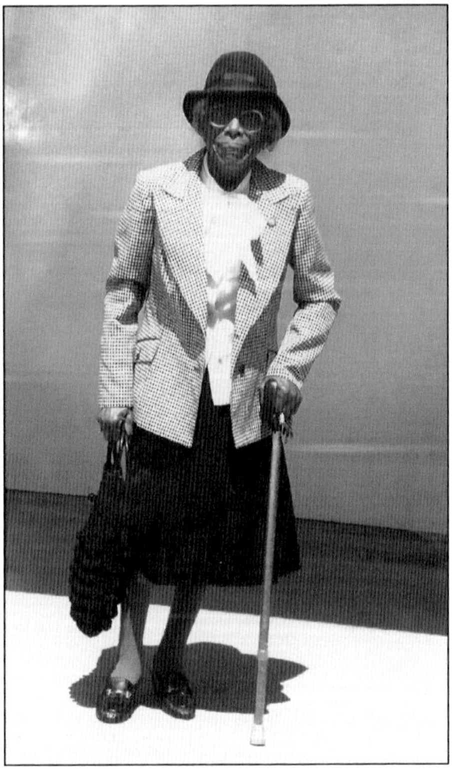

Shown here is Beatrice Brown Quarles, who was born in 1906 in Wynnsboro, North Carolina, and died in 2002 at the age of 96. She married Albert "Ratt" Quarles, and they lived on Piney Road. She worked for the Wilcox family for 27 years and was sexton at St. John Baptist Church for over 20 years. (Mary R. Cooper.)

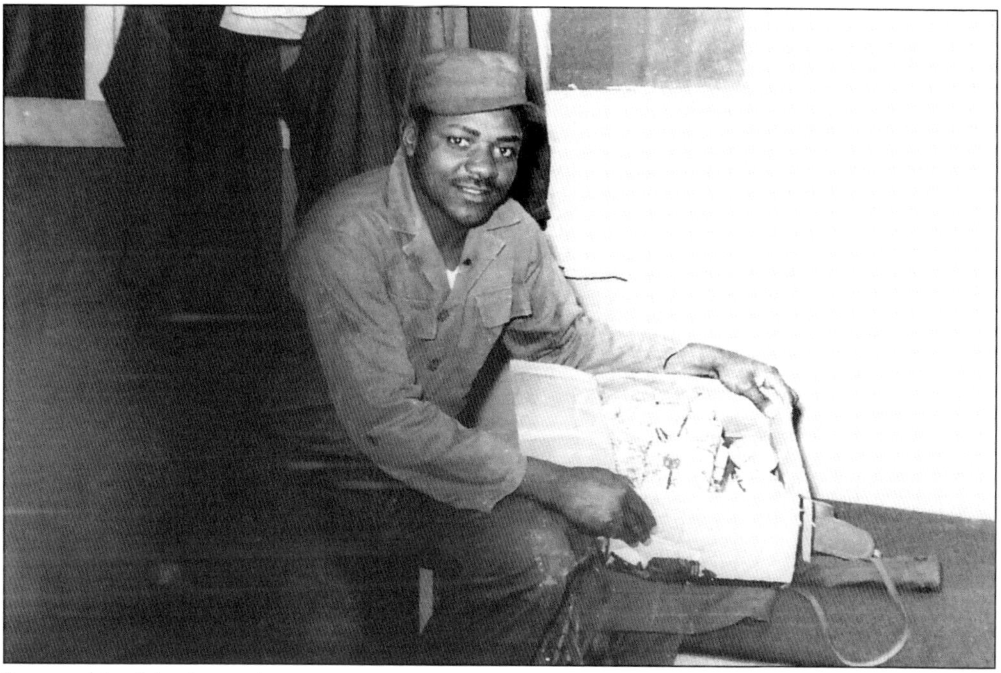

Featured in this picture is Roosevelt Harrison Jr., who was born in February 1930. He served as a corporal in the U.S. Army during the Korean War from 1951 to 1953. He formed his own business, Roosevelt Construction Company, in 1960, where he worked for 41 years until his death in 2001. (Annie Harrison.)

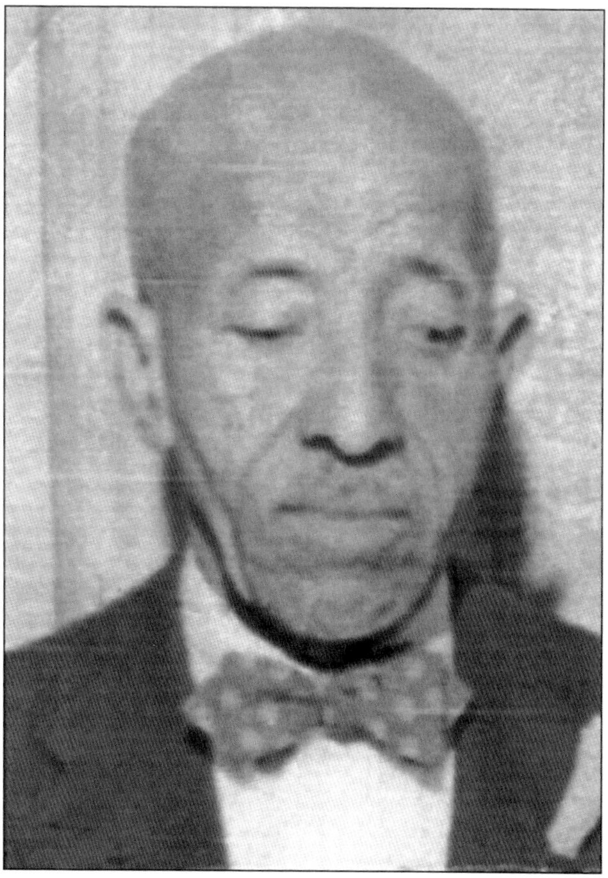

Deacon Harvey H. Johnson (1887–1974), born to Lavinia Claiborne and Virginius T. Johnson in Henrico County, was one of seven children residing on Strawberry Farm as tenant farmers. He married Janie Johnson and taught music at Prof. George Howell's music studio and at Hampton Institute, his alma mater. (Harriet Henderson Gilchrist.)

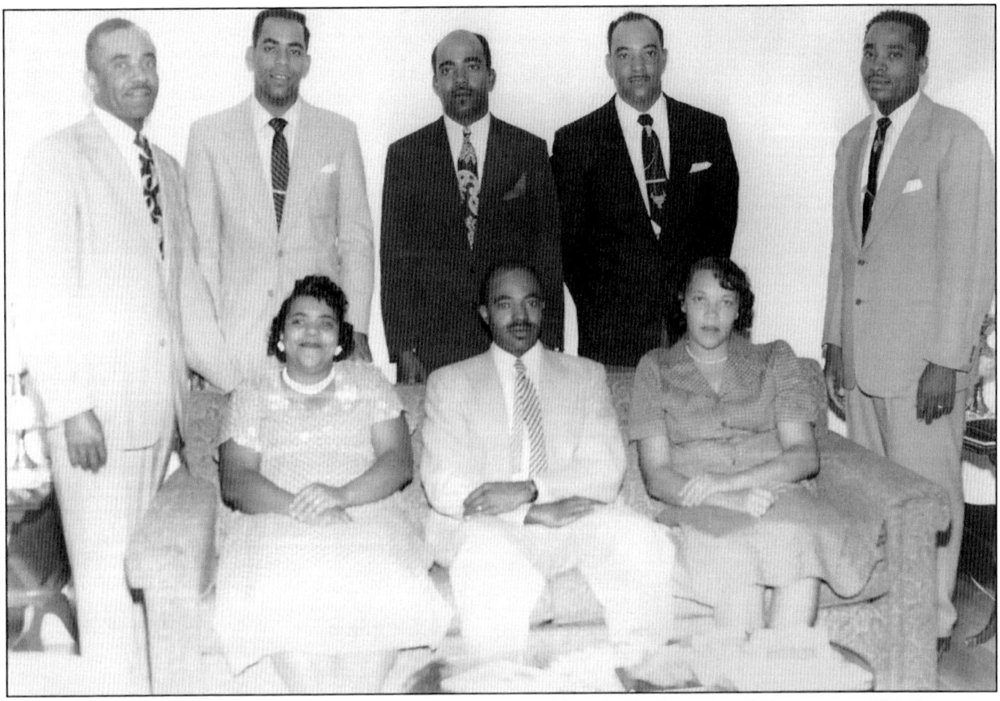

These are the eight children of Hezekiah and Betty Hubbard of Cheatwood Avenue in Washington Park. The siblings (order unknown) were Hezekiah, Ulysses, Ernest, Daniel, William, Lawrence, Ruth, and Helen. (Mable D. Hubbard.)

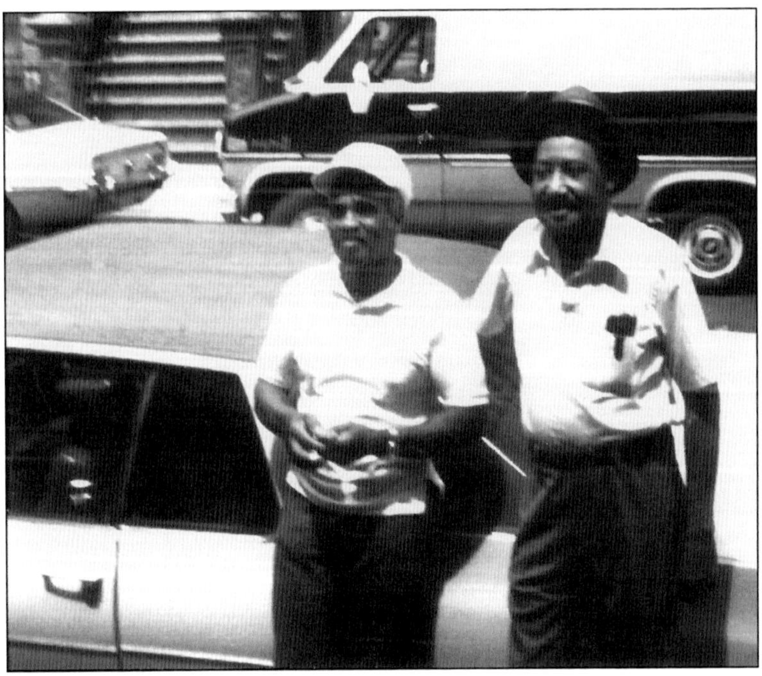

Pictured here are James Washington Jr. (left) and his father, James Washington Sr. The Washingtons are descendants of the Randolph Town community and have worked to keep the memory of that community alive. (James Washington Jr.).

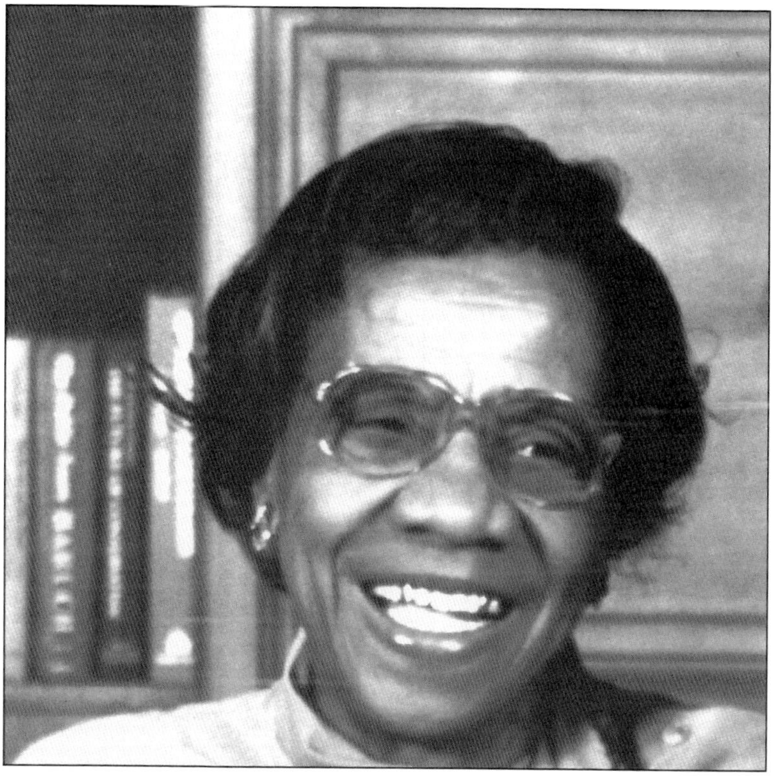

Seen here is Mary Saunders Washington, mother of James Washington Jr. and also a descendant of the Randolph Town community. (James Washington Jr.)

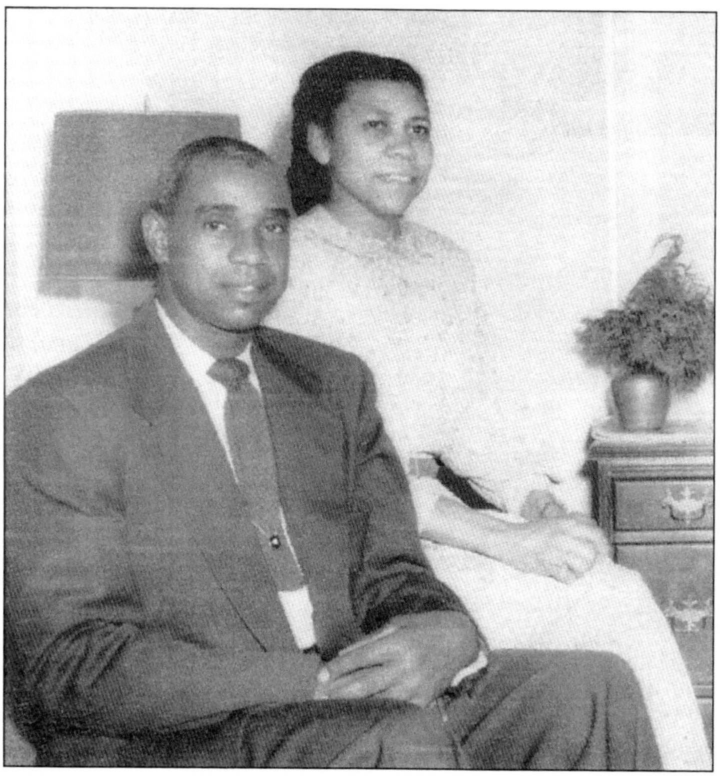

In this photograph are William and Angie Haskins Hawkes. Angie (1906–2007) was born in the Gravel Hill community to Charlie and Bettie Haskins and was baptized at Gravel Hill Church. The Hawkeses lived in the Washington Park community and were active at St. John Baptist Church. (Margaret H. Brown.)

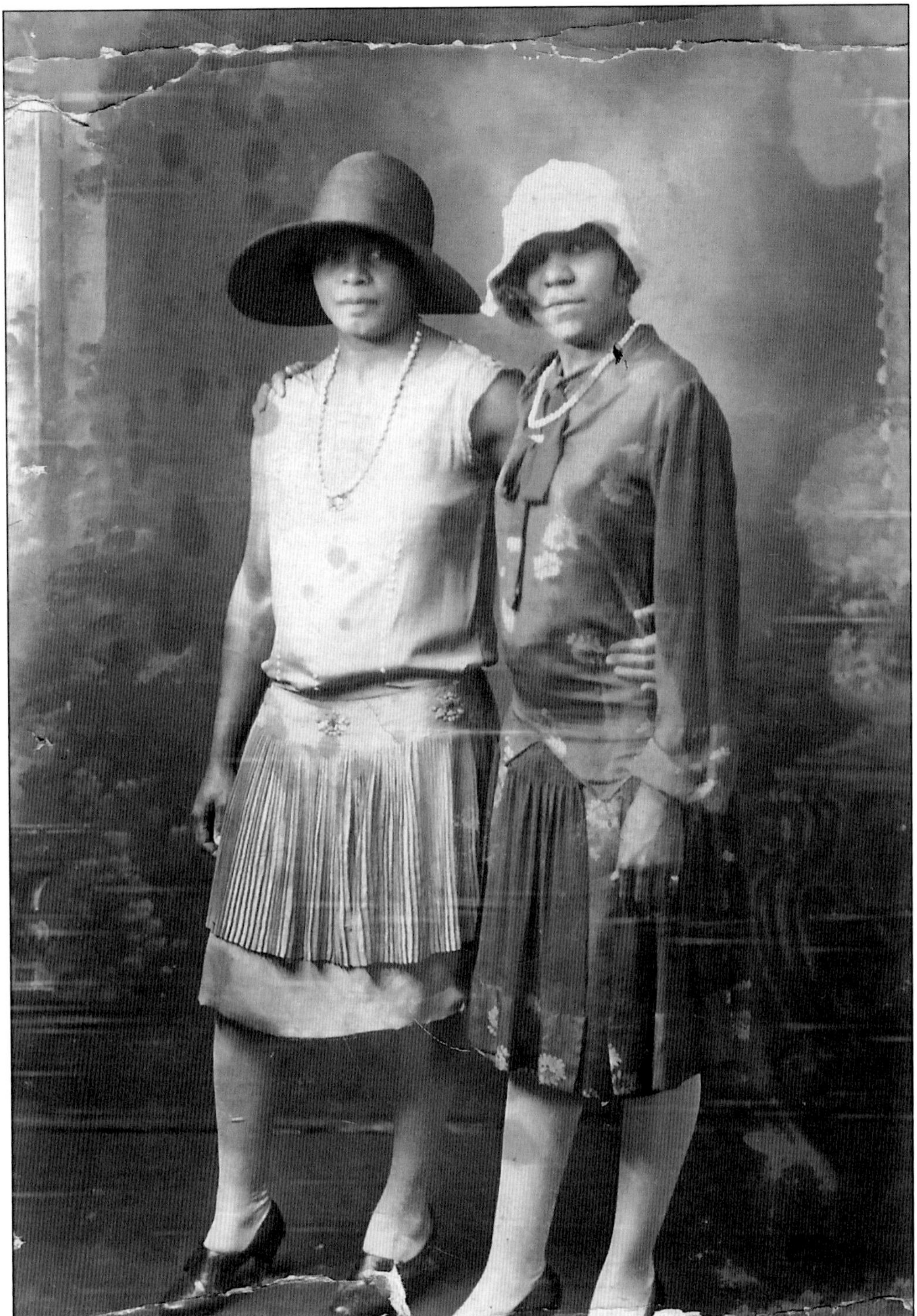

This is a picture of two stylish ladies in the 1920s. Allie (last name unknown) is pictured with Angie Haskins (at right). (Margaret H. Brown.)

Six

WESTWOOD

Another older community, originally called Westwood Village, dates back to June 10, 1870. It is reported that many founders of this community came from nearby plantations and other plantations in Virginia. After the Emancipation Proclamation in 1863, many enslaved persons were allowed to leave their plantations and come to this place.

The 1870 census showcases family names such as Carter, Coles, Holmes, Leecost, Lewis, Nixon, Parrish, Pemberton (Pendleton), Phillips, Robinson, Twine, and Warrick. The 1880 census reveals new names, indicating that more people had settled in the area: Barbour, Brown, Corbin, Lee, Martin, Peebles, Pitts, Price, Simmons, Warden, White, Winston, and Woodson. The Westwood community is located in the 5400 block of Patterson Avenue and is enclosed by Dunbar Street to the east and Glenburnie Road to the west. The one square block that is Westwood has nestled a small conclave of hardworking, progressive descendants of former enslaved and free persons.

There were members of the community who felt the need to assemble for bible study and the preached word. In 1872, they gathered at the residence of Robert Pemberton (Pendleton) in a log cabin, according to his great-great-granddaughter Jean Curtis. This group included Watt Parrish, Robert Pemberton, Robert Barber, George Holmes Sr., Charles Carter, and Charles Warrick. These men helped establish Westwood Baptist Church on Glenburnie Avenue in 1876. Three trustees—Nelson Parrish, John Price, and Andrew Young—secured the deed to a half-acre of land for $25 in August 1876, and they built Westwood Colored Baptist Church. The first pastor was Rev. George Daggett of Georgia. The cemetery was established in the rear of church. Although the headstones have been removed, the remains are still there.

The community grew and became established with the construction of the church and the creation of organizations and associations. In 1900, Westwood School was developed where the community playground now sits on Marian Street. Some teachers were M. L. Allen, Amanda Nixon, S. G. F. Holmes, and Ethel C. Holmes. Westwood School closed in 1948, as Henrico County allowed Richmond to annex the community. In the 1940s, the city wanted to rezone the community and develop it into a park. Many community leaders organized to defend Westwood. Rev. Alfred M. Waller, pastor from 1945 to 1948, spoke at a court hearing, as did civic leader Rev. W. L. Ransome and Dr. B. H. Martin, a white medical doctor. Westwood won the court case and prevented the development of the community into a park. During 1946 to 1948, mayor Horace Edwards was instrumental in getting city water, sewage, and streetlights for Westwood.

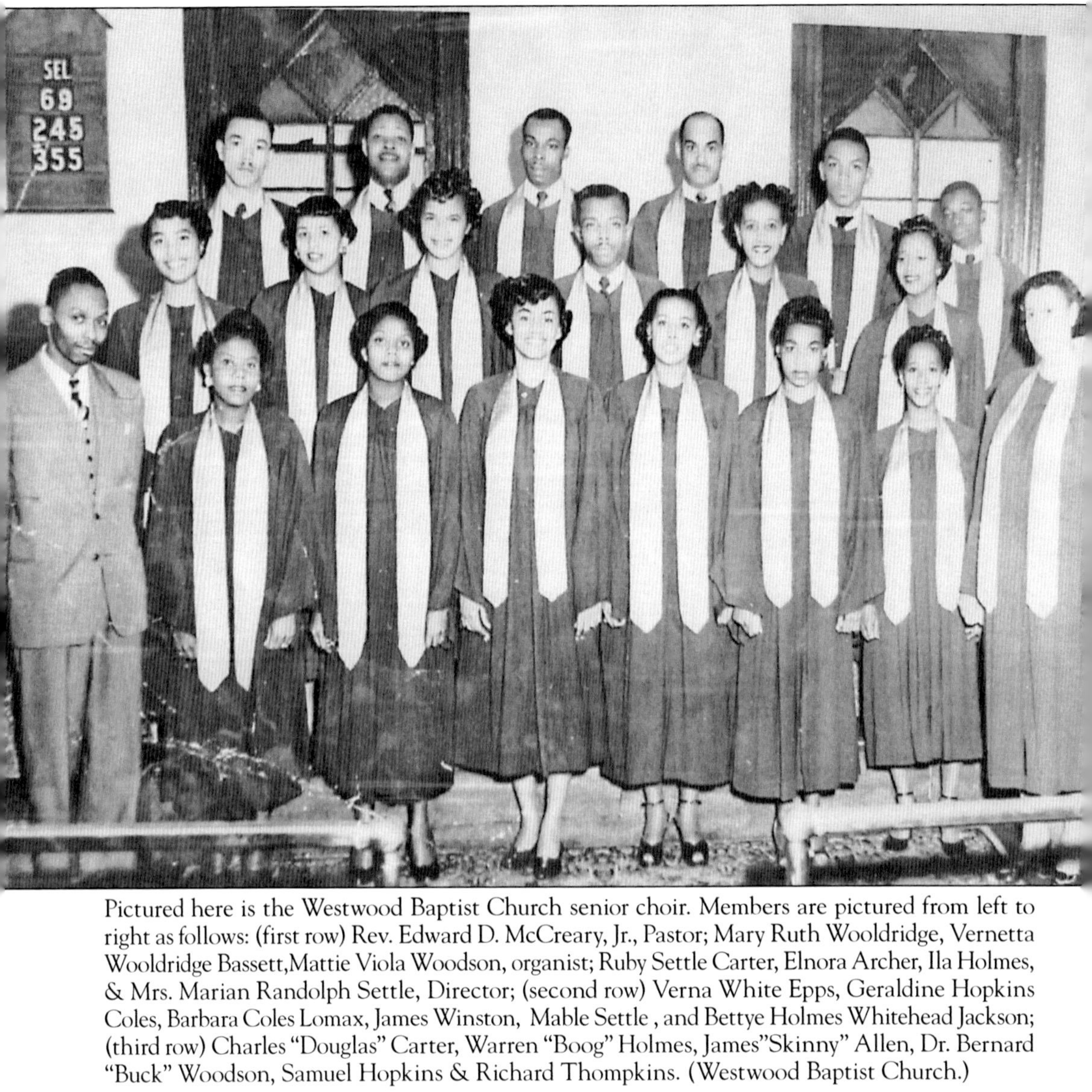

Pictured here is the Westwood Baptist Church senior choir. Members are pictured from left to right as follows: (first row) Rev. Edward D. McCreary, Jr., Pastor; Mary Ruth Wooldridge, Vernetta Wooldridge Bassett,Mattie Viola Woodson, organist; Ruby Settle Carter, Elnora Archer, Ila Holmes, & Mrs. Marian Randolph Settle, Director; (second row) Verna White Epps, Geraldine Hopkins Coles, Barbara Coles Lomax, James Winston, Mable Settle , and Bettye Holmes Whitehead Jackson; (third row) Charles "Douglas" Carter, Warren "Boog" Holmes, James"Skinny" Allen, Dr. Bernard "Buck" Woodson, Samuel Hopkins & Richard Thompkins. (Westwood Baptist Church.)

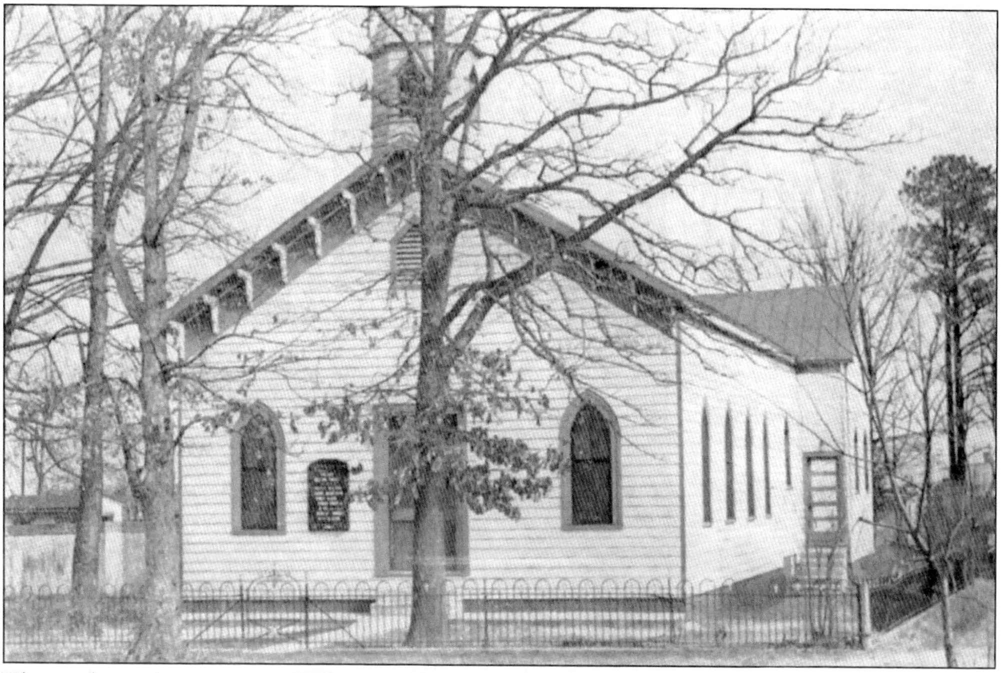

This is the early structure of Westwood Baptist Church, organized in 1874. Its style is reflective of the architecture of many churches structured in the late 19th century. Early parishioners recall being baptized in Jordan's Branch on Staples Mill Road. (Westwood Baptist Church.)

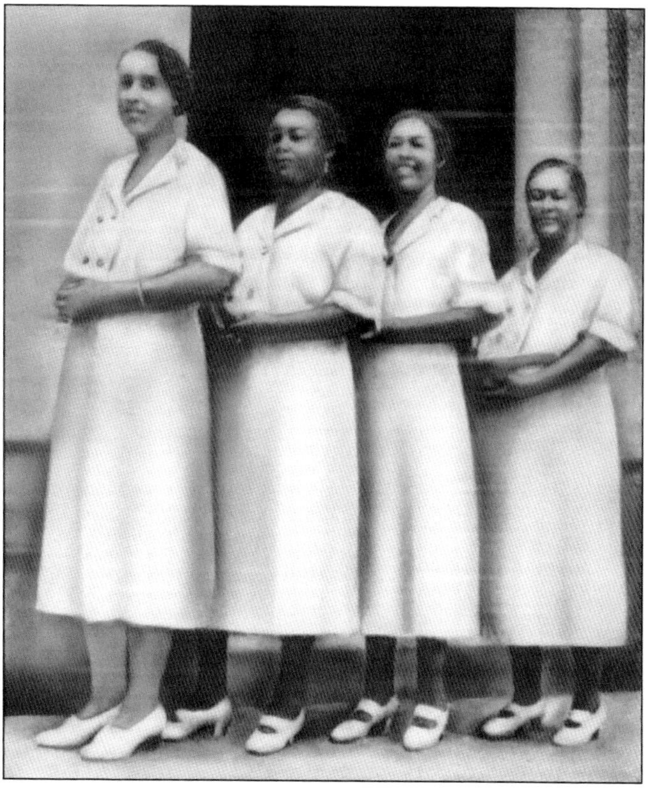

These are the singers of the renowned Westwood Female Quartet, who made history from 1933 to 1945 as one of the first female quartets to become famous for their outstanding musical ability. They are, from left to right, Marian Randolph Settle (manager and operatic soprano), Hattie Henderson (secretary and second soprano), Rebecca Coles White Henderson (treasurer and contralto soprano), and Ethel Coles Holmes (president and second contralto). Lorene Strause was the first accompanist, and Lillian Phyllis Randolph Dance was the second accompanist. Andrew Henderson provided transportation for the group. (Billy Randolph.)

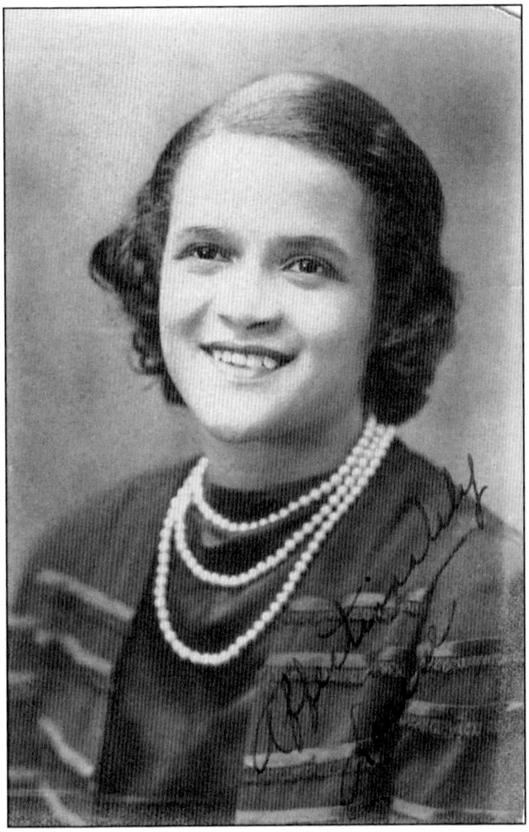

Naomi Lorene Strause Seay Plummer, born and raised in Westwood on Glenburnie Street, was the first accompanist to the Westwood Female Quartet. She also enlisted in one of the first black WAAC (Women's Army Auxiliary Corps) units during segregation, retiring in 1968. (Billy Randolph.)

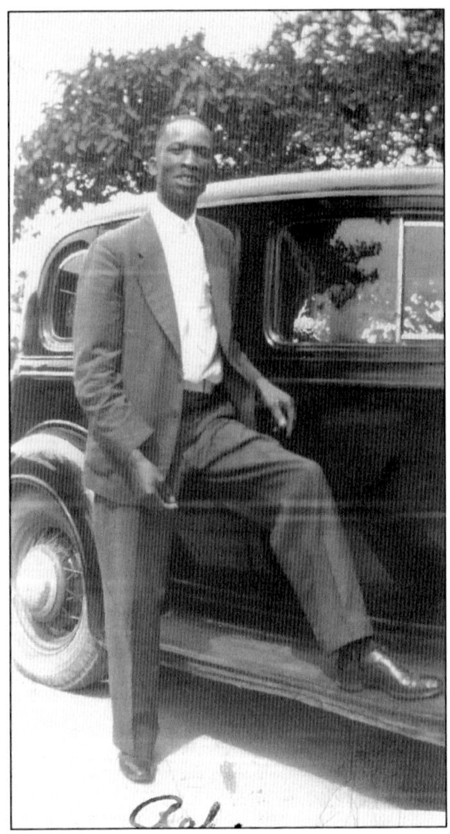

Pictured here, Rev. G. A. Boykins was the business manager for the Westwood Female Quartet and later provided transportation for the group. His wife, Kathleen, taught English at Maggie L. Walker High School. (Billy Randolph.)

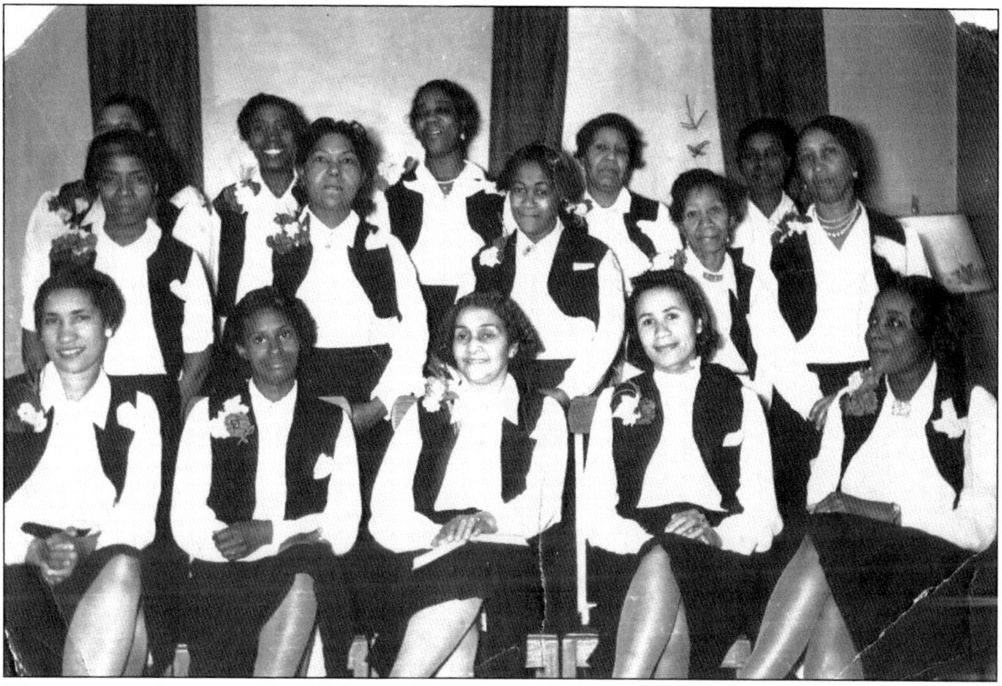

This picture taken around 1945 shows the Westwood Thrifty Club (a savings club). Members are pictured from left to right as follows: (first row) Geneva Liggons, Hester Allen, Lennie Anderson, Inez Taylor, and Lizzie Courtney; (second row) Julia Allen, Eva White, Ethel Homes, Betty Holmes, and Janie Twine; (third row) Elsie Barbour, Grace Leecost, Annie Courtney, Lillie Holmes, and Pauline Robinson. (Nora "Sister" Liggons Hopkins.)

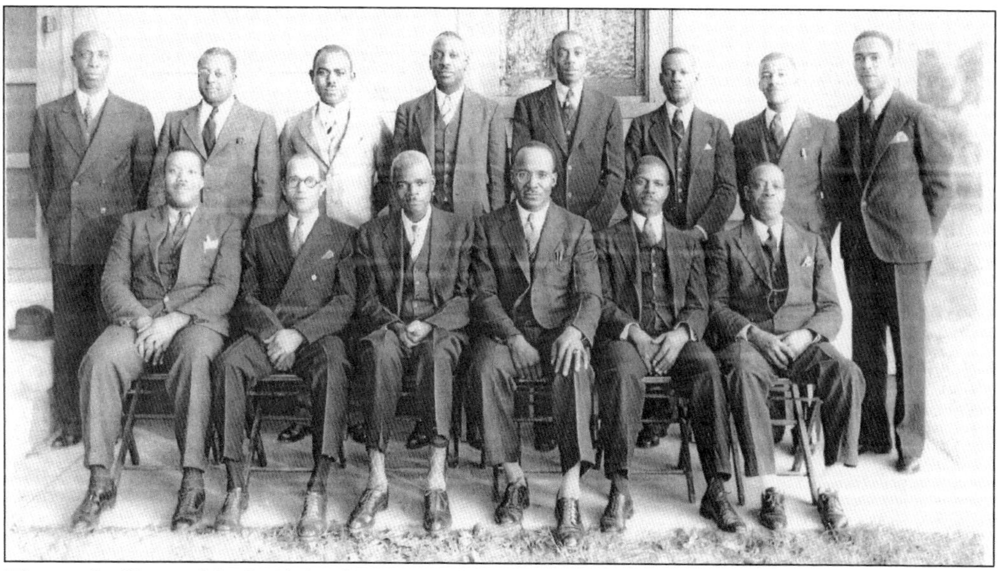

This is the Young Men's Club of Westwood, a civic and social organization, around 1938. The following members are shown from left to right: (first row) Walter Wooldridge, Eddie White, Wesley Smith, Arthur Flournoy, Joe Cephas, and Oscar Holmes; (second row) Phillip Winston, Kenneth Robertson, James Johnston Sr., Ulysses Smith, Andrew Henderson, Leonard Warden Sr., Frank Anderson Sr., and Louis White. (Lennie Anderson Thornton.)

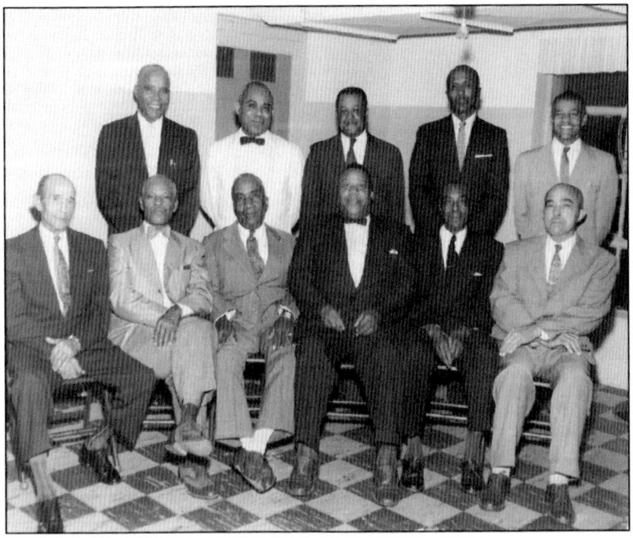

This is the Westwood Men's Club around 1945 in the fellowship hall of Westwood Baptist Church. This is an older group of the Young Men's Club of Westwood. The following members are shown from left to right: (first row) Eddie White, Leonard Warden Sr., Edward Woodson, Walter Wooldridge, Andrew Henderson, and Samuel Burleigh Jr.; (second row) Eddie Flournoy, James Johnston Sr., Kenneth Robertson, Isaac "Ike" Williams, and Frank Anderson Sr. (Ruth Truman Winston.)

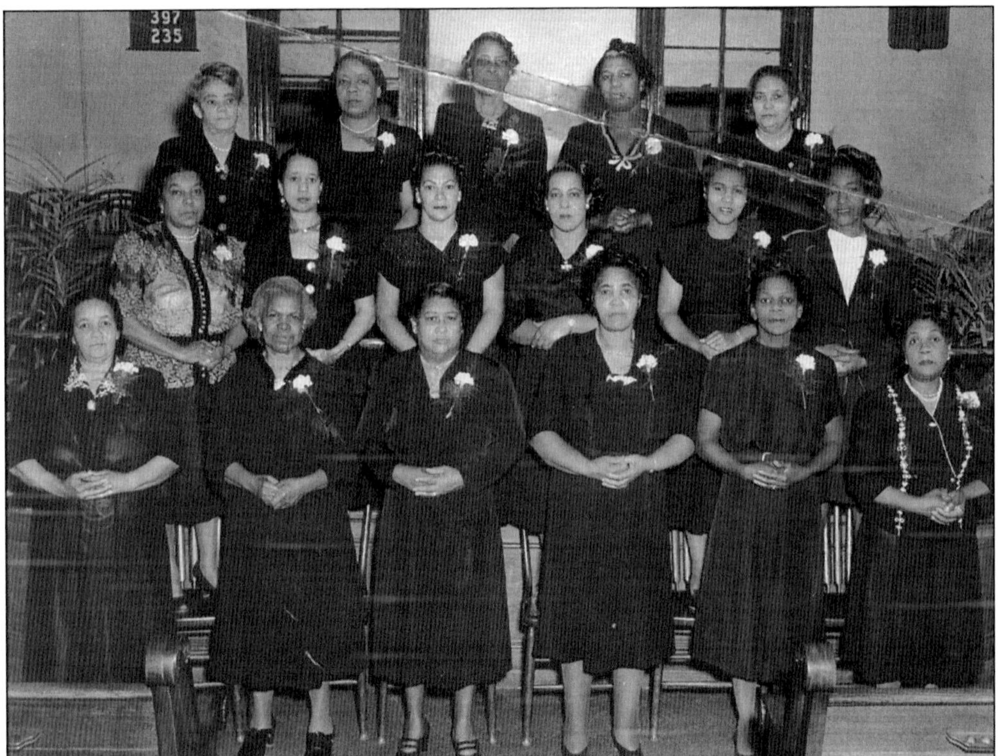

This photograph of the Young Women's Club of Westwood was taken around 1930 at Westwood Baptist Church. The following members are shown from left to right: (first row) Henrietta R. Strause, Betty Warden Parrish, Sarah Carter Warden, Rebecca Coles White Henderson, Ruth Smith Wooldridge, and Berta Woodson; (second row) Clara Moss White, Helen Johnston, unidentified, Lucy Parrish Anderson, Martha Price, and Elaine Anderson Robertson; (third row) Emma Bradford Woodson, Paige Flournoy, unidentified, Bessie Price Corbin, and Jimmy Cunningham. (Lennie A. Thornton.)

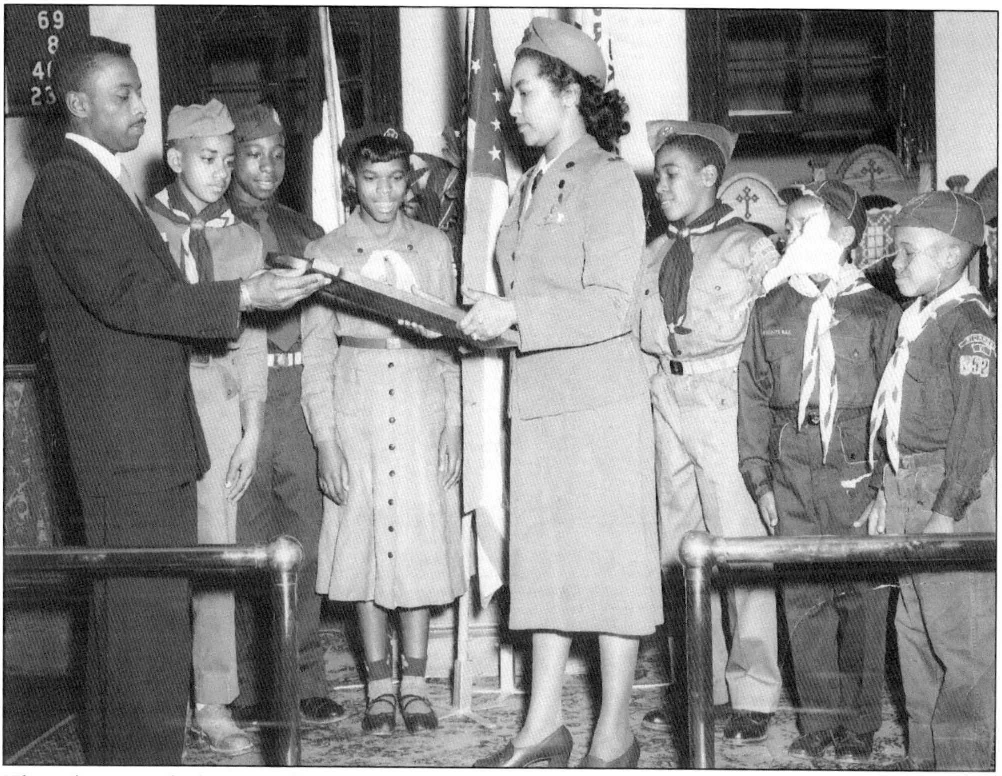

This photograph features the Scouting tradition in Westwood. Henrietta Green from Scout headquarters is giving a plaque to troop leader James "Sonny" Winston. Scouts featured from left to right are Abbot Lambert, Ronald White, Hazel Barbour, Frank Anderson Jr., Leon Robertson, and John Pretlow. Henrietta A. Green earned a bachelor's degree from Virginia Union University and a master's of education from Virginia Commonwealth University. She worked with the Scouts and Richmond public schools for 22 years. (Franceno A. Diggs.)

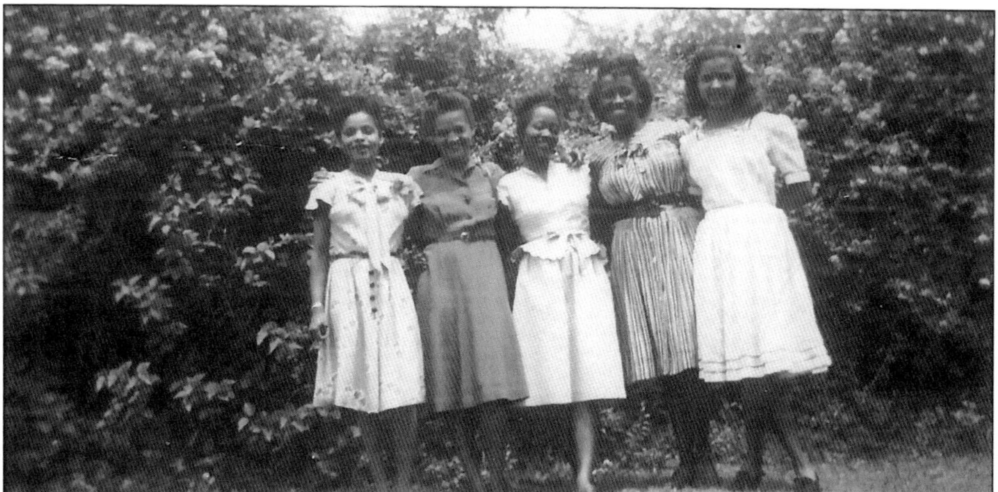

This picture features "The Debs of Westwood" in the 1930s. These were five of Westwood's prettiest young ladies. From left to right are an unidentified young woman, N. Lorene Strause, Bettye Holmes, Mable Settle, and Odessa Cunningham. (Billy Randolph.)

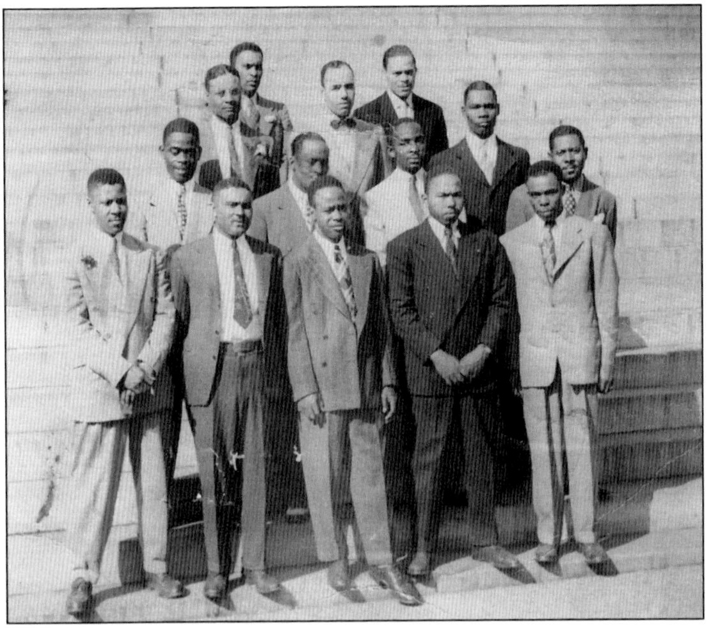

This photograph taken around 1950 shows the handsome young men who made up the first Count's Club. From left to right are the following members: (first row) Warren Holmes, Alvin Anderson, Oscar Holmes, Ernest White, and James Allen; (second row) Ernest Giles, Leonard Warden Jr., Abe Feldon, and Samuel Byrd; (third row) Monroe Nixon, Tommy Jones, and Delaware Giles; (fourth row) Edwin Price and Freddie Fleming. (Lavinia H. Dabney.)

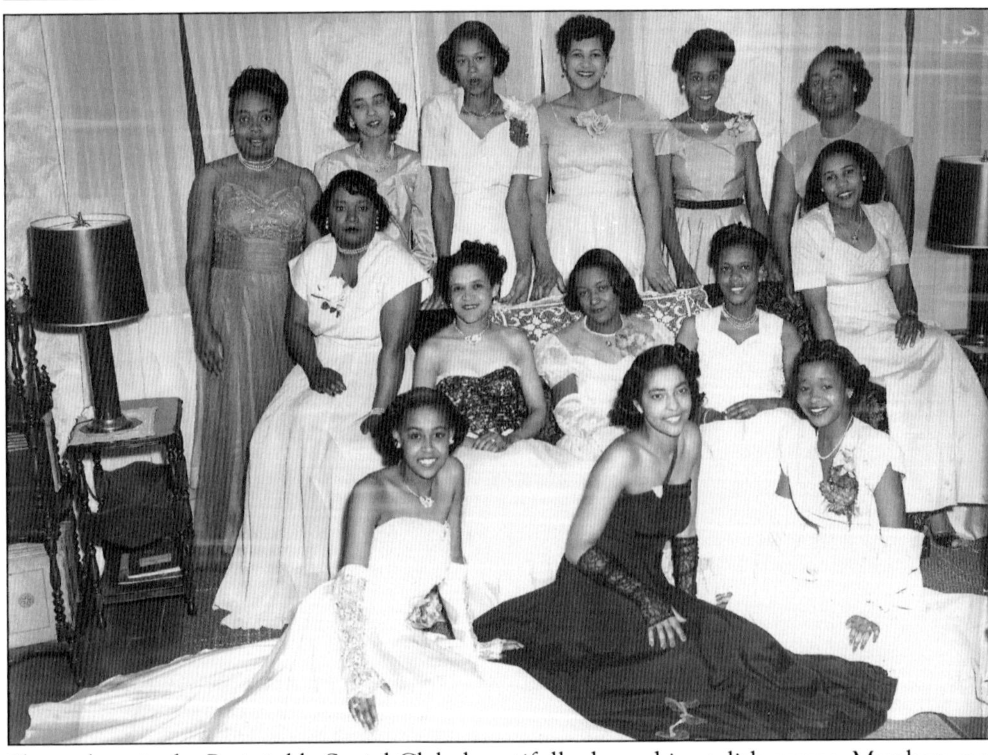

Shown here is the Periwinkle Social Club, beautifully dressed in stylish gowns. Members met monthly from house to house, enjoying good company and playing cards with one another. From left to right are the following members: (first row) Ruby Settle Carter, Henrietta Anderson, and Bettye Holmes; (second row) Nannie Warden, Naomi Lorene Strause, Lucille Warden Loving, Minnie Fountain Holmes, and Martha Price; (third row) Susie Truman, Wilhelmina Warden, Lucy Woodson, Marilyn Cunningham, Mable Settle, and Isabelle Giles. (Bettye H. Jackson.)

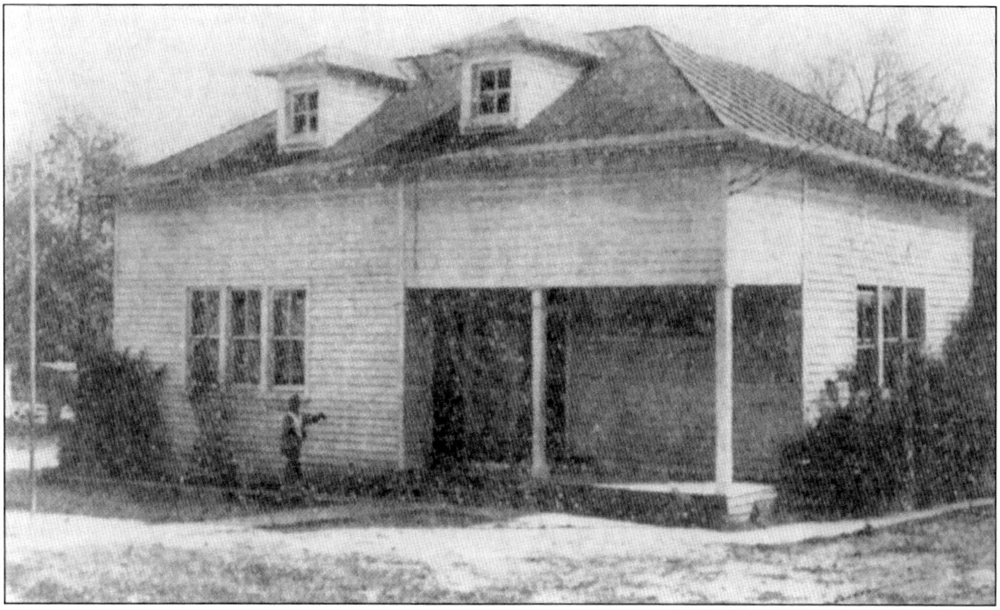

This is Westwood Elementary School, located on Leonard Street (now Marian Street), which educated the African American children of the community. (Lennie A. Thornton.)

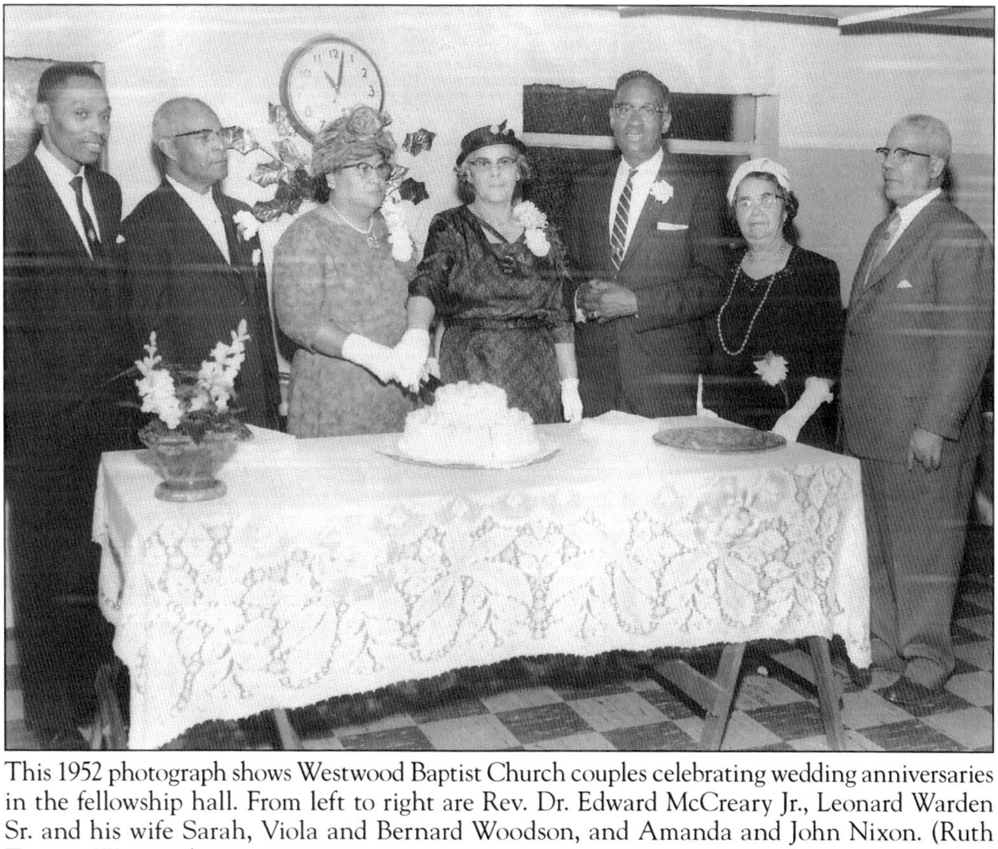

This 1952 photograph shows Westwood Baptist Church couples celebrating wedding anniversaries in the fellowship hall. From left to right are Rev. Dr. Edward McCreary Jr., Leonard Warden Sr. and his wife Sarah, Viola and Bernard Woodson, and Amanda and John Nixon. (Ruth Truman Winston.)

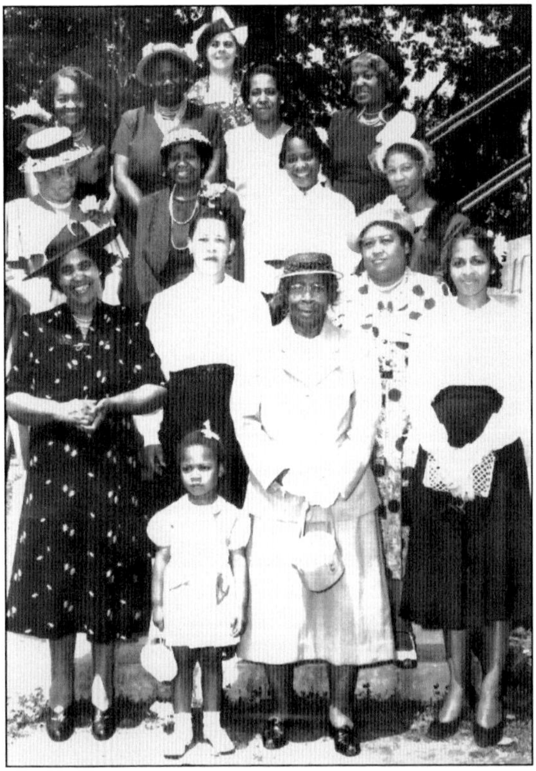

This photograph features the Missionary Society of Westwood Baptist Church. From left to right, they are as follows: (first row) Rebecca Coles Henderson, Daisy Jane Cooper (child), Sabre Pines, and Ethel Buford; (second row) Mary Bibbs Day and Sarah Carter Warden; (third row) Emma Bradford Johnson Woodson, Lillie Holmes, Grace Hopkins, and Martha Bibbs Davenport; (fourth row) Elaine A. Robertson, Berta Turner, Lucy Parrish Anderson, and Sarah Carter; (fifth row) Viola Crump Woodson. (Warrick Taylor Sr.)

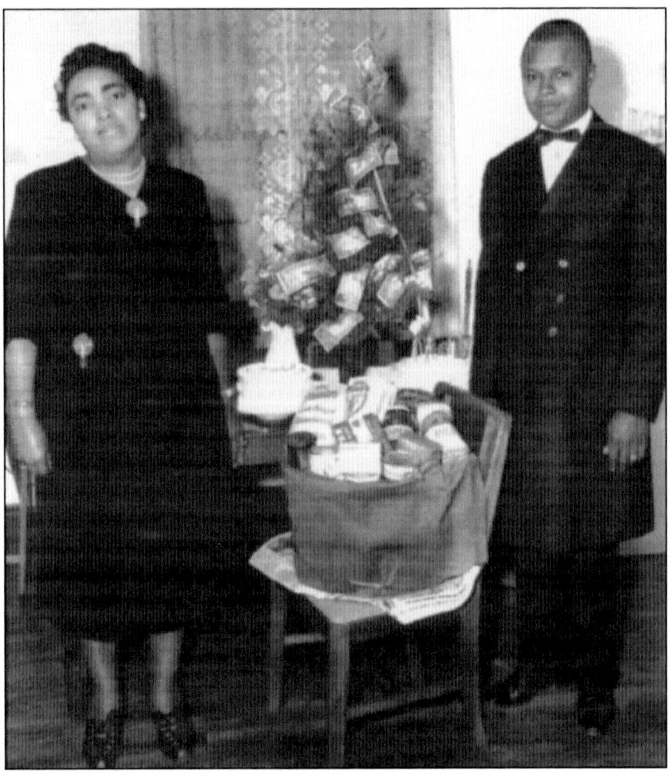

Rev. Albertis and Virginia "Jen" Lewis Mason (from Westwood) are pictured here on their first wedding anniversary. As an anniversary present, the congregation presented the couple with a money tree, a cake, and a tub full of non-perishable food. Note the Domino sugar, Pillsbury flour, and Lipton tea. This is how the church paid a portion of pastors' salaries in the black community. (Abraham Lewis Sr.)

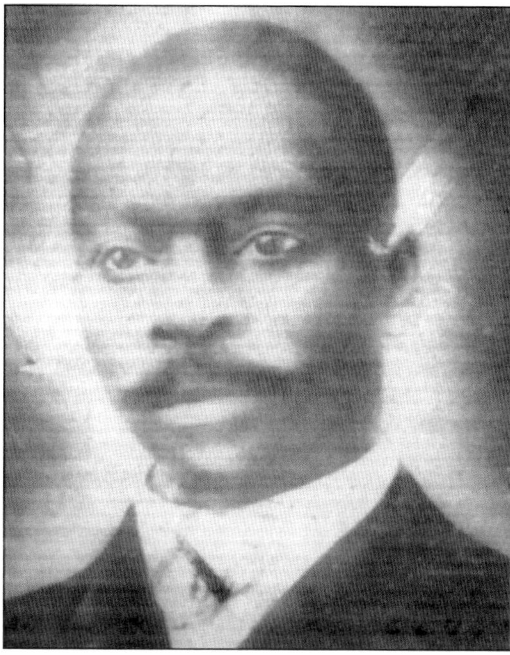

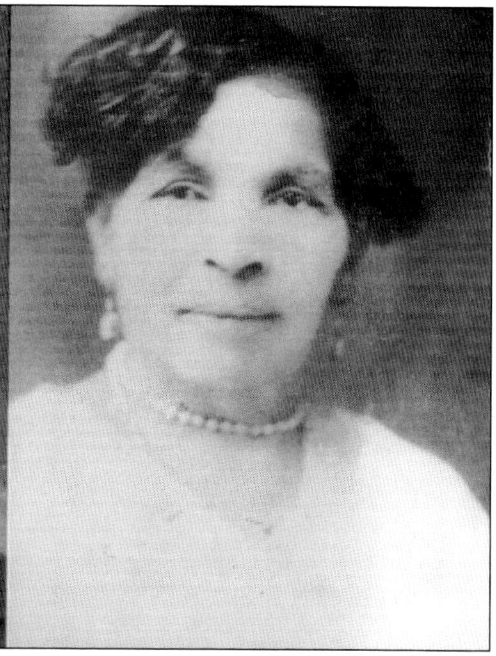

Pictured here are Mary White and Jefferson Lewis Sr. The couple lived at 5310 Marian Street and had five children—Virginia, Ellwood, Althenia, Jefferson Jr., and Abraham. Jefferson Lewis Sr. became a deacon and directed and sang in the choir at Westwood Baptist Church. His wife Mary was a homemaker. (Abraham Lewis Sr.)

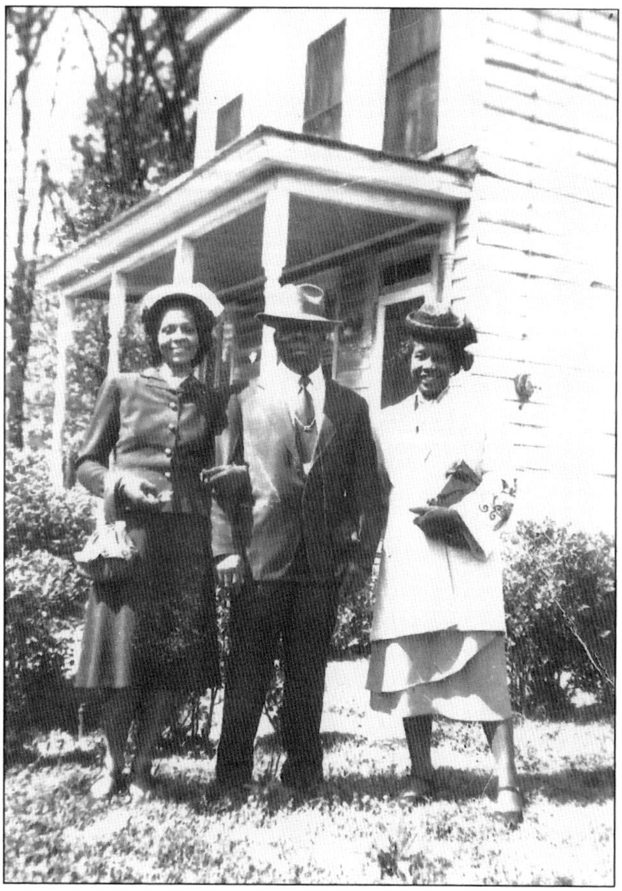

Ethel Turner Lewis Buford (left), Edmund Pemberton, and Grace Hopkins pose in front of Edmund's house on Leonard Street (which later became Marian Street) after Sunday church service. (Kathleen Hopkins Valentine.)

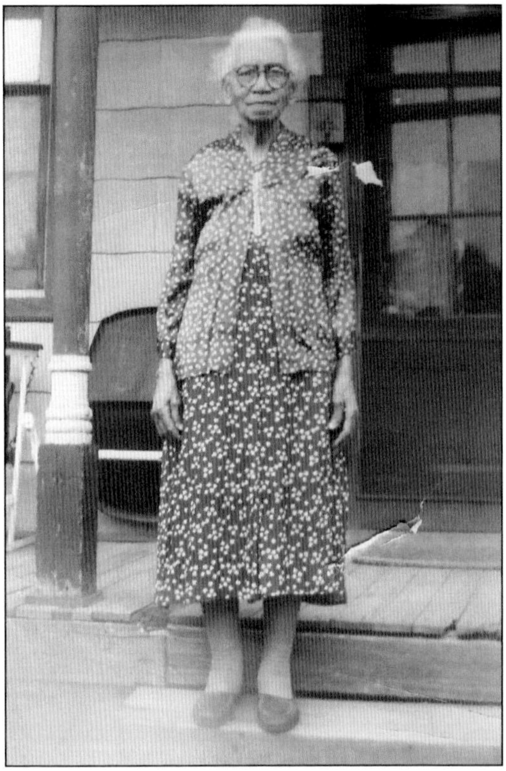

This is Martha Daisy Ford Bibbs (1873–1964), wife of Charles H. Bibbs. She had one sister, Lula Ford McCargo, and two brothers, Peyton Ford and Nelson Ford. Martha worked as a washerwoman, taking in washing from three or four white families. She worked extremely hard, spending long hours bent over a zinc tub using a scrub board. (Marian Davenport.)

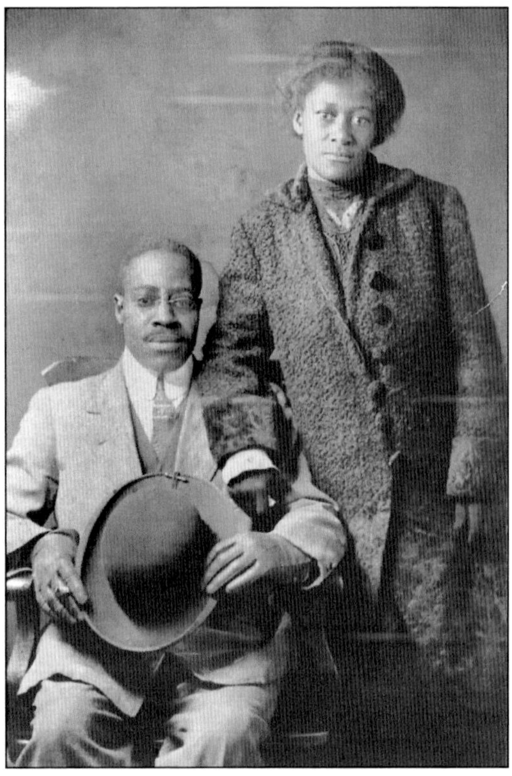

This is Deacon Oscar Warren and Ethel Coles Holmes, both of whom were born in Westwood. Oscar worked for 39 years at Liggett-Meyer Tobacco Company. They lived at 5411 Leonard Street (later Marian Street) and were parents to nine children—Belle, Revelle, Harold, Pernett, Lavinia, Warren, Bettye, Ila, and Oscar. Ethel was the community midwife, sang second contralto alto for 17 years in the Westwood Female Quartet, and took in washing for several white families. (Lavinia H. Dabney.)

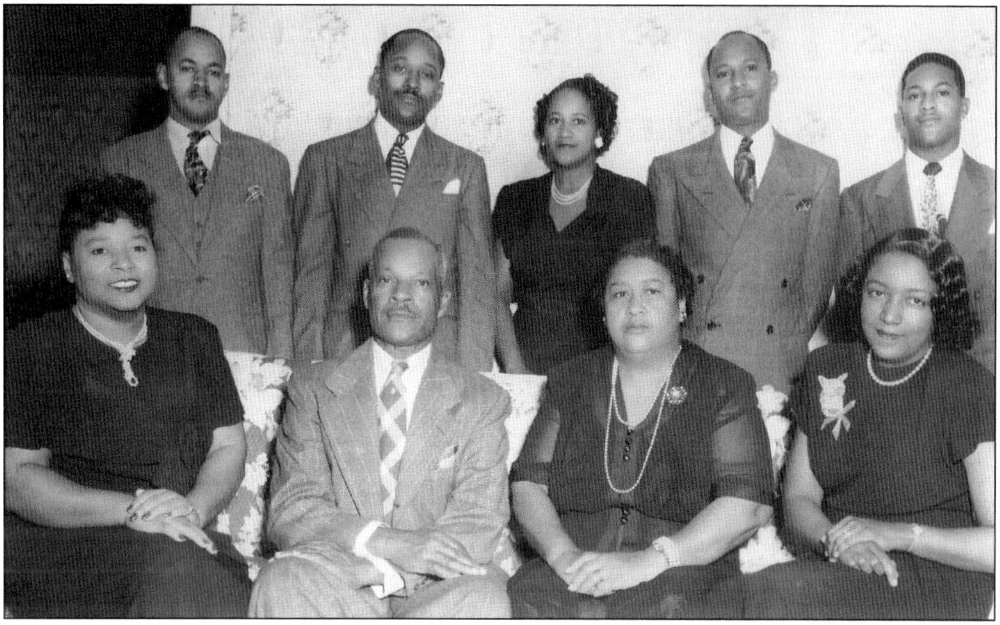

Leonard Warden Sr. would walk through the fields from Glenmore to Zion Town to court Sarah Jane Melinda Carter, the only girl of 14 children born to Albert and Mary Lewis Carter. Leonard Sr. was the son of George and Frances Warden, who settled in Glenmore. Pictured here with their seven children they are, from left to right, as follows: (first row) Nannie, Leonard Sr., Sarah, and Lucille; (second row) Clifford, Leonard Jr., Mary Frances, George, and Albert. (Mary Frances W. Lambert.)

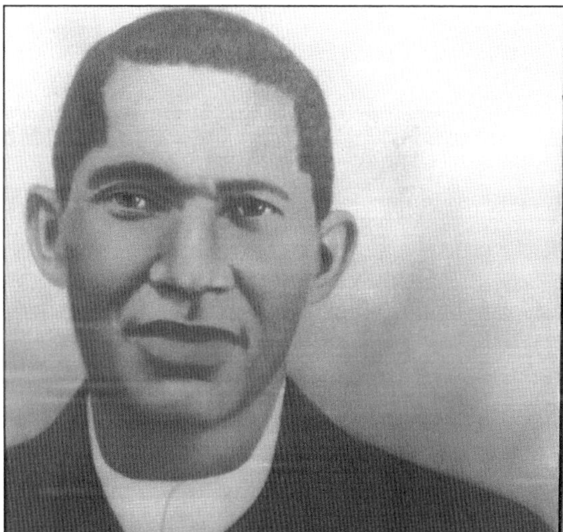

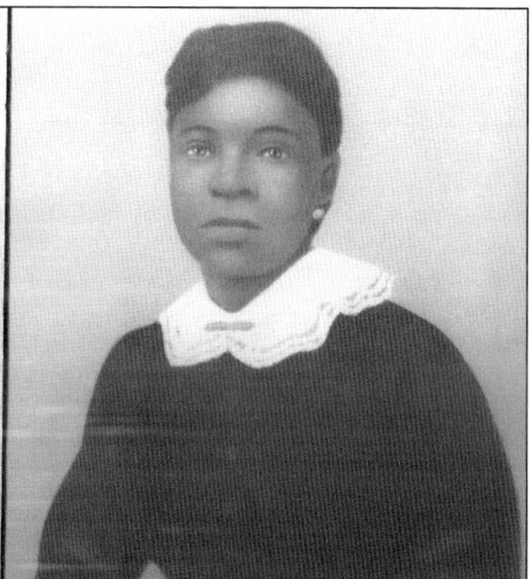

Tucker and Lavinia Price Coles married in 1885. Coles, born 1855, died in the 1920s. He was the son of William and Cordelia Coles. There was a brother named Emmanuel Coles who lived in Varina. Lavinia Price (1864–1913) was the daughter of John Price (1825–1925) and Susan Piper Price (1831–1920). Tucker and Lavinia Coles farmed land and had five children—Willie, Ethel, Rebecca, Harvey, and Cornelius. Upon William Coles's death, Cordelia married Charles Carter. They had one son, Thomas Carter, the half-brother of Tucker and Emmanuel. Thomas Carter, of Westwood, married Emma Pope. (Lavinia H. Dabney.)

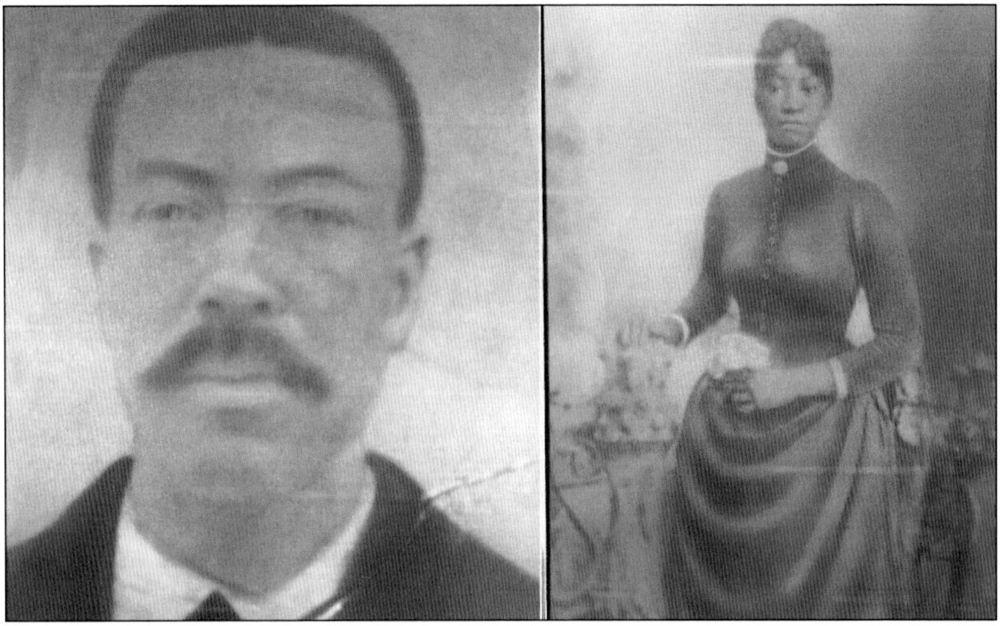

Pictured here are Bettie Thomas and George Warren Holmes Jr. (1867–1921). He was one of the 10 children born to Phoebe and George Holmes Sr. It is unknown when Bettie was born to George and Ellen Swann Thomas, but it is known that she died in 1943. George Jr. and Bettie's five children were Oscar, Lillie Ann, Helen Jane, Caroline, and Milly Holmes. (Helen H. Burrell.)

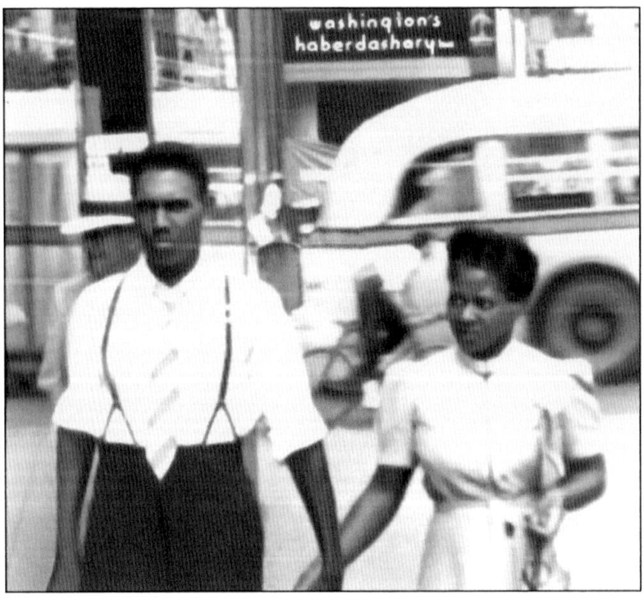

This photograph shows the 1940 elopement of Ernest Adolphus and Lavinia Malyne Holmes Dabney in Washington, D.C. Ernest was born in 1915 in Pryor's Court, an area of Quioccasin. Lavinia (1918–1999) graduated from Armstrong High School and attended Virginia State Normal School for one year. She was lifelong member of Westwood Church, where she sang in the choir and acted as chair of the deaconess board. She established a Girl Scout troop at Quioccasin Church and worked with the NAACP field office. (Ernest A. Dabney.)

Westwood residents would lend their talents to other communities. Beatrice "Bea" Bush was born in Westwood to Dock and Willie Hardy Bush. She married Jack Jackson and moved to Boston, Massachusetts. She had a beautiful contralto voice and studied at the Boston Conservatory of Music. This picture shows her performing in an opera in Boston in 1956. (Betty H. Jackson.)

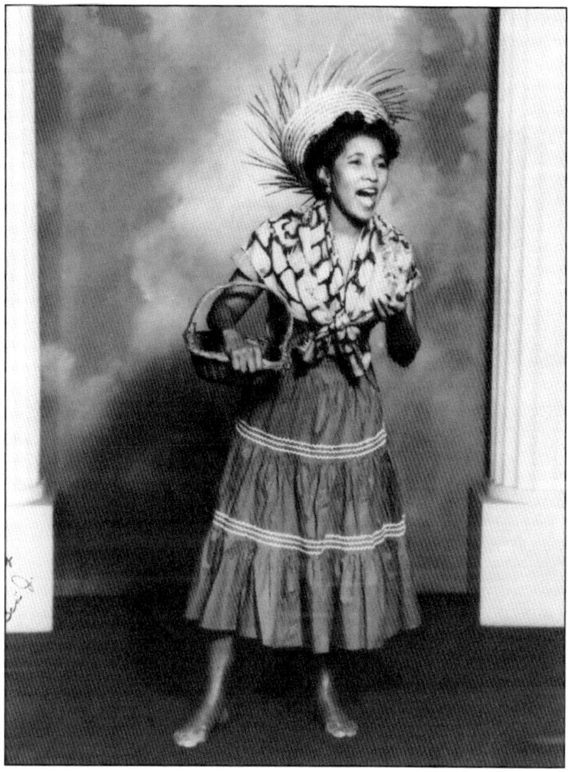

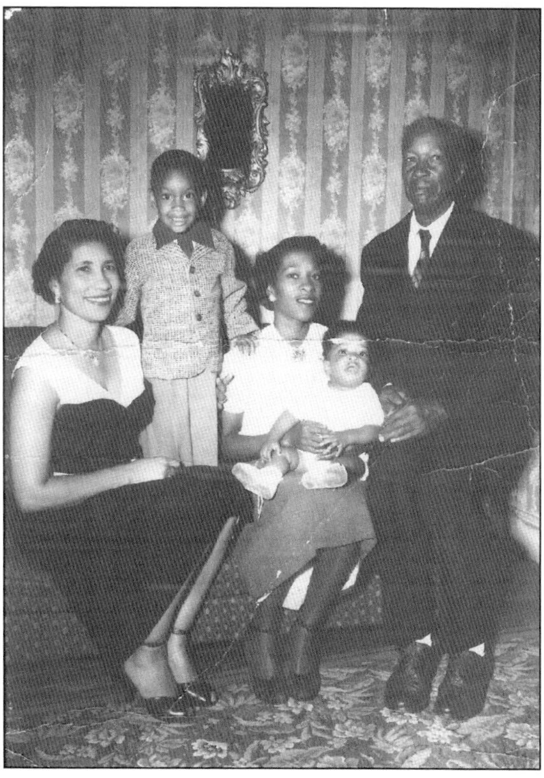

Four generations of the Bush family pose in this photograph from around 1955. Pictured from left to right are Geneva Bush Liggons (an early member of the Westwood Female Quartet), Samuel Hopkins Jr., Nora L. Hopkins, Michael Hopkins, and Dock Bush. Dock worked for the Richmond, Fredericksburg, and Potomac Railroad for over 25 years. Not pictured is Dock's wife Willie Hardy Bush. (Nora L. Hopkins.)

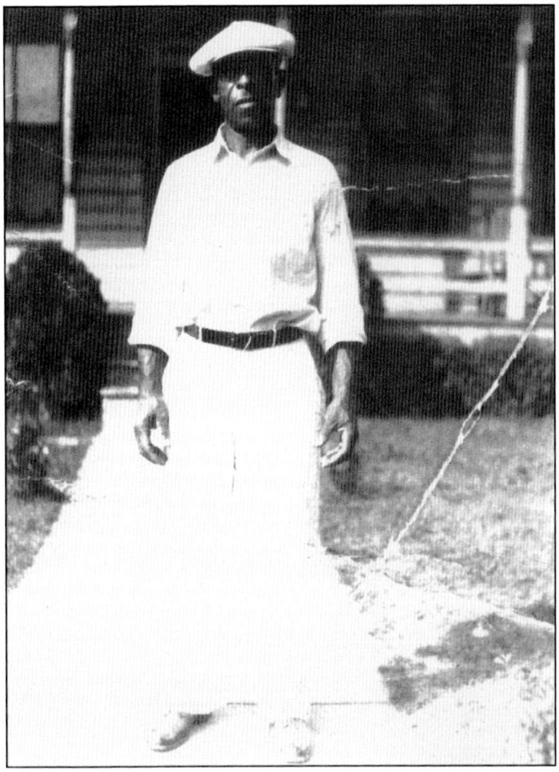

This is Luther Daniel Parrish (1880–1942), son of Nelson and Lucy Jane Holmes Warrick Parrish. Parrish Street is named for their family. Luther Parrish married Bettie Elizabeth Warden in 1900, and they had five children, Shadrach, Meshach, Abednego, George Daniel, and Lucy Jane Parrish. (Lennie A. Thornton.)

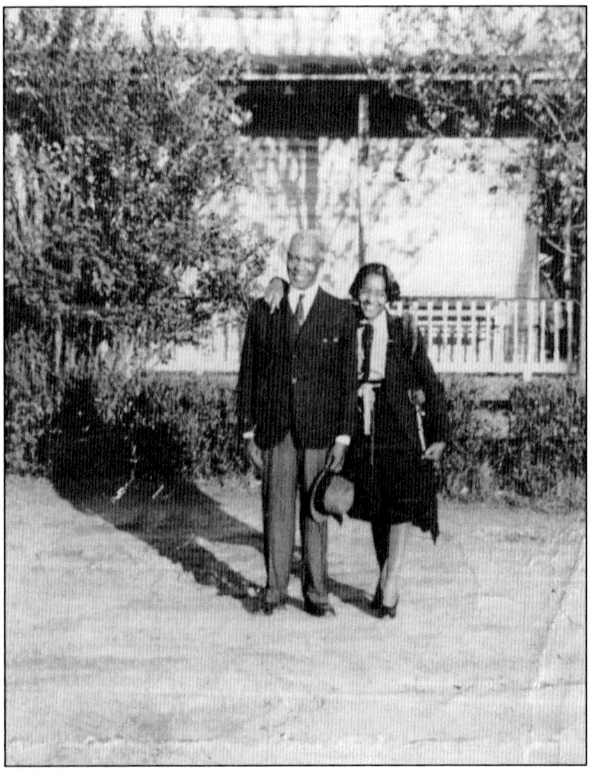

Isham T. "Papa Dooley" Anderson is seen here with his daughter Elaine. He was employed at the Bellwood Defense Plant for the federal government for 26 years. He came to Westwood from the Eastern Shore of Virginia with his wife, Lennie Hoskins Anderson, and their eight children, Marguerite, Frank, Verna, Garland, Elaine, Lucille, Alvin, and Henrietta. Elaine was a deaconess, Girl Scout leader, and sponsor of the Baptist Young People's Union. She was married to Kenneth Robertson. (Verna "Bumpsy" White Epps.)

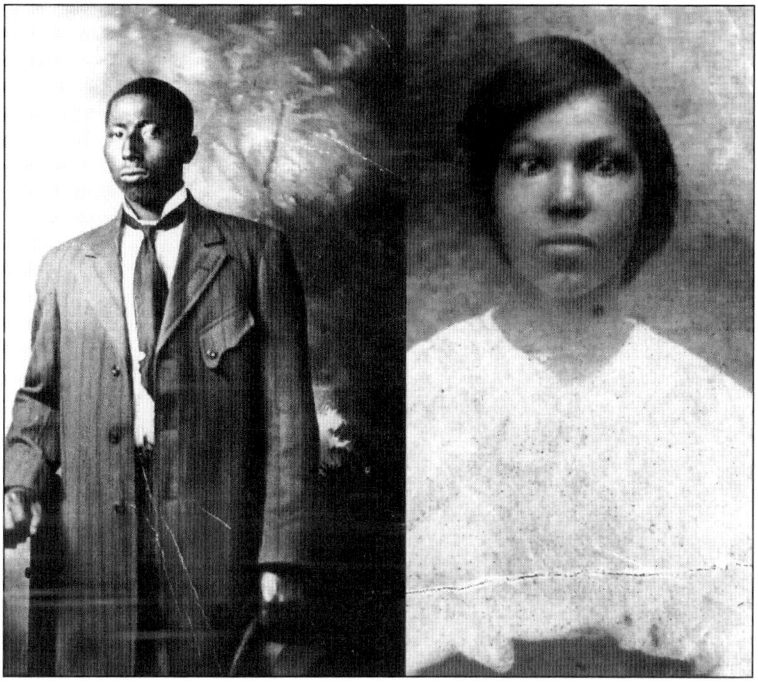

Pictured here are Carter and Eva White. Carter was born in 1893 to Joe and Mariah White. He married Eva, who was from the Pilgrim community. They lived on the corner of Parrish and Marian Streets and had eight children—Alice, Lerlean, Curtis, Carter Jr., Freddie, Purcell, Charles, and Ernest. (Vivien "Nickie" W. Rozzell.)

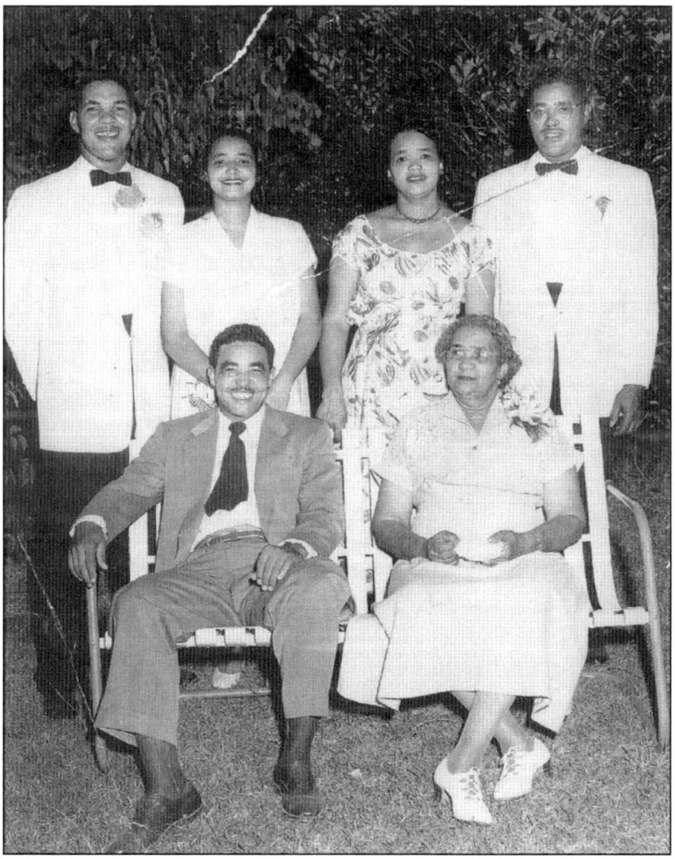

The Cunningham family celebrates the occasion of Roosevelt Cunningham's marriage to Rebecca White on Glenburnie Road in the 1940s. Pictured from left to right are the five children of the Cunningham family and their mother: (first row) Miles and his mother Jimmy; (second row) Roosevelt, Odessa, Dorothy, and E. J. The Cunningham family migrated to Westwood from Oglethorpe, Georgia. Father Johnny worked for the Richmond, Fredericksburg, and Potomac Railroad for many years and died in 1932. Johnny and Jimmy had additional children—Emma, James, Mattie, Roberta, and Gertie Bea. (Dorothy Cunningham Brown.)

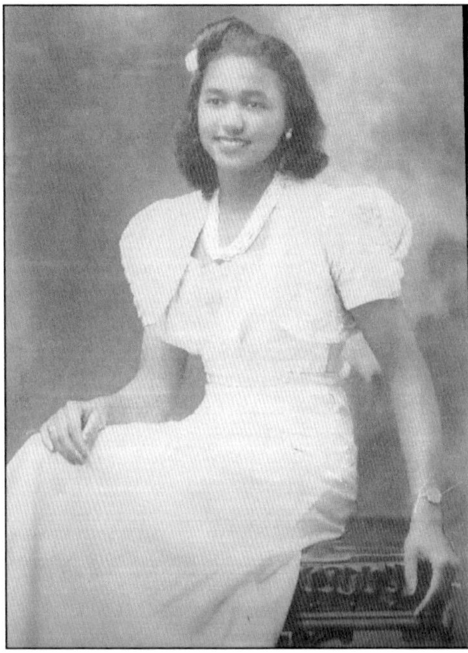

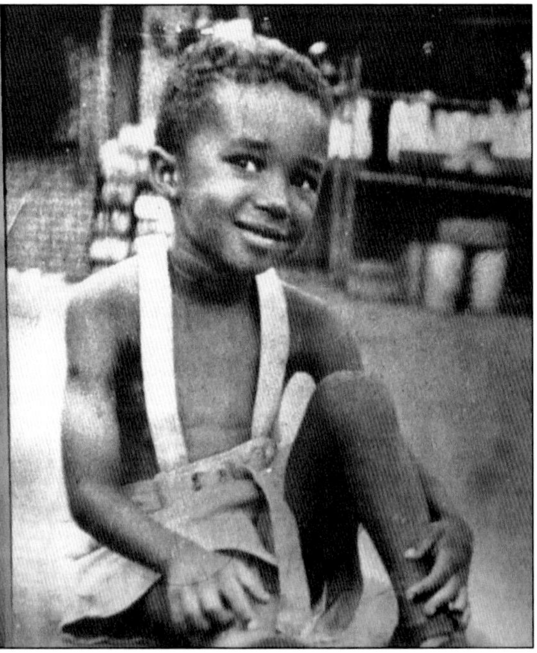

Mattie Cunningham Ashe (1922–1950) is pictured here with her famous son, tennis champion Arthur Ashe Jr. Mattie was born in Westwood to Johnny and Jimmy Cunningham. She married Arthur Ashe Sr. and they had two sons—Arthur Jr. and Johnny. Mattie was a strikingly beautiful woman who faced an untimely death at the age of 28. She is buried in Woodlawn Cemetery in the north section of Henrico. Little Arthur began playing tennis in Brookfield Gardens and attended high school in St. Louis, returning home to Westwood during many summers and weekends to visit family. He received a tennis scholarship to UCLA in 1963, the same year he became the first black player ever chosen for the Davis Cup team. He won the U.S. Open and became the first African American man to win Wimbledon. He was inducted into the International Tennis Hall of Fame in 1985. Ashe married Jeanne Moutoussamy in 1977. Mother and son were buried in Woodlawn Cemetery upon their deaths. (Dorothy C. Brown.)

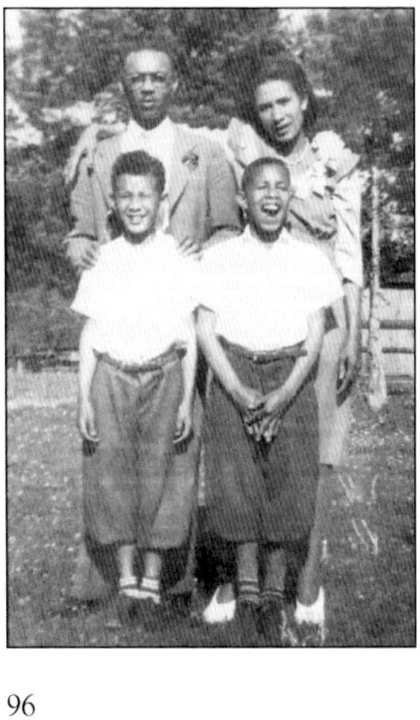

Pictured here are James O. and Inez Warrick Taylor with their sons Warrick ("Wawa," at left) and James ("Jimmy," at right) in the yard of their home. James Taylor died young. His wife Inez (1914–2007) was born in Westwood to Mary Virginia Cooper and Samuel Warrick. Inez had three brothers, Glen, Preston, and Oliver. For many years, Inez worked for Mary Tyler Cheek, a well-known humanitarian and philanthropist. Later she trained to become a nurses' assistant and worked private duty cases. (Warrick D. Taylor Sr.)

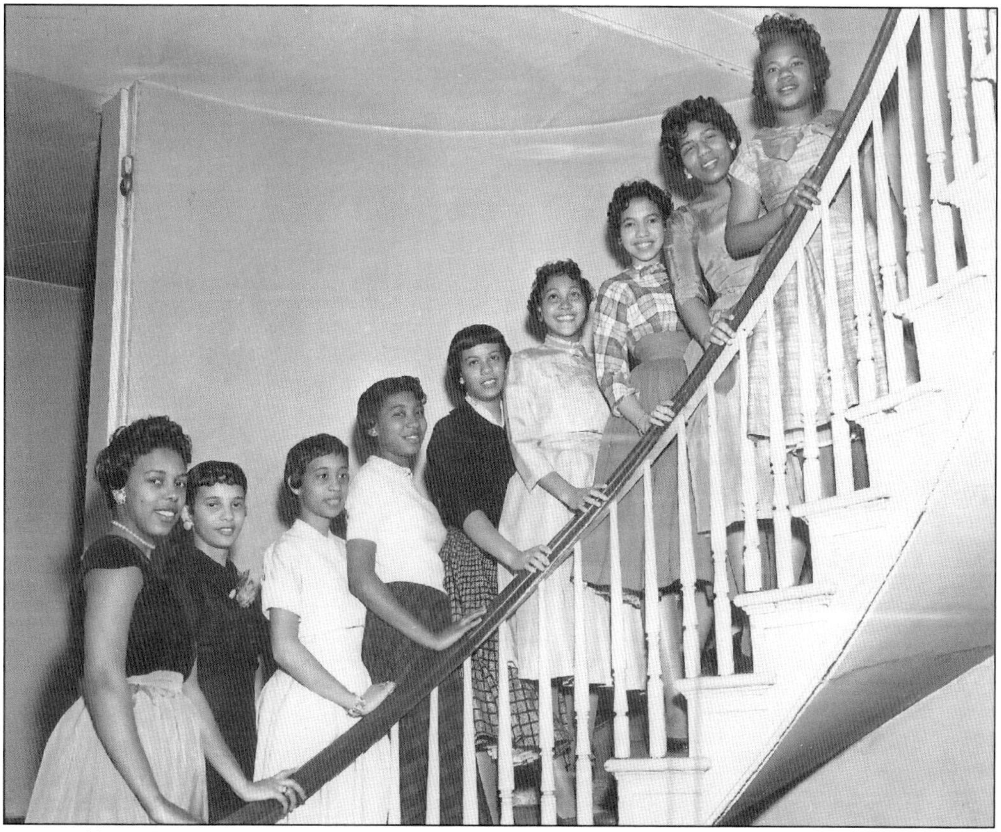

Pictured here from left to right are 1957 debutantes at the Zeta Phi Beta sorority cotillion, Elaine Johnson, Barbara Thornton, Roberta Anderson, Dorothy Wyatt, Barbara Taylor, Brenda Dabney, Sheila Jacobs, Jacqueline Winfree, and Sandra Burrell. Their sponsor was Audrey Bradford Robinson. (Brenda Nichols.)

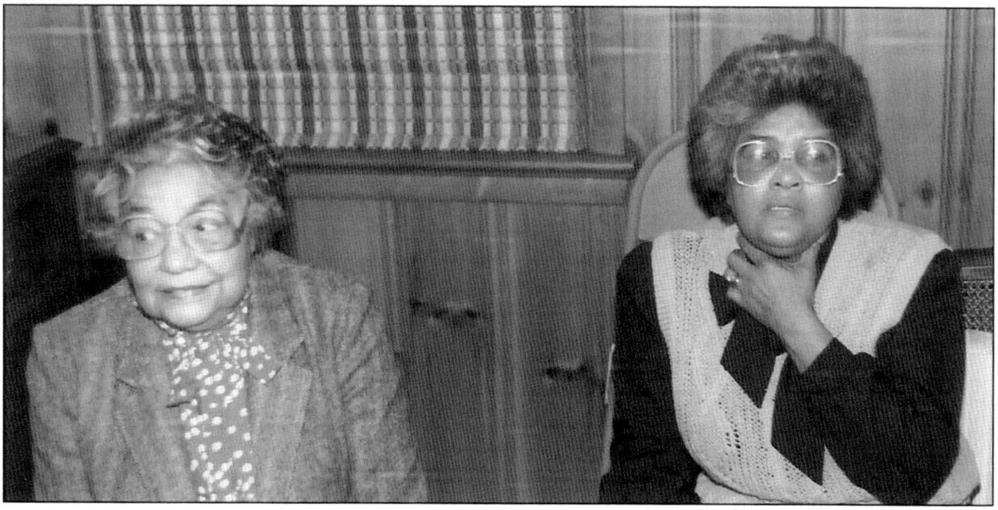

Verna Anderson White enjoys an afternoon with her daughter Rebecca White Cunningham in this photograph. Her husband, Louis White, and daughter Verna "Bumpsy" W. Epps are not pictured. (Dorothy C. Brown.)

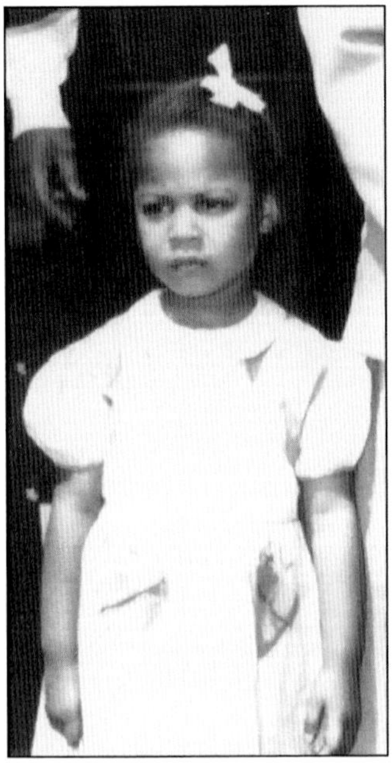

As Westwood continued to thrive in the 1950s, three of its children would participate in the massive resistance period of public school integration. Pictured here is Daisy Jane Cooper Johnson, daughter of Elizabeth Cooper of Marian Street. She was one of six applicants who, with their parents, filed a petition to attend all-white schools, three at Westhampton Elementary School. By the time the petition was granted, she was eligible to attend Westhampton Junior High School, becoming its first African American student. The 1958 legal petition—*Warden v. Richmond School Board*—would become a landmark. She became the first African American graduate of Thomas Jefferson High School in 1966. She attended Virginia Union University. (Warrick D. Taylor Sr.)

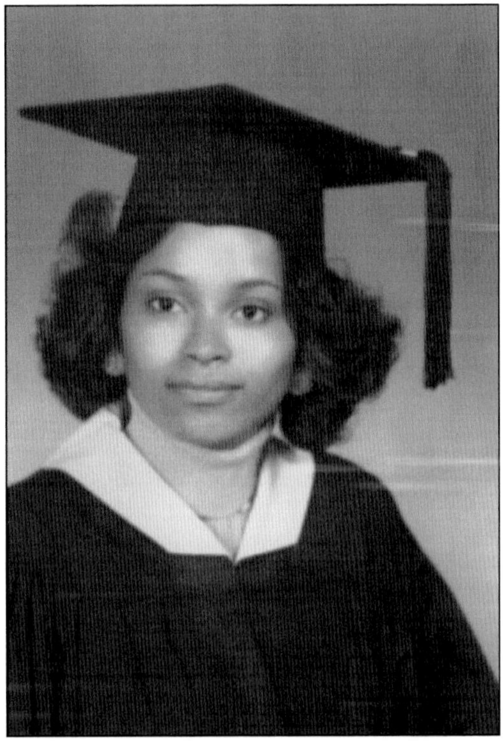

These courageous young ladies are the pride of the Westwood community. Pictured here are Lorna Renee Warden (right) and Wanda Irene Dabney Zanders (below). Lorna and her parents, Wilhelmina R. and Leonard Warden Sr., were the chief plaintiffs of the 1958 petition to integrate Westhampton Elementary School. Lorna's parents petitioned for her to attend the all-white Westhampton Elementary. (Mary Frances Warden Lambert.)

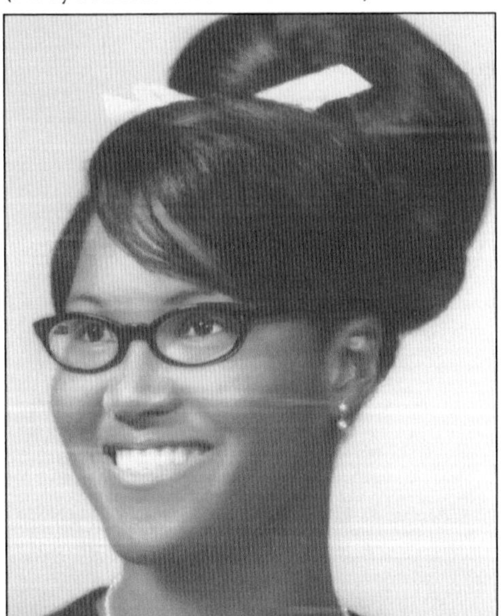

Wanda Dabney, born in 1950, lived with her parents, Lavinia Holmes and Ernest Dabney. During the waiting period, Wanda's parents built a home in Pryor's Court on Ridge (later Eastridge) Road. As they moved there along with sister Brenda, Wanda entered Douglas Freeman High School. Still in a minority of 10 black students among a student population of 1,500, Wanda graduated in 1966, ranking 51 of 500 seniors. She graduated from American University in Washington, D.C., and Virginia Commonwealth University. Wanda died unexpectedly in 2008. (Ernest and Lavinia Dabney.)

Seven

Bandy Field Pilgrim Brookland

Bandy Field was located on Three Chopt Road near Patterson Avenue. In the 1800s, this area was known as Greenville, named after plantation owner Benjamin Green. There were only a few African American families in Bandy Field—the Bradford, Brown, Burleigh, Byrd, Johnson, Pryor, Truman, and Young families.

The Pilgrim community is nestled on West Broad Street Road in the far west end of Henrico County. It is bordered by Broad Street and Penick (now Glenside Drive), Bethlehem, and Basie Roads. This is a community that has remained intact. Some of its early inhabitants were the Adams, Burrell, Campbell, Coleman, Coles, Fleming, Garner, Hicks, Kenney, Mitchell, Robinson, Starke, Twine, and Winston families. Pilgrim Journey Baptist Church originated in 1887, when a group of neighbors affiliated with the Elijah Community Hall began to meet. Leaders were Reverends John Burton, Sherman Morse, James Garner, and Phillip Poindexter, along with Randall, Lizzie, Lucy, and Martha Burrell. The first pastor was Rev. Andrew Jackson. It was destroyed by fire and rebuilt twice. In 1960, the church sold the land on Broad Street Road. Pilgrim created the four-room Union School, located on West Broad Street Road, which housed grades one through six. After completing their schooling at Union, students matriculated at the Virginia Randolph Training (later High) School. Some of Union's early teachers were Alice Thompson and Irene Gee.

The Brookland community, founded around 1860, was located across from Westwood on Broad Street Road, approximately two blocks headed west from what would become Willow Lawn Shopping Center. Most of the residents attended Good Hopewell Baptist Church, formed in 1868. The first pastor at Good Hopewell was Rev. John E. Fountain. Brookland's first residents were the Allen, Berry, Corbin, Hollow, Johnson, Payne, Perkins, Price, Thompkins, Twine, and Tyler families, according Lillie Etta Corbin, who was born in Brookland. This little neighborhood sat between two thriving communities—Westwood and Pilgrim. Children from Brookland walked to Pilgrim in order to attend Union School.

It is important to mention that another community once existed in this area of Henrico County. Burrelltown, located on Forest Avenue, was a residential community made up of the Burrell, Bradford, Johnson, Snead, and other families. Burrelltown has completely disappeared; however, many Burrelltown residents married into families of Bandy Field, Brookland, Pilgrim, and Westwood, as well as other African American communities in Henrico County.

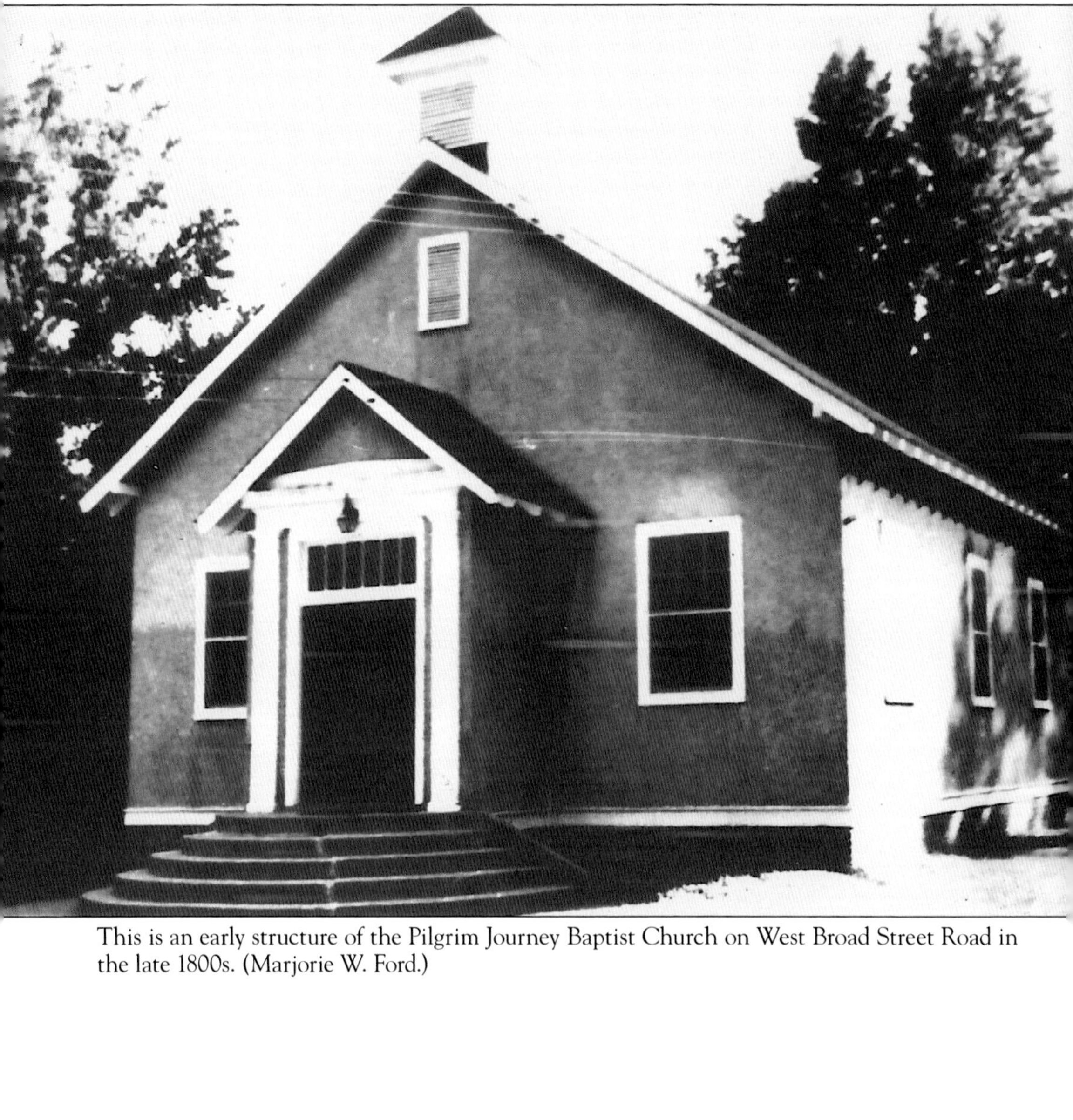

This is an early structure of the Pilgrim Journey Baptist Church on West Broad Street Road in the late 1800s. (Marjorie W. Ford.)

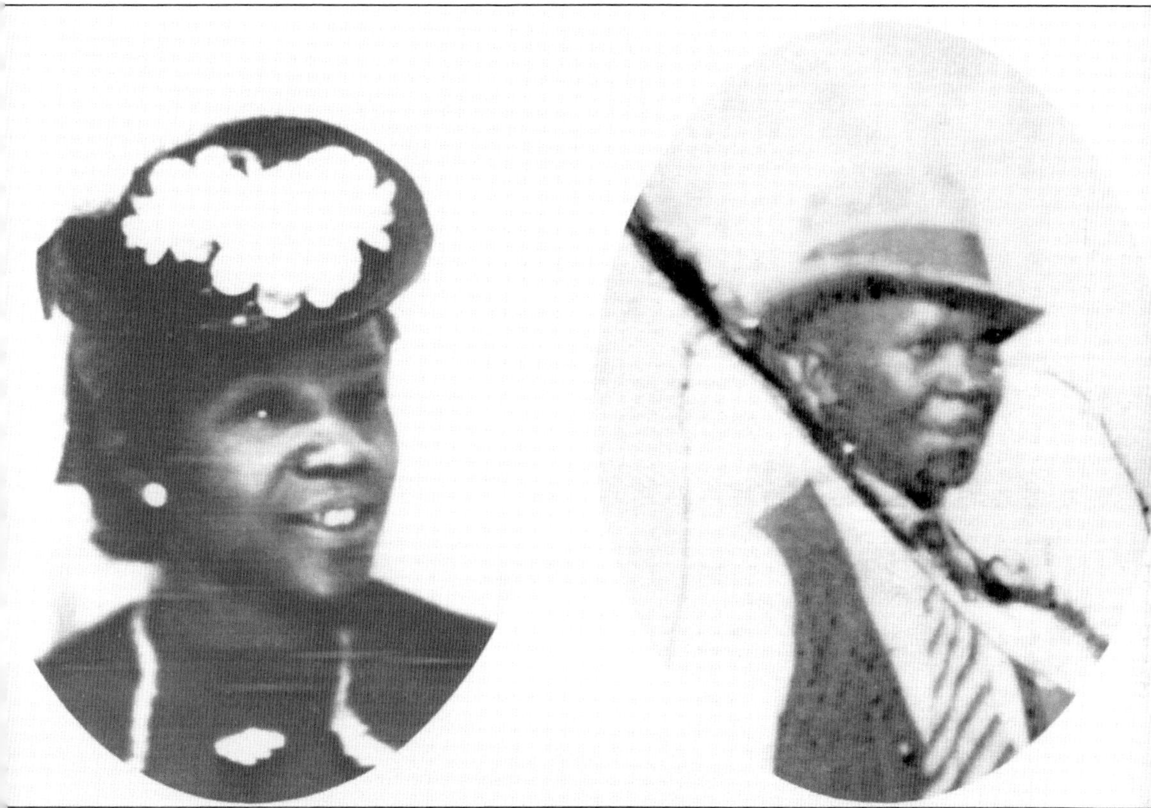

Pictured here are Rosetta Rock (1900–1947) and Baylor Winston (died in 1950) of Pilgrim. They courted while she attended Hartshorn Memorial College on Leigh Street in the city of Richmond. Rosetta was the daughter of John Rock, a West Indian, and Florence Virginia. Baylor's parents were Baylor and Phyllis Burrell Winston of Burrelltown. Rosetta and Baylor had nine children—Thelma, Agnes, Marjorie, Daisy, James, Florence, Ruth, Bernard, and Vernelle. (Marjorie W. Ford.)

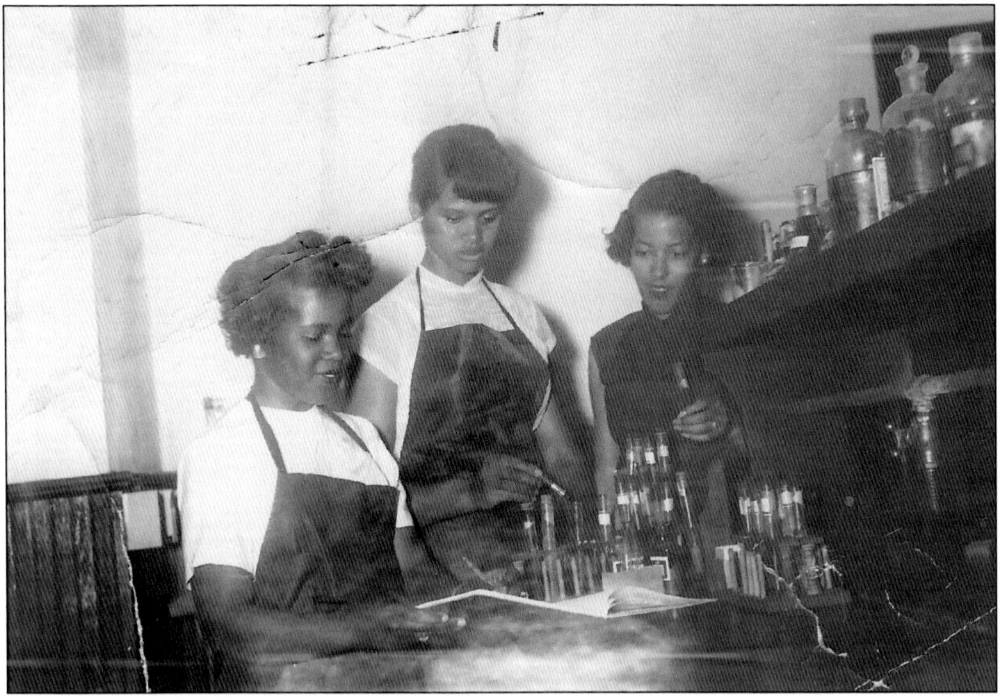

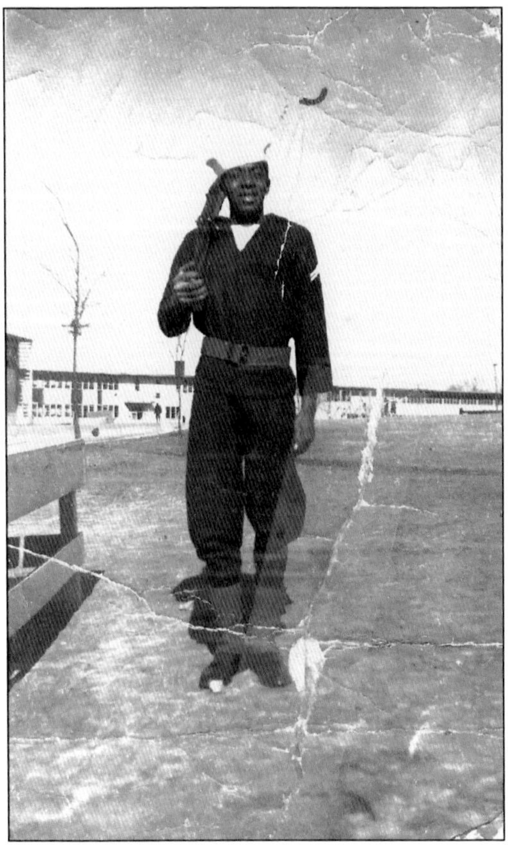

Florence Virginia Winston Harris, above at left, teaches chemistry to two unidentified students at Southampton Training School in Courtland, Virginia. A product of the Pilgrim community, she graduated from Virginia State College with a bachelor of science degree in biology and chemistry in 1952. She taught at Virginia Randolph Elementary School in Glen Allen for 20 years, retiring at age 55. (Florence V. W. Harris.)

Pictured at left is Florence's husband, William Bradford Harris, whom she wed in 1954. He graduated from Virginia Randolph in 1948 and entered the U.S. Navy in 1950. (Florence V. W. Harris.)

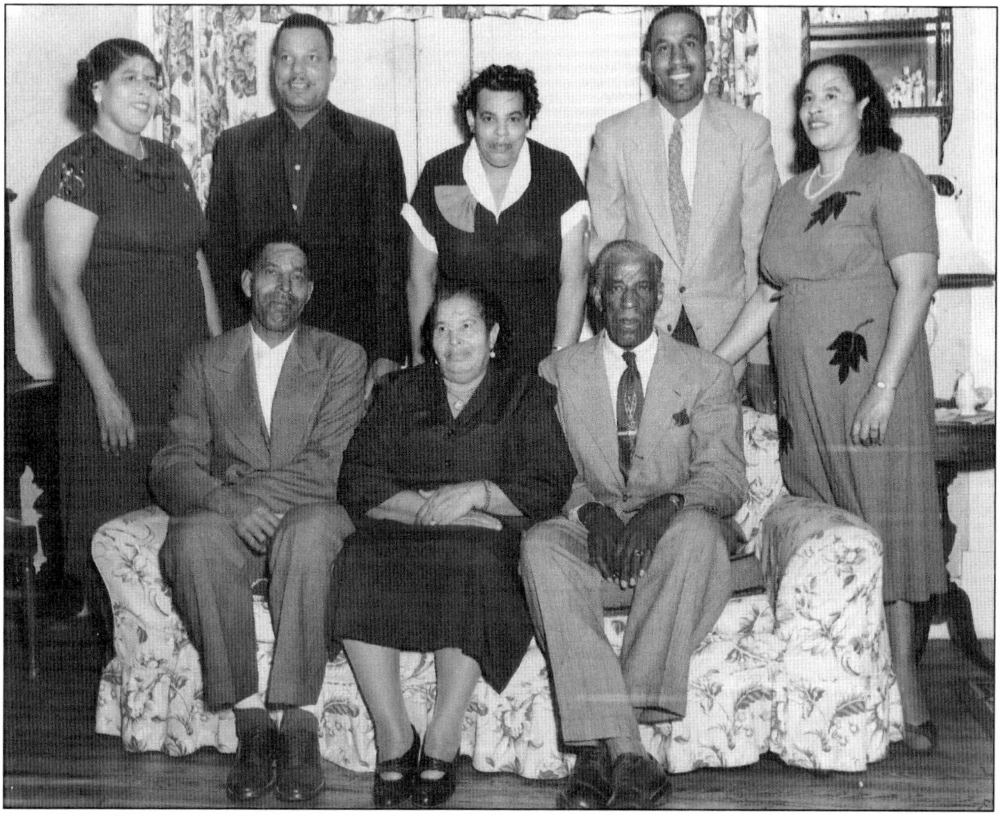

Louise Rock (1894–1987) and Willie Lee Coles (1894–1987) are pictured here with their children. The popular Coles family moved from Randolph Town to Pilgrim around 1949, settling at 2809 Bethlehem Road. From left to right, they are as follows: (first row) James Melvin, Louise, and Willie Lee; (second row) Elizabeth Coles Kenney, Louis Sr. ("Bubba"), Irene Coles Thompkins, Harvey, and Blanche C. Christian Anderson. Daughter Lavinia C. Bassett is not shown. Louise was a homemaker, and Willie Lee was the owner of the successful W. L. Coles and Sons Construction. (Connie and Ralph Christian Jr.)

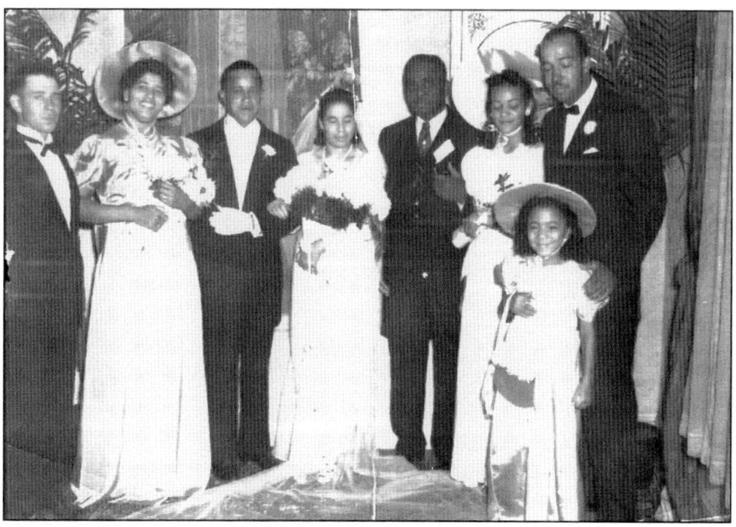

This is the wedding of Blanche Coles and Herman Christian at Pilgrim Journey church in 1940. Rev. John E. Fountain officiated. From left to right are James Christian, Elizabeth C. Kenney, the groom and bride, Reverend Fountain, Inez W. Christian, Raymond Bassett, and flowergirl Jean Christian. (Connie and Ralph Christian Jr.)

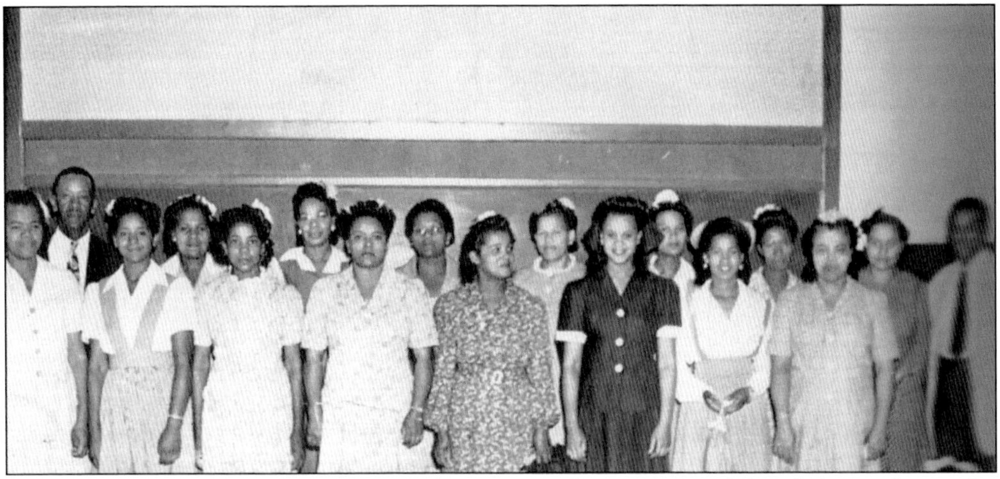

The Pilgrim community sewing circle is shown around 1950. Pictured from left to right are the following: (front row) Mable Saunders, Bessie Henley, Bertha Wright, Doris Dean, Pearl Fleming, Ruth Lloyd, Eleanor Kenney, and Josephine Harris; (second row) Horace, Elnora, and Hattie Fleming, Emma Burrell, Phyllis Johnson, Kate Randolph, Ida Twine, and Alvina and Bruce Bozeman. (Pilgrim Journey Baptist Church.)

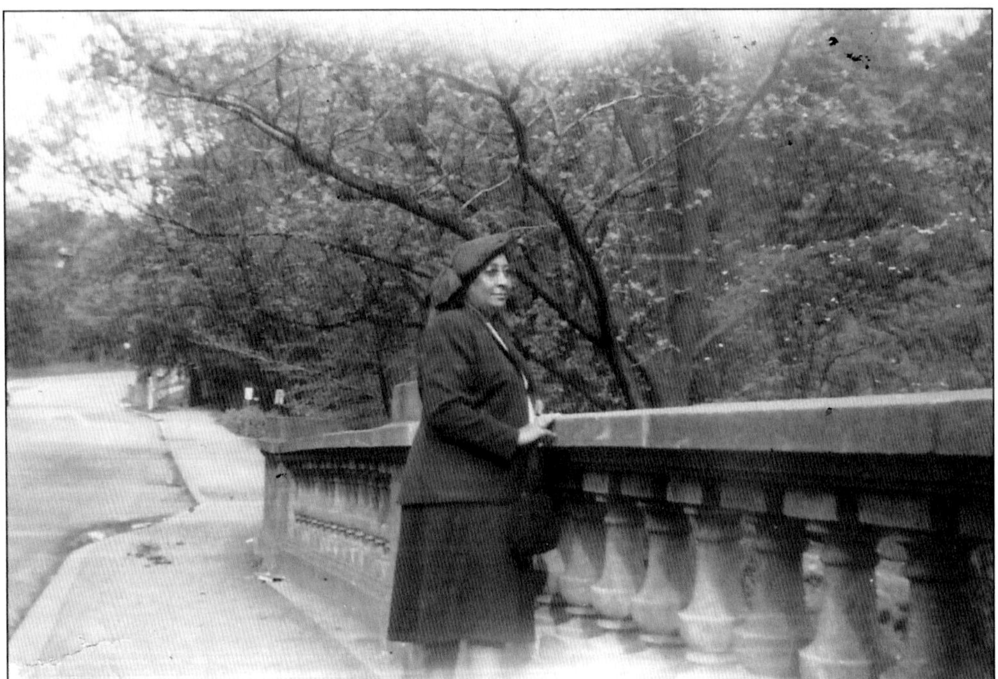

Irma Gee, a teacher at Union School on Broad Street Road, is pictured standing on a bridge around 1949. (Connie and Ralph Christian Jr.).

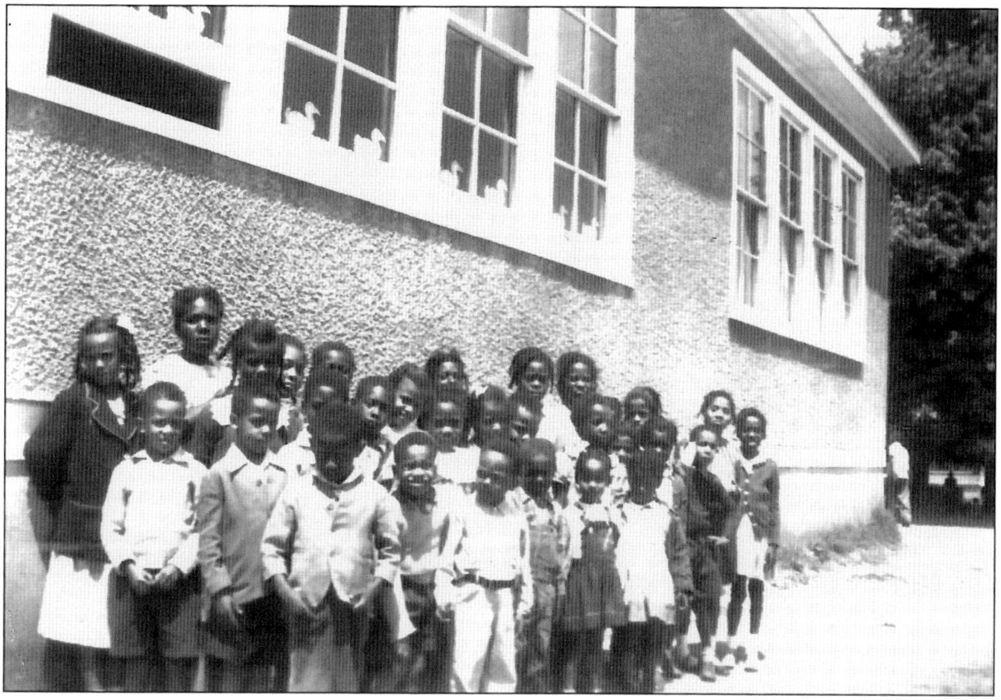

Students stand in front of Union School in the 1940s. (Connie and Ralph Christian Jr.)

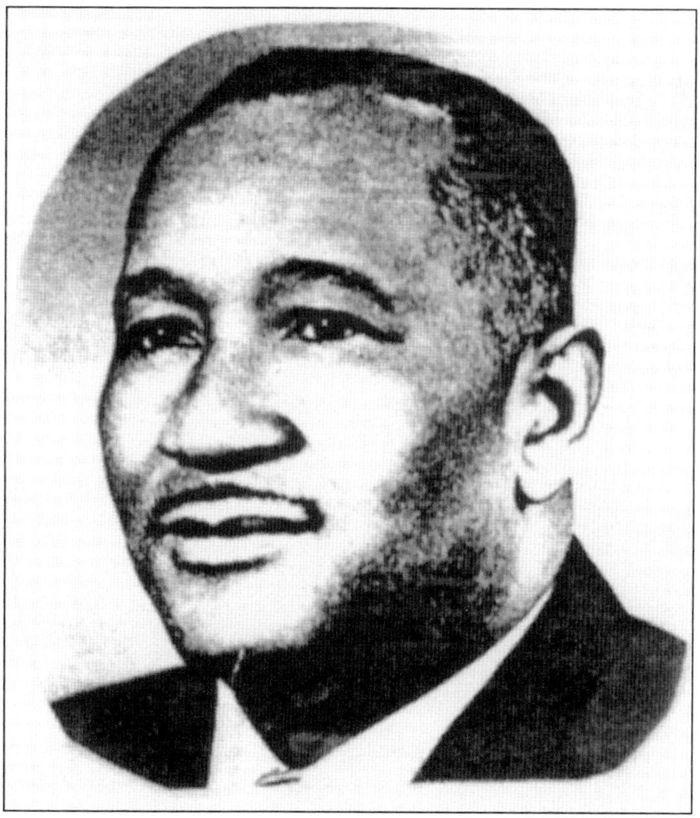

Pictured here is Dr. Maryland Taft Fleming, born in Pilgrim in 1908 to Claude S. and Sarah J. Fleming. He is the youngest of eight children. In 1929, he married Hattie Cunningham, and they had five children. Fleming was baptized into the Pilgrim Journey Baptist Church and in 1932 was licensed and ordained there by Rev. John Fountain. He was pastor of several churches, most importantly Zion Baptist Church, located in south Richmond, where he served for 25 years. He earned a bachelor of divinity degree at Virginia Union University. (Pilgrim Journey Baptist Church.)

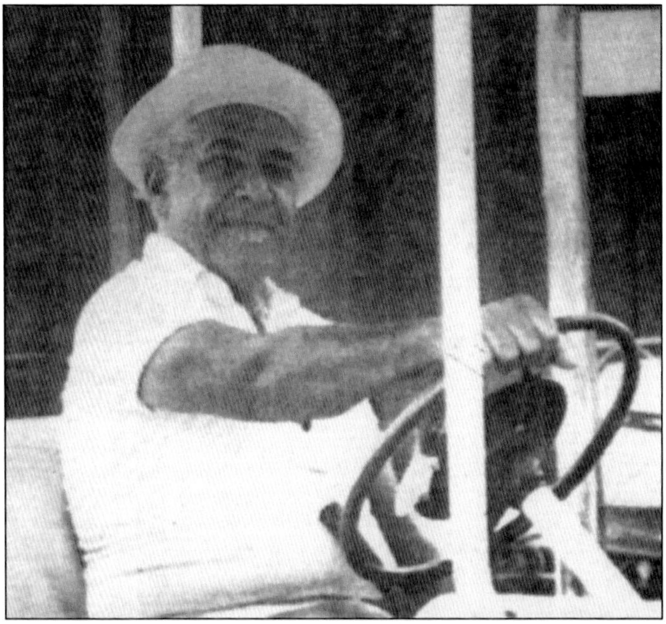

Thomas Kenney is pictured on a golf cart on his 100-acre golf course. Born 1923 in Pilgrim, he attended Virginia Randolph and Virginia Union University. He first married Clara Theresa Pervall of Providence Park, and they divorced. He sold his parents' land and in 1955 purchased the Spring Lake Country Club on Mountain Road (named by its original owner Eddie Morse of Zion Town), which was a golf course used by black golfers during segregation. Later, he and his second wife, Johnetta C. Kenney, sold the land. (Thomas W. Kenney.)

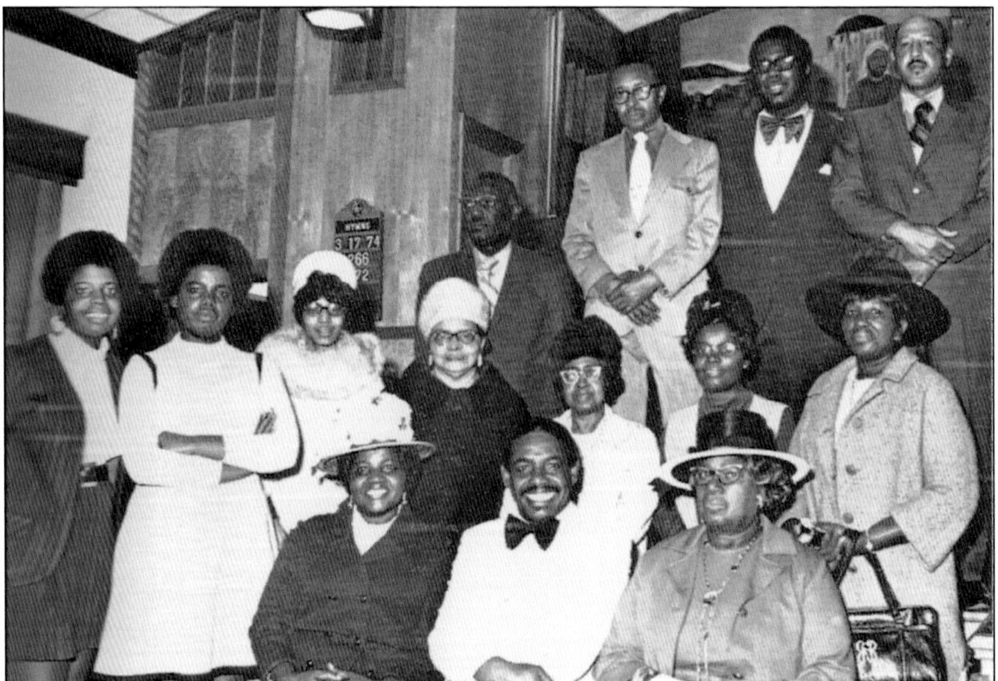

Bessie Price Corbin (1896–1988), seated at right on the first row, and Marshall Corbin Sr. (died 1937) moved from Brookland to Pilgrim. They are shown here with their seven children, Doris, Elizabeth, Lillie, Marshall Jr., Avis, Berkley, Helen, and Bessie's stepson, Isaac. Bessie went to work for the C. F. Sauer family, and Marshall Sr. worked at the Richmond, Frederick, and Potomac Railroad. After her husband's death, Bessie eventually moved back to the Westwood community, where she was born, and she was employed by philanthropist Mary Tyler Cheek. (Pilgrim Journey Baptist Church.)

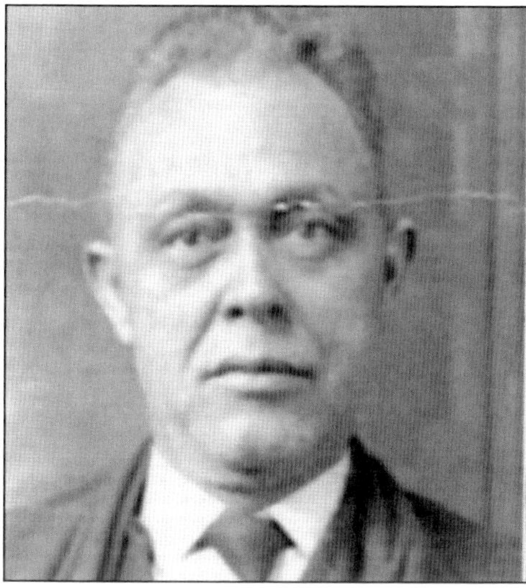
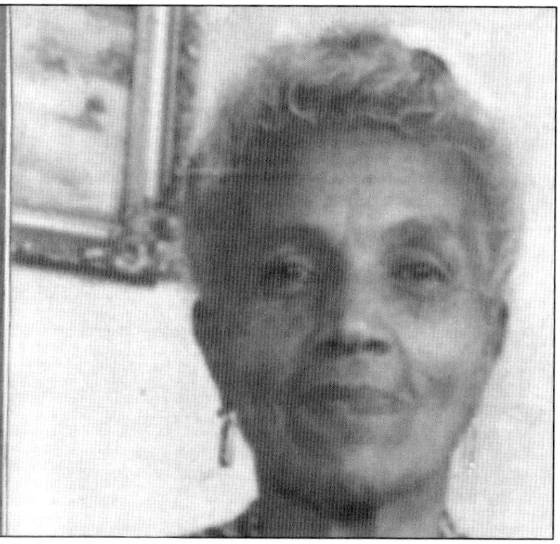

Pictured here are Rev. Samuel Lafayette Burleigh Sr. and his wife, Nannie Brown, of Greenville (Bandy Field). Samuel was a minister and member of Westwood Baptist Church, and Nannie was the daughter of Peggy Thomas and Samuel Brown. They lived on Three Chopt Road with their five children, Samuel Lafayette Jr., Ruth, Elizabeth, Pearl, and Moses. The Burleighs were the only family with a telephone in Greenville, so they charged 5¢ per call, payable up front, for others to use it. (S. L. Burleigh III and Dell B. Johnson.)

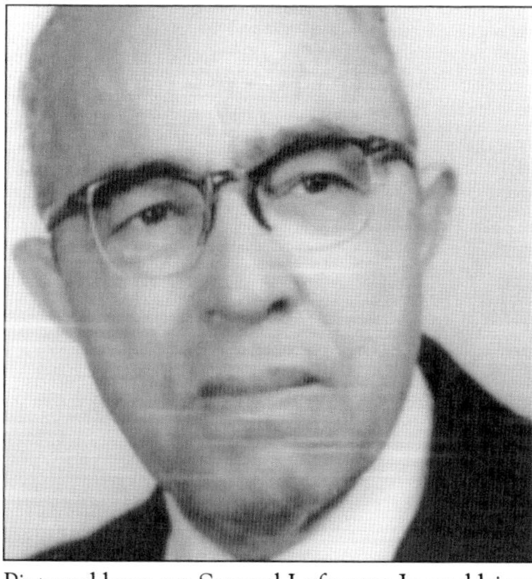
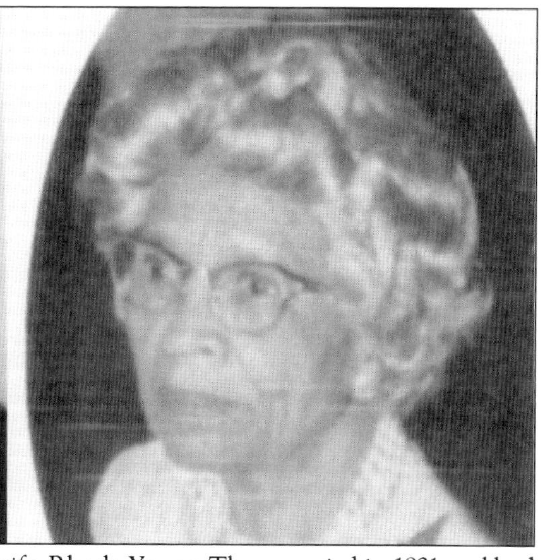

Pictured here are Samuel Lafayette Jr. and his wife, Rhoda Young. They married in 1921 and had two children, Samuel Lafayette III and Dell B. Johnson. Rhoda was born in Hampton, Virginia, in 1894 to John and Patience J. Young. She attended the Whittier School/Paine College in Augusta, Georgia. She trained in nursing at Dixie Hospital, an all-black nursing school, graduating from Hampton Institute in 1916. She married Samuel Lafayette Jr. in 1921, working at the Medical College of Virginia Hospital and retiring in 1958. Deacon Samuel Lafayette Burleigh Jr. (1894–1981) was born in Providence, Rhode Island. He finished Virginia Randolph Training (High) School, and graduated from Hampton Institute/Armstrong-Slater Memorial Trade School in 1917, majoring in carpentry. He was discharged after service in World War I and worked as a mail carrier from 1920 to 1959, serving Rural Free Delivery Route 2, eastward for 27 miles from Three Chopt Road to Meadow Street. (S. L. Burleigh III and Dell B. Johnson)

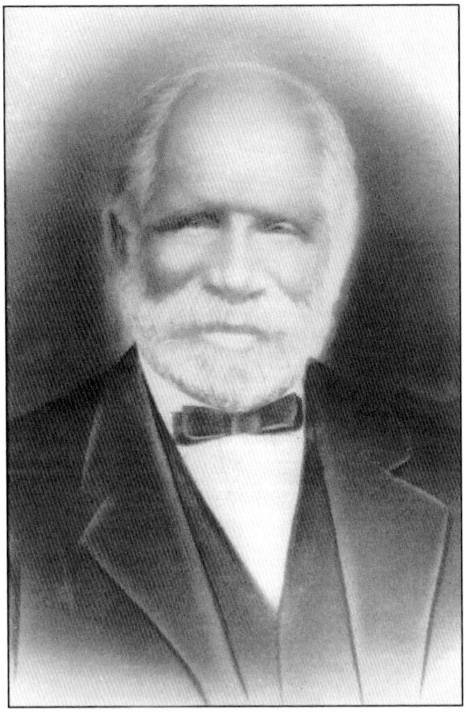

This is Moses Bradford, who was born in 1835 and buried in Bandy Field. Bradford married Eliza "Ellen," born in 1840. They had six children: Isaac, Edna (born in 1882), Archie, Florence, Noah, and Moses Jr. (1869–1936), who fought in the Spanish-American War and was honorably discharged after being seriously wounded. (Helena and Ellen Fountain.)

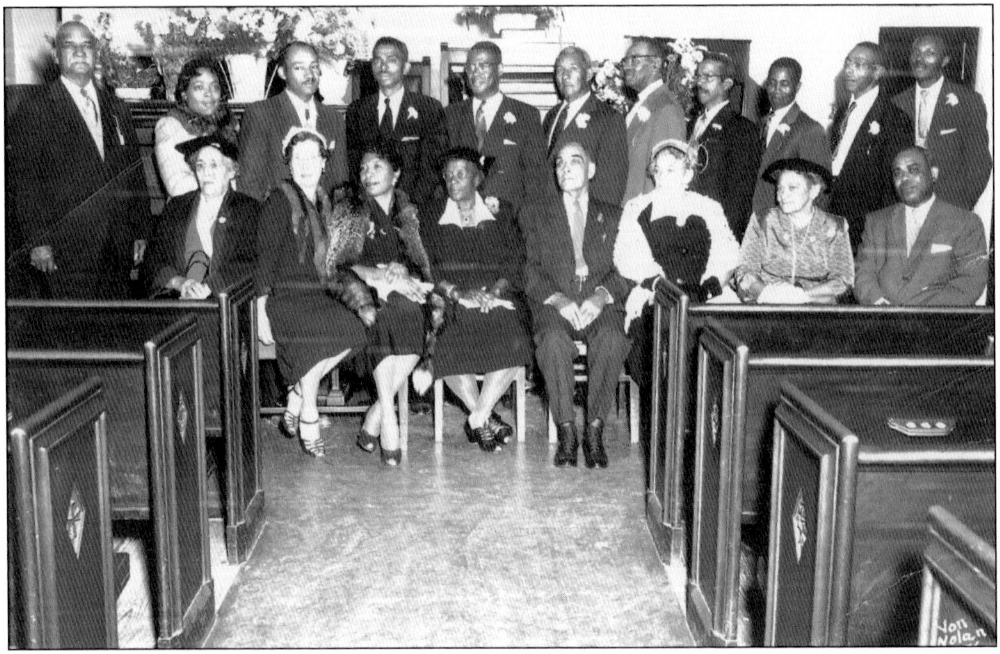

Deacon David Bradford Jr., the nephew of Moses Bradford, was honored as church clerk at Pilgrim Journey Church. Pictured from left to right are the following: (first row) Lucy Jones, Leone Young, Johnnie Fogle, Eva C. Bradford, Deacon David Bradford Jr., Emma Bradford Woodson, Grace Bradford Truman, and James Johnston; (second row) Archie Bradford, Susie Truman, William Truman, Robert Campbell, Rev. Ernest Fogle, James Winston, Horace Fleming, Alex Kenney, Lewis Blanchard, Ernest Burton, and George Starke. (Ruth T. Winston.)

Eight

Glen Allen

The Glen Allen community, located in northwest Henrico County, was originally known as Mountain Road Crossing and was the hunting ground of the Chickahominy tribe of Native Americans. In 1864, the community was named Glen Allen after the late Benjamin Allen, whose widow, Sue, later married Capt. John Cussons. Some of the first African Americans in the area were the Andersons, Burleighs, Goodes, and Witchers. Mount Olive Baptist Church was formed in Yellow Tavern when a few black people left North Run Baptist Church in 1867. The church purchased 1.18 acres of land and recorded the name "Mount Olive African Baptist Church" in the Henrico County Courthouse. In 1896, Rev. James Binford became the pastor of Mount Olive, serving 40 years. St. Peter Baptist Church was founded in 1882 on donated land with Rev. Timothy Harris as its first pastor.

In 1882, Springfield Baptist Church was formed with Rev. A. H. Jackson as its first minister. Deacon Isham Grief Houston, born in 1851 in Manakin, Virginia, was a shoemaker by trade. He purchased land between Short Pump and Sadler Roads and deeded it to the church. The building was erected in 1887 at West Broad Street Road. Some families in the Springfield Church were Abrams, Buckner, Burton, Chiles, Green, Miller, Minor, Morse, Pryor, Richardson, and Taylor.

Moses Johnson and Jake Lewis founded Mount Vernon Baptist Church in 1892. Land was purchased for the church in 1904, and Rev. Calvin Anderson was its pastor until 1908. Landowners J. T. and Lucy Francis founded Francistown in the early 1800s. The Chandler, Cosby, Cousins, Dandridge, Garrison, Hayes, Jasper, Lewis, Meadow, Moore, Perry, and Sutton families populated Francistown. Its borders were Springfield and Hungary Roads.

The Coal Pit School, named after the nearby Springfield Coal Pits, was built on Francistown Road in 1905. The school had two rooms (grades one through three in the front room and grades four and five in the back room) and two teachers—Lloyd D. Thompson and Mary Valentine. By 1913, the enrollment was 46 students, and an active Parent-Teacher Association flourished. Echo Lake Park was a popular place for blacks to be from 1920 to the 1940s. Rev. Jacob Lewis purchased the park but sold the land in the face of financial problems. Jesse Pryor Jr., John Chambers, Herman Melton Sr., Eddie Morse, A. D. Price Jr., and Sam Stewart purchased the park and organized Echo Lake, Inc., in the 1920s. Churches such as Mount Olive, Mount Vernon, and Abner used the lake for baptisms. During segregation, the park flourished, but by 1948, most activity had subsided. It is presently owned by Henrico County.

George Washington Gee, born in 1891 to Littleton and Henrietta Gee of South Boston, Virginia, was a brick mason and a contractor. After the death of his wife, Julia, he relocated to Henrico County, where he married his second wife, Lloyd D. Thompson, and purchased 33 acres in 1950. He also built the Middleton-Gee and Thompson Heights subdivisions and the historic present Quioccasin Baptist Church.

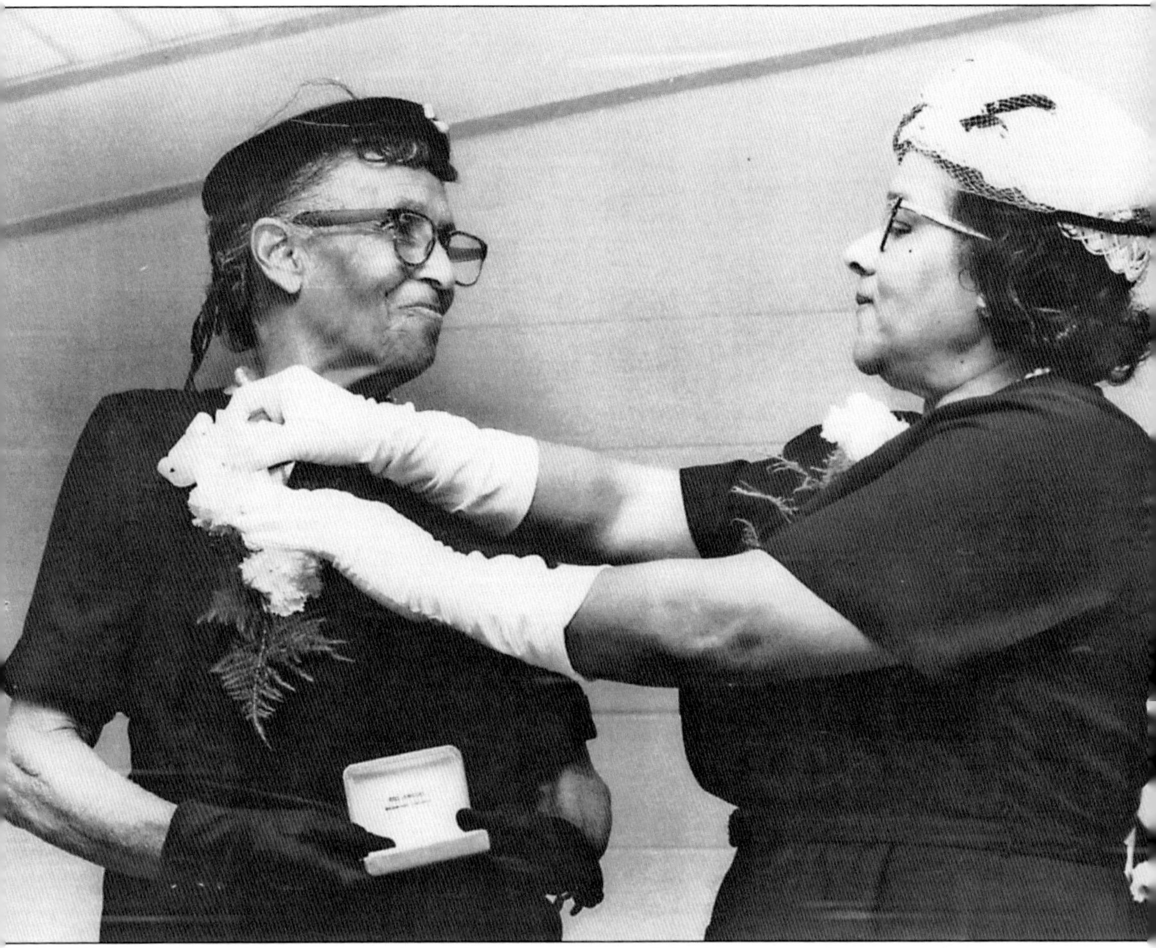

Priddy Cosby (left), was president of the Virginia Randolph Foundation, formed in 1954. Mrs. Cosby was founder of the scholarship fund. She was honored at the 12th annual meeting of the association. The scholarship endowment exceeds $10,000. Lynwood W. Harris, a teacher at Virginia Randolph Elementary School, is pinning the corsage and the endowment pin in the early 1960s. (Hilda Johnson Cosby.)

This is the original Mount Olive Baptist Church, founded in 1867. The present-day congregation continues to worship on the original site. (Eugene Mallory.)

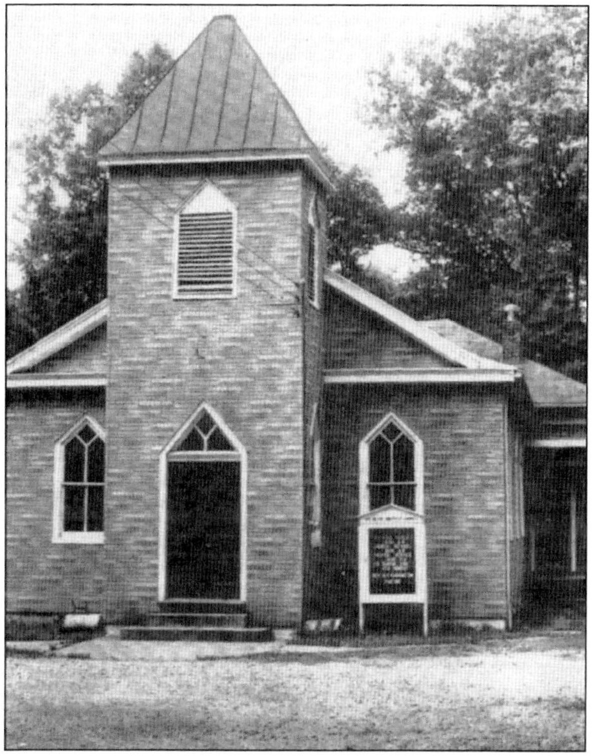

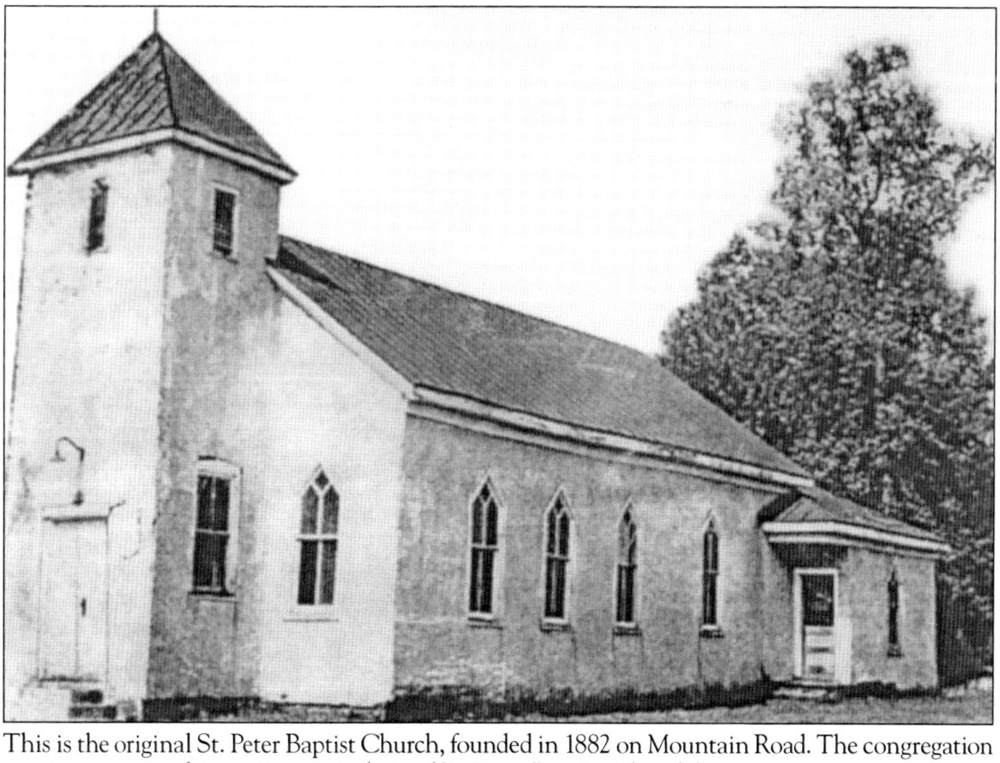

This is the original St. Peter Baptist Church, founded in 1882 on Mountain Road. The congregation continues to worship on its original site. (St. Peter Baptist Church.)

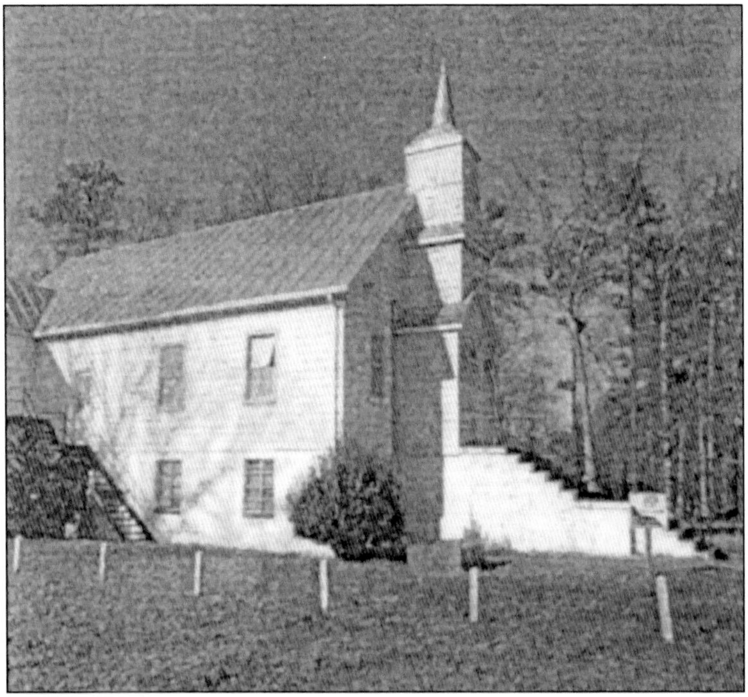

This is Springfield Baptist Church, founded in 1882, and located off West Broad Street Road. (Donald Houston.)

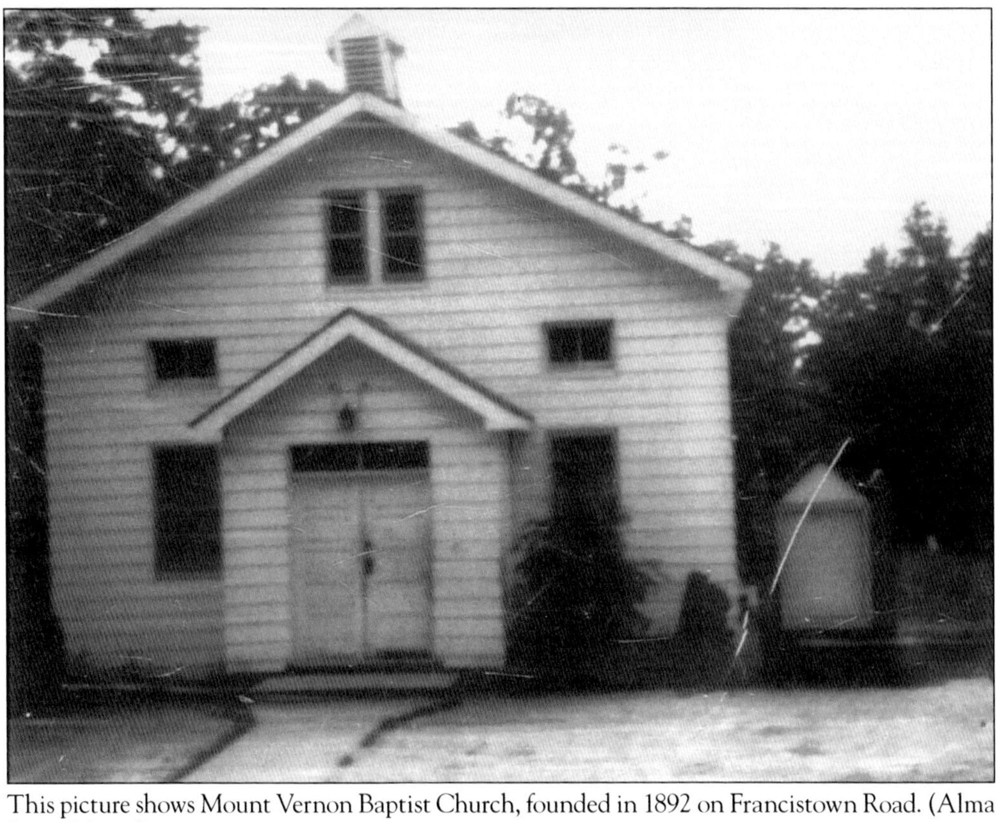

This picture shows Mount Vernon Baptist Church, founded in 1892 on Francistown Road. (Alma Lewis Hayes.)

Pictured here are members of the Hayes family. Pvt. James M. Hayes (left) served in the U.S. Army, enlisting in 1944 during World War II. He served a tour of duty in Okinawa and the Philippines and was honorably discharged in 1946. His wife, Alma Lewis Hayes, is pictured with sons James Jr. (at left), Edward, and Kenneth H., whom she is holding on her lap. Later they would add five more children to their family. (Alma Lewis Hayes.)

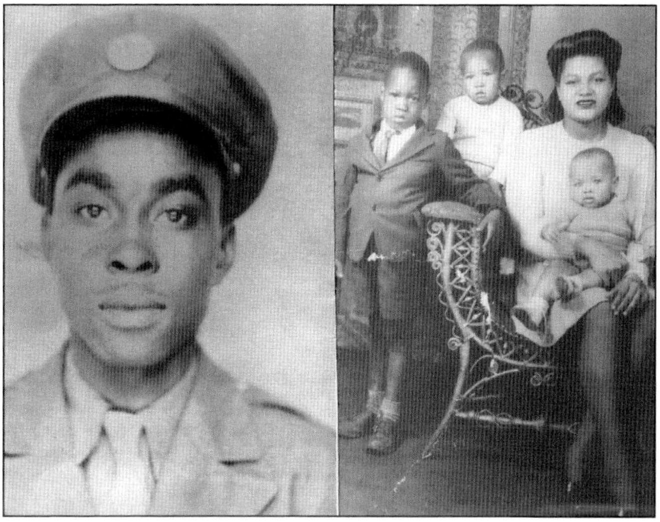

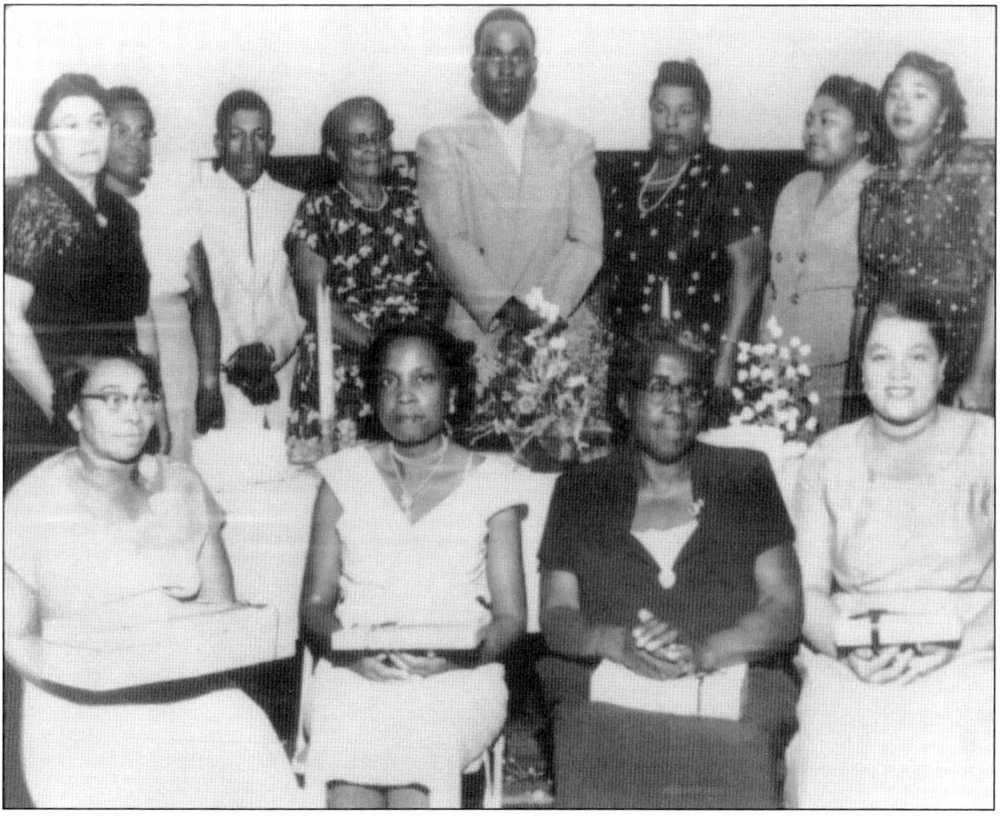

Coal Pit School was named after a coal mine located between Francistown and Springfield Roads. This 1946 picture shows members of its active PTA. Pictured from left to right are the following: (first row) Matilda Woodson and Mary, Fannie, and Alma Hayes; (second row) Marie Hython, Inez James, Russell Cosby, Fannie Johnson, James Hayes, Grace Cousins (who was a midwife), Aurelia Jackson, and Dorothy Shelton. (Alma Lewis Hayes.)

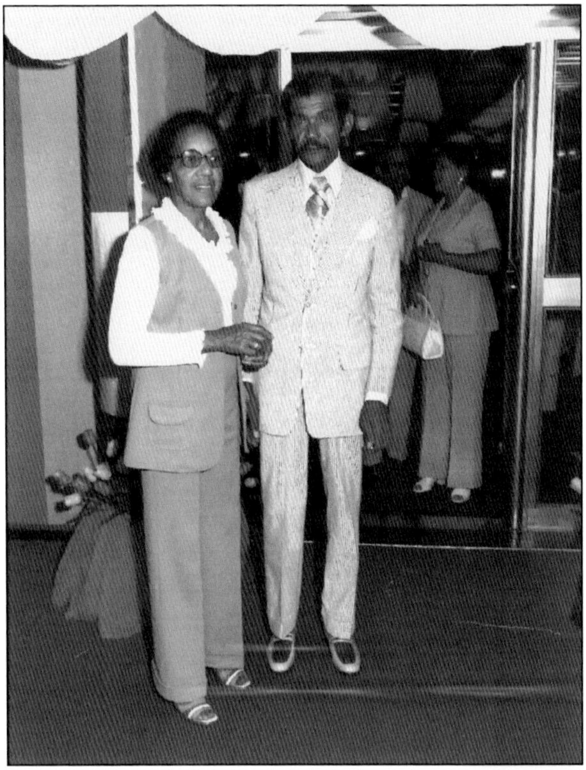

Pictured here are James Lee (1914–2000) and Louise D. Dandridge (1917–2006). In 1950, they purchased 13 acres, on which they raised cows, horses, pigs, geese, and chickens, and named it Dandridge Farm. James was born in the St. James neighborhood of Goochland County. He worked at the Alcohol Beverage Control Board for 35 years and had a small refuse service for 15 years. Louise was born in Pryor's Court, Quioccasin, and worked at Reynolds Metals for 25 years. After retirement, she worked as a party caterer at the Reynolds family home. (Dionne Dandridge Sr.)

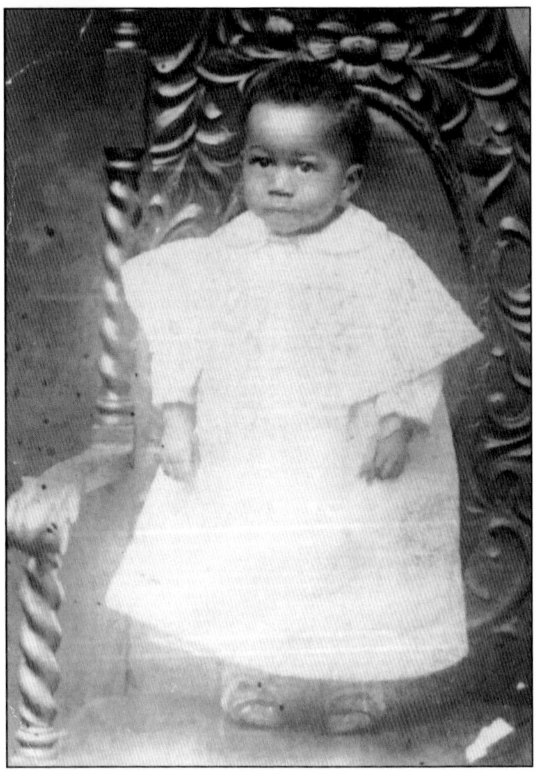

Infant Queen Victoria Perry Goode, born in 1918, is shown in this beautiful decorative chair. She was one of two children born to Mattie Booker and Charles Perry, who lived on Francistown Road in Glen Allen. She married Samuel Goode of Mecklenburg, Virginia, and they had 10 children. (Victoria Perry Goode.)

Pictured here is Bennie Mallory (1914–1985). He served in the U.S. Army Air Corps and was married to Gladys Isabelle Harris Mallory (1917–2004). The family lived in Yellow Tavern until they moved to Mountain Road, where they bought 20 acres of land. The land was divided between four brothers to farm, and some was sold for the establishment of the Virginia Randolph School. (Eugene "Boo" Mallory.)

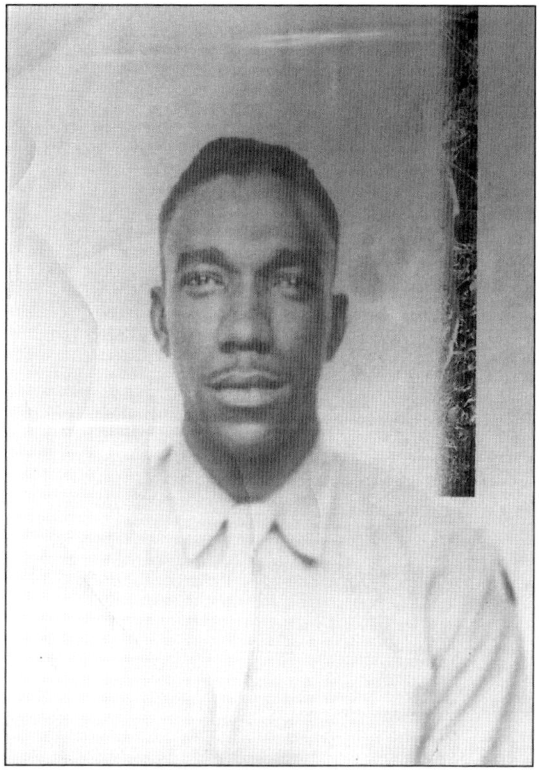

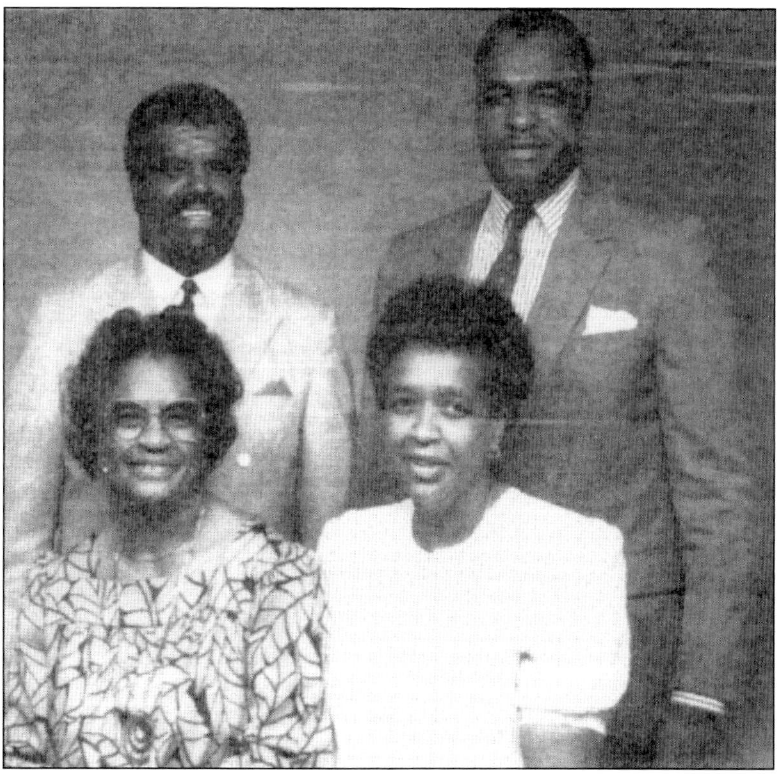

Gladys Harris Mallory (bottom left) is pictured with her daughter Jean and sons Eugene (top left) and Alvin. Gladys was employed by Henrico County Schools and retired from Douglas Freeman, where she worked as a dietician. (Eugene "Boo" Mallory)

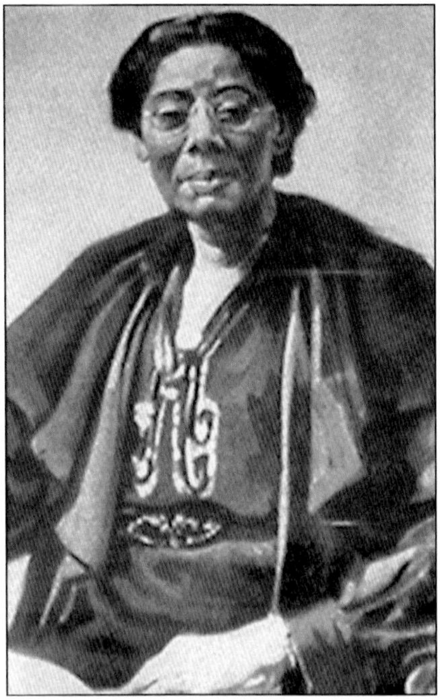

Pictured here is Virginia Estelle Randolph (1874–1958), daughter of former slaves Sarah E. Carter and Edward N. Randolph and sister to Mary, Emma, and Sarah Randolph. In 1892, after her formal training and teaching experience, she opened the Mountain Road School for black children in Henrico County, where she included vocational education alongside traditional academic subjects. In 1908, Randolph became the first Jeanes Supervisor Industrial Teacher, tasked with improving rural school communities and promoting vocation education for black children. She developed the first in-service teaching for rural black teachers in Virginia, with a goal of improving the curriculum, and established the first Arbor Day program in Virginia. In 1915, she established the Virginia Randolph Training School for vocational education, and she later expanded the campus with dormitories and other buildings. Two educators, Warner Jones Sr. and William Cosby, were her best students. She was beloved by her niece Aurelia Davis and nephew Henry Davis Jr. (Henrietta McMickens.)

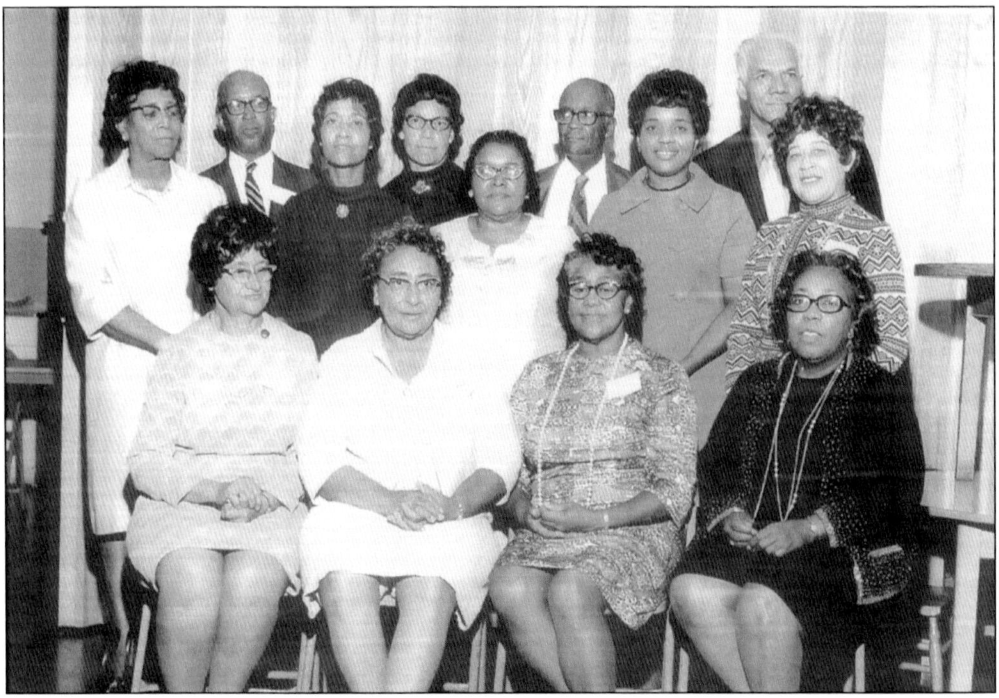

Shown here is the annual meeting of the Henrico Teachers Association Federal Credit Union, which was chartered in May 1957, during segregation in Henrico County. Pictured from left to right are the following: (first row) Blanche J. Andrews, Irma Gee, Sarah Lightfoot, and Sadie C. Sears; (second row) Mary Thompson, Helen Guthrie, Lynwood Harris, Anna Washington, and Clorrie Brown; (third row) William Cosby Sr., Hilda Cosby, Matthew Robinson Sr., and Warner Jones Sr. (Hilda Cosby.)

HBO's 2004 miniseries *Something the Lord Made* featured actor Mos Def as Vivien Thomas, who was forced to experience humiliating segregation in the medical field at Johns Hopkins. A similar form of segregation occurred to Herman Melton (1892–1973), a shining star of the Glen Allen community pictured here in his laboratory. A graduate of Virginia Randolph High School, Melton worked at the Medical College of Virginia as a technician for 41 years during segregation. He washed tubes and bottles and attended neurology and pathology classes. He sliced both animal and human tissues and prepared about 10,000 microscopic slides every year, aided by three assistants. He built gadgets for the lab, including an automatic solution dipper and compressor (described in a trade journal and credited to him). Melton also had a lab in his home where he performed tests for the Virginia State Department of Health. He was married to Julia Price, and they had four children—Camilla, Julia (wife of William Thornton), Herman Jr., and Herbert. (Julia Melton Thornton.)

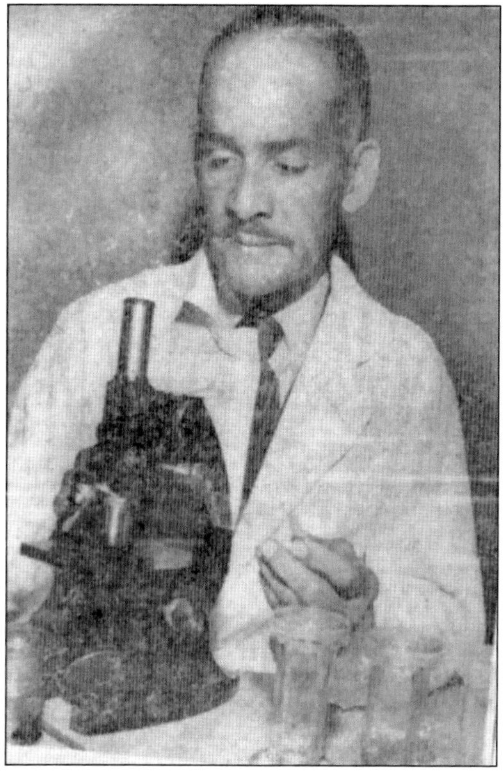

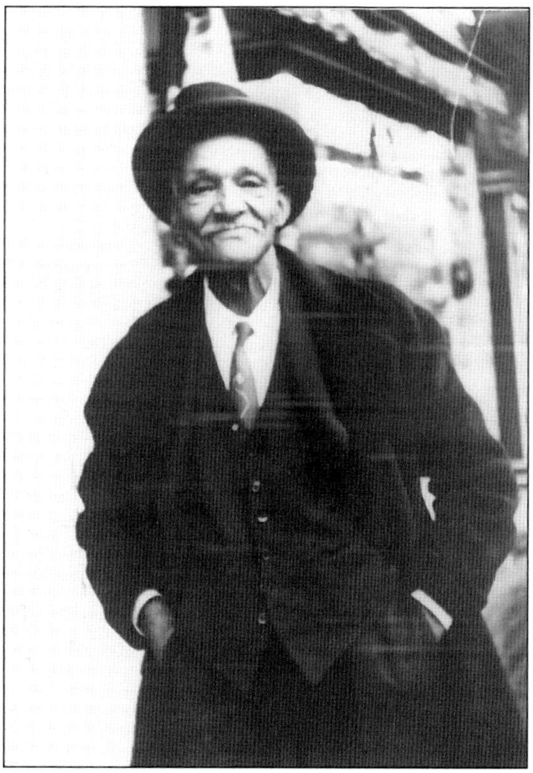

This is William Franklin Jones (1878–1960), son of Henry Clay Jones (1842–1920) and Martha Jane Johnson (1852–1912), who had 14 other children. For 47 years, he was an owner and operator of the family business, Jones Lumber Mill, located off of the old Hanover (now Jones) Road. William Jones married Josephine of the Mattaponi Native American tribe, and they had four children, Blanche, Newton, Warner Sr., and Nora. (Warner Jones Jr.)

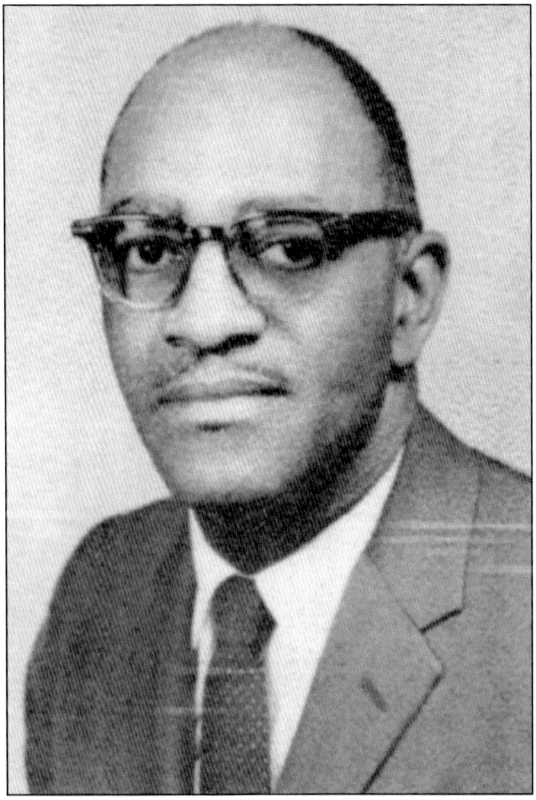

Pictured here is Robert A. Bracey Jr. (1912–1977), son of Martha and Robert A. Bracey Sr., who moved to Glen Allen from Petersburg, Virginia, when he was a child. Robert was educated at Virginia State College, where he earned both his bachelor's and master's degrees. He married Mable Wallace Bracey and had an illustrious teaching career from 1934 to 1976 in Greensville and Henrico County schools. He became supervisor of veterans' training for the Virginia Department of Education and served as principal of Virginia Randolph High School. He retired from Hermitage High School. (Robert A. Bracey III.)

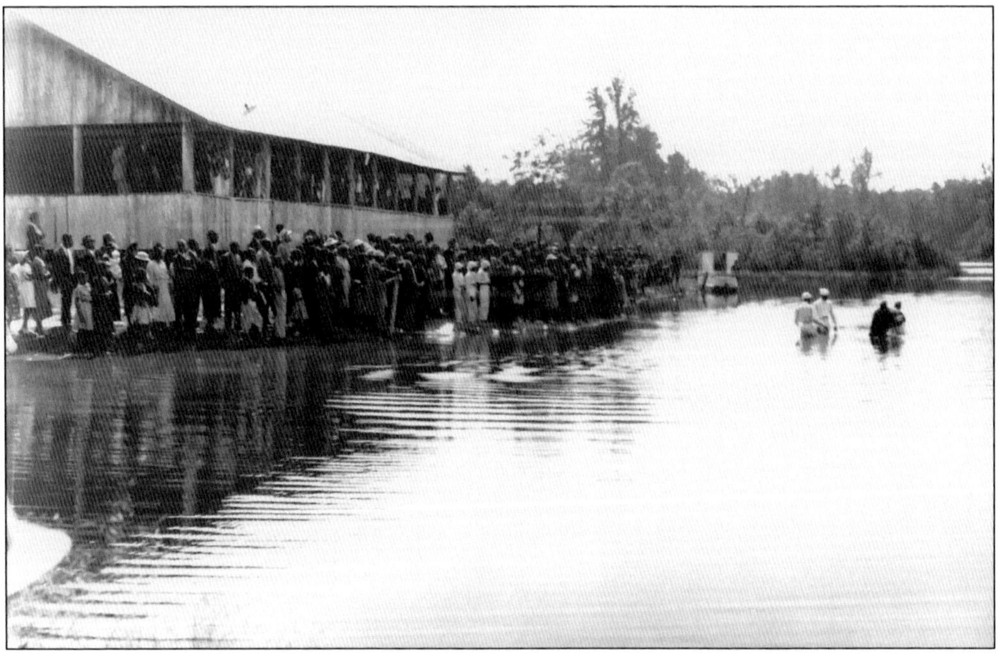

This picture shows a baptismal at Echo Lake around 1930. Notice the "mourners" in white. Several black churches in Glen Allen performed baptisms at the lake prior to building edifices with pools. (Julia Melton Thornton.)

Nine

Quioccasin Back Neighborhood Zion Town

The history of Quioccasin coincides with the American Civil War. William Vandervall was walking through a wooded area and discovered a tree near the church building inscribed with the Native American word *Quioccasin*, which means "beautiful place." Quioccasin was chosen to be the name of the new church, community, and road (which remains a main thoroughfare). The Quioccasin community is bordered by Pemberton, Three Chopt, and Ridge Roads. Pryor's Court is located on Ridge Road. The Bryant, Dabney, Dobson, Jackson, Johnson, Jones, King, Lomax, Lyles, Moss/Morse, Overton, Price Edward, Pryor, Sparkman, Talley, and Vandervall families inhabited this community. William Vandervall persuaded the county to build Zion Town School on lower Ridge Road, and later a five-room school was built called Quioccasin School.

Zion Town, which means heavenly city, is 1 mile directly west of the University of Richmond on Ridge Road, half a mile north of River Road. It was named by Henry Pryor (1825–1900), a former slave on Higginbotham Plantation who purchased 5 acres for $200 in 1872 from E. A. Green. He was forced to purchase the land twice, because he could not produce the deed. Unfortunately, there is no picture of Henry Pryor, a carpenter and community leader who inspired confidence among those who knew him. Pryor had the torso of a giant and the lower extremities of a child, but he had great physical prowess. He married Panola "Piney" Thomas and lived in a house with his mother, Bettie Pryor, born in 1803. They had six children—Bettie, Jesse Jr., Moses, Anne Pryor, Thomas Henry, Martha—and Piney had another daughter, Panola Thomas, from her previous union to John Thomas Sr.

In the bend of Ridge Road was the Thompson family farm of 50 acres, owned by William David and Ella Davenport Thompson. Their daughter, Lloyd Delma Thompson, married George W. Gee, and later they developed Thompson Heights. Zion Town had three stores for its residents: Cauthorne's Market, Ledbetter Store (owned by Pete Henley), and Lukard Market. The families of Zion Town were Byrd, Carter, Dandridge, Fenner, Fountain, Jackson, Lambert, Lewis, Morse, Norrell, Pryor, and Thomas.

According to Welford Burrell, a local family historian, other neighborhoods were Lane Road, Flat Branch, Sleepy Hollow, Back Neighborhood, and Thompson Heights. Back Neighborhood was home to several families: Carter, Johnson, Lewis, Talley, Taylor, Truman, Warren, and Woodson. The Quioccasin and Westwood communities shared a cemetery on Quioccasin Road since the 1920s. The J. S. Pryor Sr. Memorial Cemetery was purchased in 1939 by descendants for family members to be buried. The Lambert family is also buried in Pryor Memorial Cemetery. The stones from the Moss/Morse family cemetery were moved and relocated with other family members.

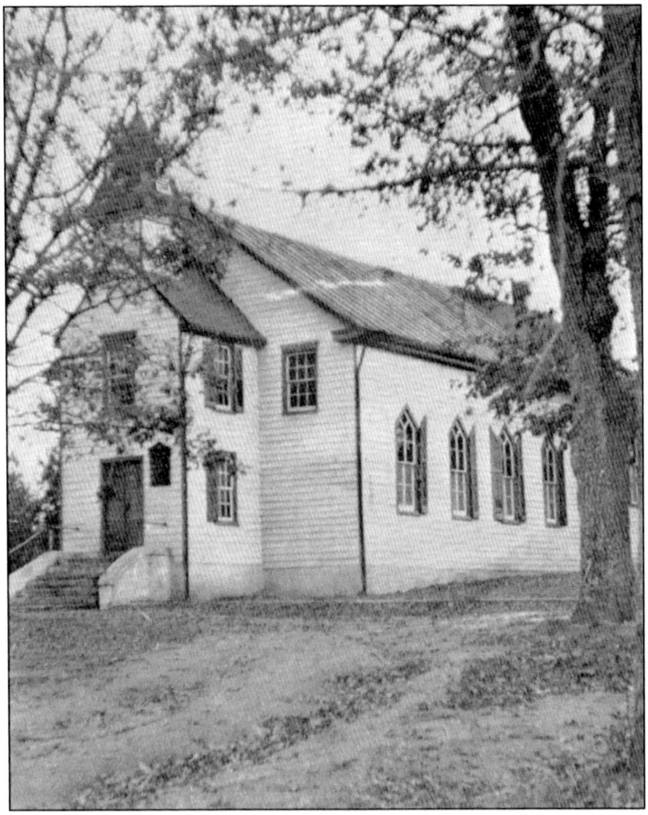

This is the second structure of Quioccasin Baptist Church, which burned down in 1951. The records show that in 1865 a group of blacks, former slaves, and Native Americans withdrew from the Deep Run Baptist Church, a white congregation. They held services at William and Rebecca Vandervall's house on Pemberton Road, where Byrd Middle School stands. The Vandervalls also donated portions of land and logs to erect a structure in 1866. Mr. Frederick Moss/Morse Sr. donated logs and hewed them out. The first service was held in 1867 with Rev. Royal Smith as pastor. Three trustees, William Bradford, Frank Jones, and F. Moss/Morse Sr., secured the deed to Quioccasin Church, known as Colored Baptist Church. (Quioccasin Baptist Church.)

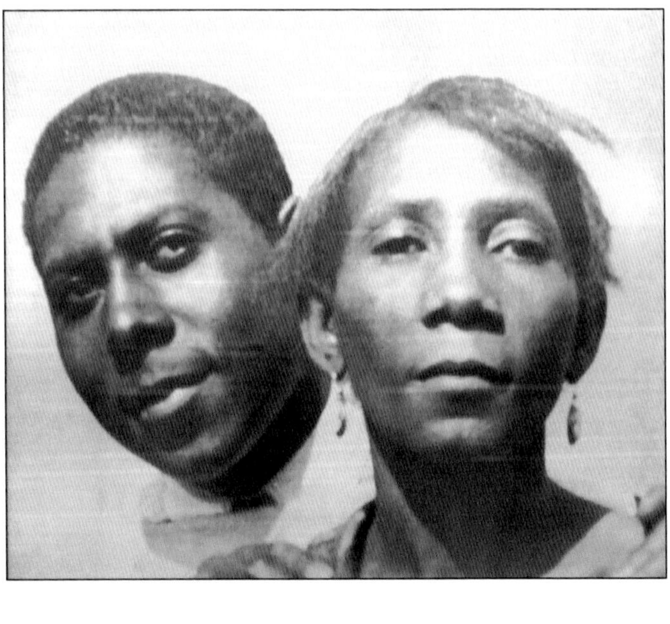

This is a picture of Samuel Morris "Zummy" Byrd and his mother, Panola "Nicey" Patterson Byrd of Zion Town. Samuel and his wife, Ruth, had three children, Sammy Jr., Vaudine, and Joan. Samuel's mother, Nicey, was the daughter of Ann Pryor and Morris Patterson. After the death of her first husband, Ann married Trimuel Fenner. Their home is off of Ziontown Road and adjacent to the Higginbotham property. A family cemetery is behind the Patterson home. (Ruth Spain Byrd.)

Pictured here are Ethel Mayo and Walter Jackson Sr. in their yard on Pemberton Road in the 1960s. Walter (1901–1966) worked for the Seaboard Coast Line Railroad for 30 years, and Ethel (1906–1992) was a homemaker. (Wilhelmina Jackson Cunningham.)

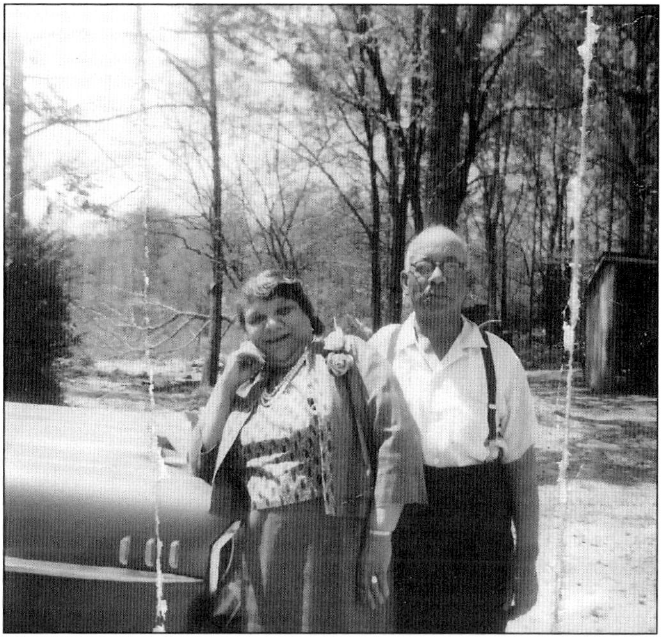

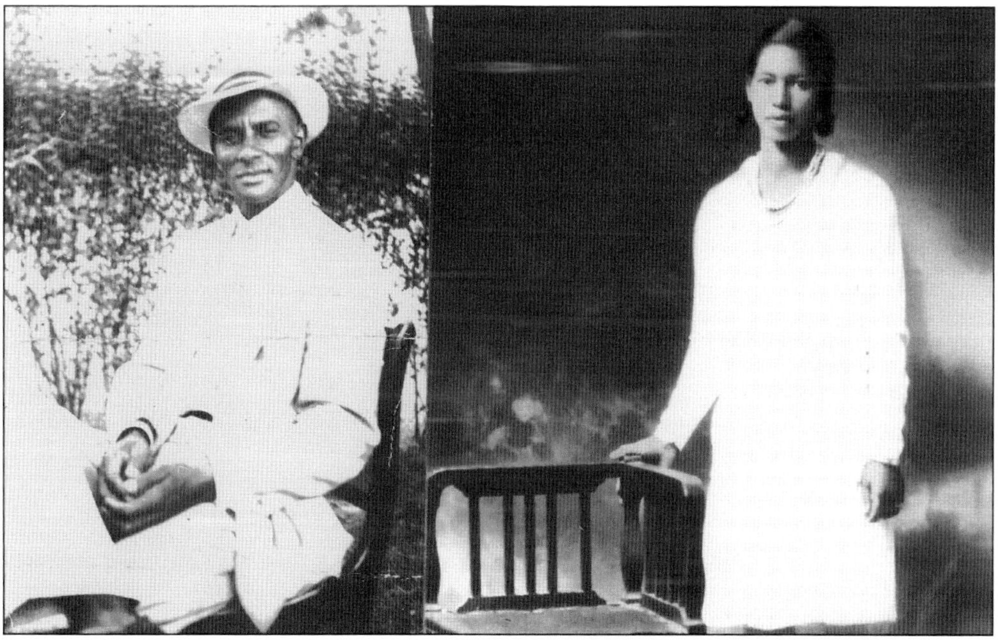

Featured here is Rev. Frank Lomax Sr. (1900–1994), born in Bon Air, Virginia (in Chesterfield County), to Spencer and Ellen T. Lomax. He worked as a butler for the family of John Coke (lawyer), was employed by Virginia Electric and Power Company, and was a sexton at Tuckahoe and Vandervall Elementary Schools in Henrico County. Reverend Lomax, licensed and ordained by Bon Air Baptist Church, later joined Quioccasin Baptist Church. He was married to Novella Fountain Lomax (1909–1991), daughter of Deacon Philmore and Hattie Roane Fountain from lower Ridge Road. She graduated from Hartshorn Memorial College and taught school. The couple had three children—Frank Jr., Louise L. Pryor, and Frederick Spencer. They moved to Pemberton Road in the 1950s. (Rev. Frank Lomax Jr. and Barbara Coles.)

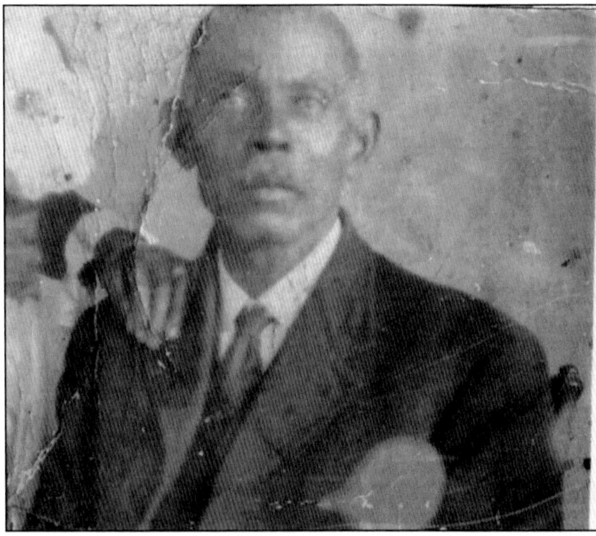

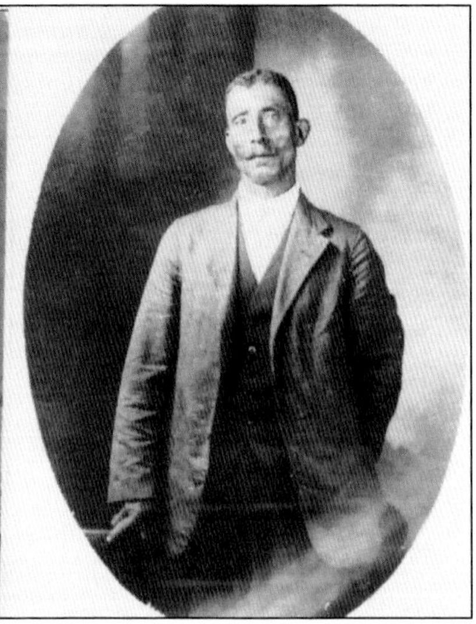

These are the Vandervall brothers. At left is William Leroy (1860–1934), teacher and principal in Quioccasin and Zion Town Schools. Under segregation, a new school for black children was built on Pemberton Road named Vandervall Elementary. After integration, it was renamed Pemberton Elementary. In 1903, William was the first black postal carrier (Rural Free Delivery No. 1) west of Three Chopt Road up River Road. He was married three times, to Mary Dandridge, Leah Houston, and Janie Briggs, and had seven children. On the right is Benjamin D. (1861–1956). Benjamin married Adelaide Johnson and worked for W. I. Johnson Sr. Funeral Home in the city. Their eight children were Ulysses, Louise, Bernetta, Martha, Gracie, Hugh, Hattie, and Leanna. (Jean V. Carter and Adelaide J. Warren.)

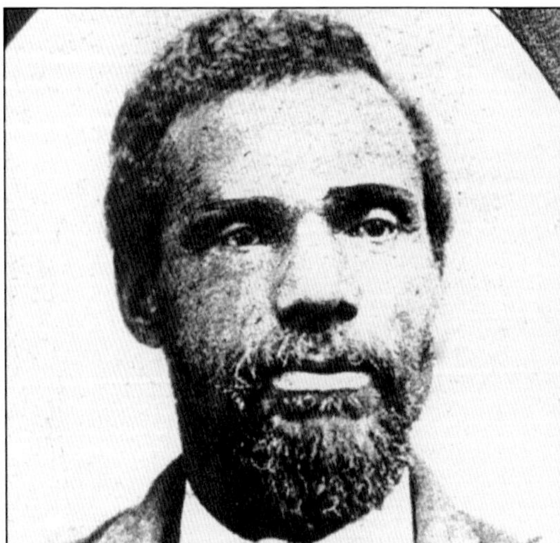

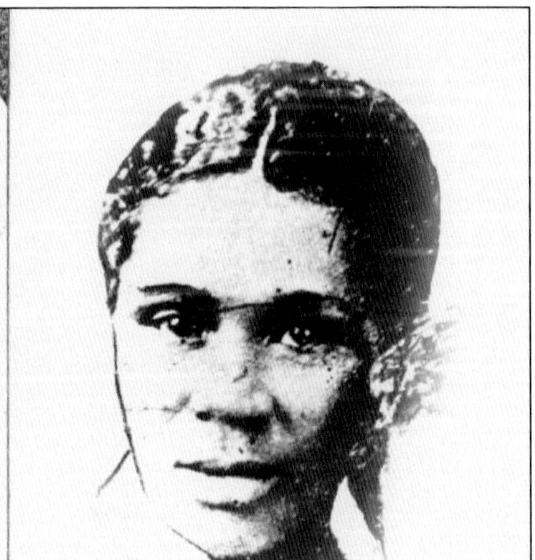

This is Frederick Morse (1829–1919) and his wife ,Caroline Major Morse (1831–1893). He was a born a freedman, and it is said that he was the son of a Native American maid and a man from the Cottrell family. The Cottrells owned Gayton Coal Mine on Gaskins Road. She was born on the Pamunkey Indian Reservation in King William County. They married in 1852, and had 13 children: Maria, Sophie, Smith, Miles, Mary, Eliza Jane, Frederick Jr., Andrew Sherman, Anna, Ella, Eva, Lavinia, and Louise. The Morse name was also spelled as Moss. They lived on Three Chopt Road at Ridge Road and owned a farm and several pieces of property in that area, where a small family cemetery still exists. This land would later house Douglas Freeman High School. (Brenda D. Nichols.)

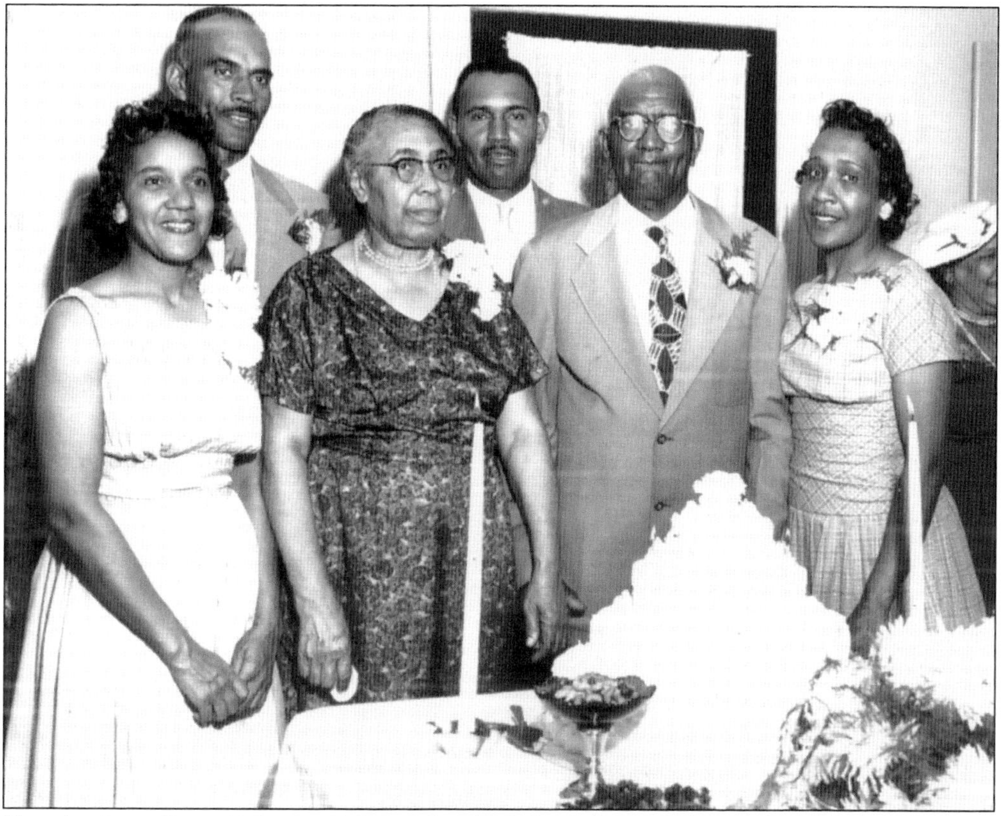

Blanche Irene Pryor Dabney celebrates her 70th birthday with her husband and children in Pryor's Court on East Ridge Road. They are as follows, from left to right: (first row) Louise Dabney Dandridge, Blanche (1889–1976), her husband Percy (1890–1961), and Mable Dabney Hubbard; (second row) Forrest and Ernest Dabney. Percy Dabney was born in King William County to Scott and Virginia Chick Dabney, and he founded the Dabney Lumber Company in 1947. He also owned an auto repair shop and a store on West Leigh Street. Blanche was born in Zion Town to Eliza J. Moss and J. S. Pryor Sr. (Ernest Dabney.)

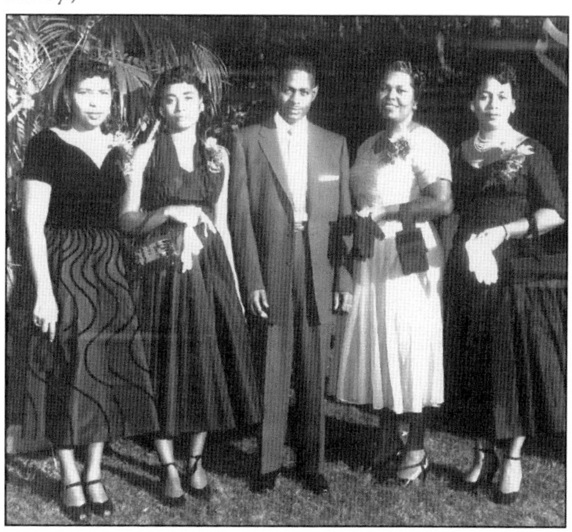

In 1947, Arthur and Carrie Jones Carter of Glen Allen purchased seven acres of land and moved to Derbyshire Road in Back Neighborhood, where they raised their four children. Pictured here from left to right are Maxine Carter, Jean Vandervall, Jean's husband Arthur, and Goldie and Mary Connie Carter. Maxine, the oldest child, worked for 54 years in Henrico County food services. Jean Carter Vandervall did domestic work for 56 years for the Whitley family. Goldie Carter was also employed by Henrico County food services. Connie worked in the medical field for three physicians. (Maxine Carter.)

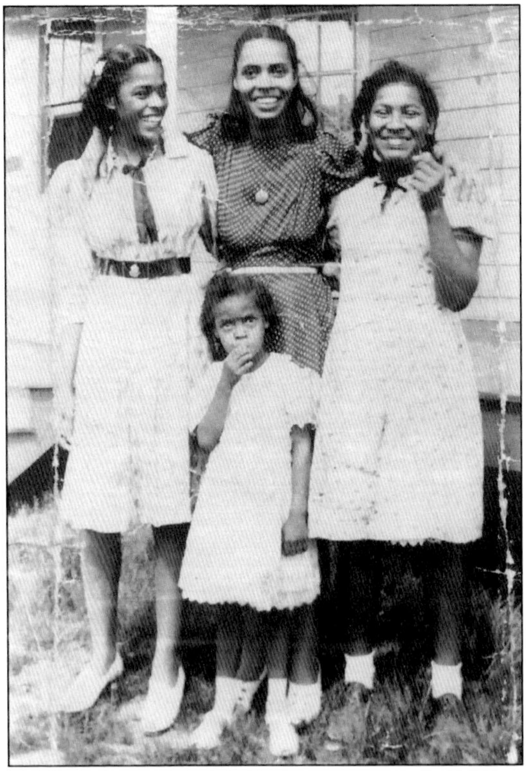

This photograph from the 1940s shows the smiling daughters and granddaughter of Harry and Leanna Vandervall Jackson. They are, from left to right, Adelaide (age 18), Lucy (age 24), Mable (age 16) and Barbara Pemberton (age 6). (Adelaide J. Warren.)

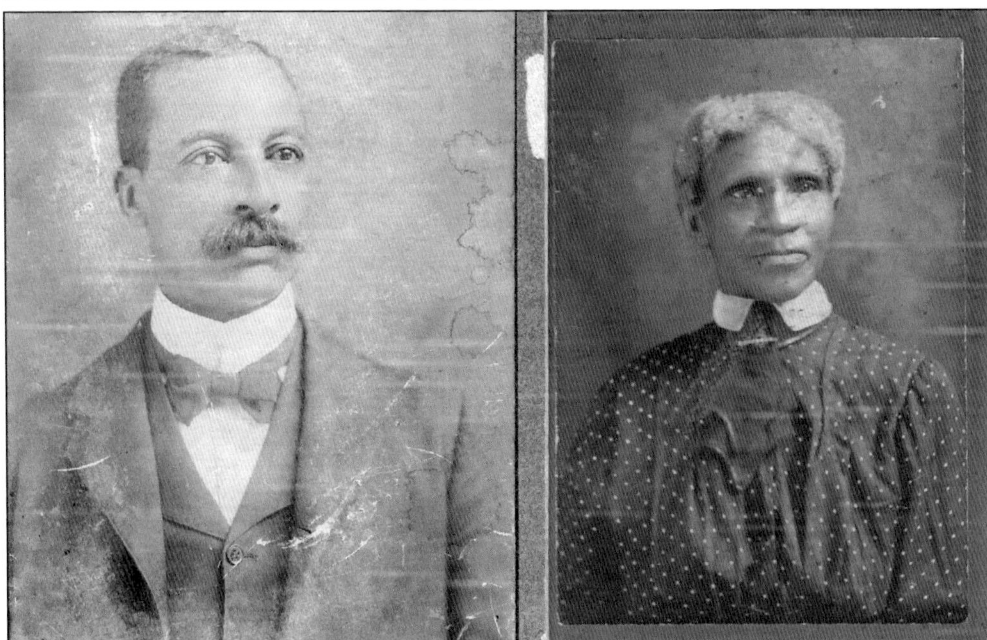

Pictured here are William David Thompson (a farmer and insurance collector) and his wife, Ella Marshall Davenport (a schoolteacher), with whom he had 14 children. They lived on River Road in the Westham area and purchased 50 acres from C. Ashburner in 1901. Initially a family farm, it was developed into the residential area Thompson Heights, named after their family. (Lucille Haskins.)

Bettie Pryor Fountain (1851–1917), pictured here, was the daughter of Henry and Panola "Piney" Thomas Pryor. She married Spencer Pemberton Fountain of Hanover County, and together they had six children. After the early death of her husband, Bettie and her children returned to Henrico County, and her father Henry Pryor lived with them until his death in 1900. Grandchildren Helena and Ellen Fountain still live in the family home. (Helena and Ellen Fountain.)

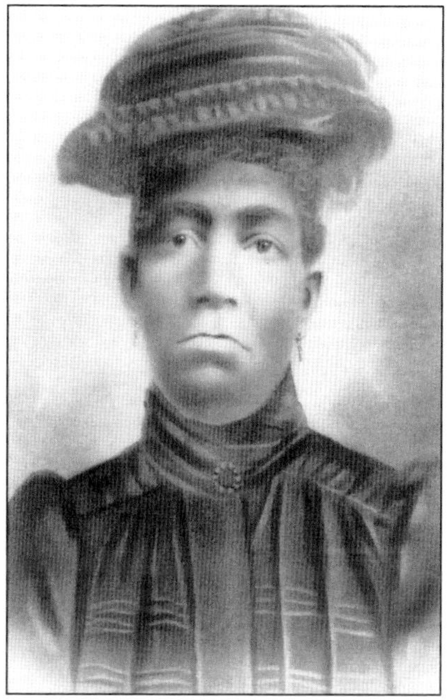

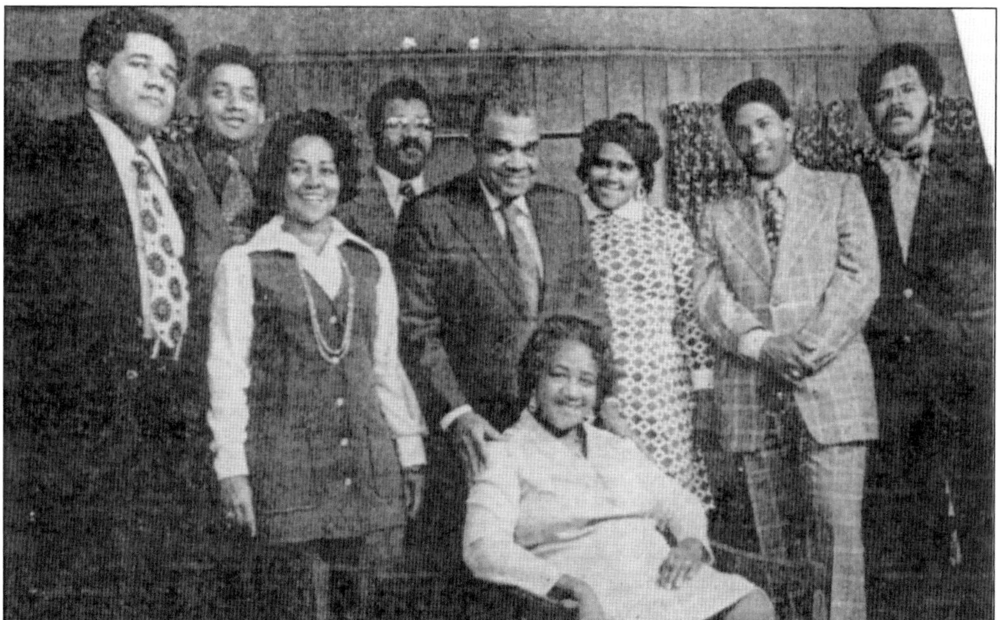

Benjamin Lambert Jr. and his wife, Frances, of Zion Town, were married in 1934. They owned Lambert Catering Service for 35 years, serving homes, clubs, and businesses, including the governor's mansion. They are pictured here with their seven children, who would become leaders in their chosen professions. They are, from left to right, Benjamin J. Lambert III (optometrist and esteemed former state senator), Abbott Jackson Lambert (Thalhimers' senior vice-president), Elizabeth L. Johns (retired supervisor of speech and hearing), John A. Lambert (accountant), Benjamin Lambert Jr., Frances (seated), Anne L. Johnson (dentist in Kansas City), Leonard W. Lambert (attorney and former judge), and Richard Andrew Lambert (owner of Scotts' Funeral Home). (B. J. Lambert III.)

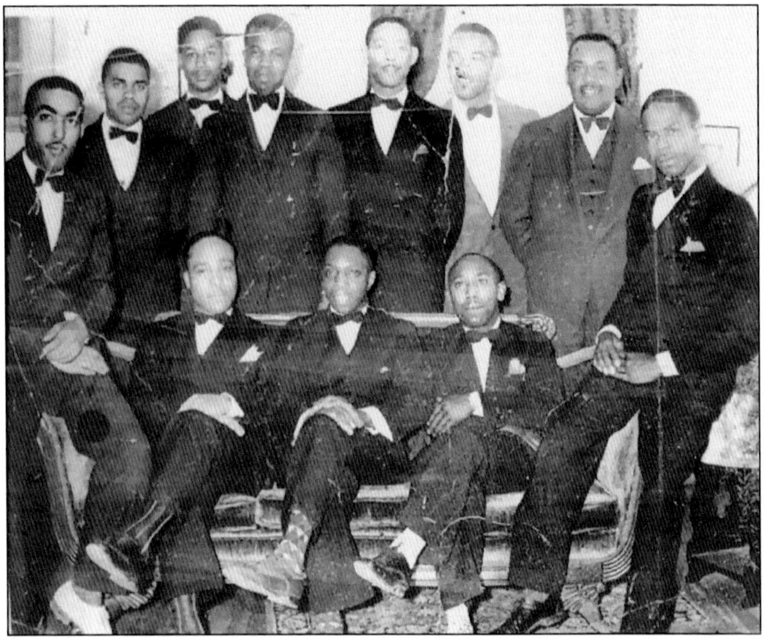

Pictured here around 1955 are the young men of Zion Town. They are, from left to right, (first row) Fredrick Morse Pryor Sr., Snowden Pryor, Willie Lewis, Herbert Dabney Sr., and George Johnson; (second row) Benjamin Lambert Jr., Cardoza Scott, Willis Norrell, Edward Taylor, unidentified, and Ellsworth R. Pryor. (Ellsworth C. Pryor Sr.)

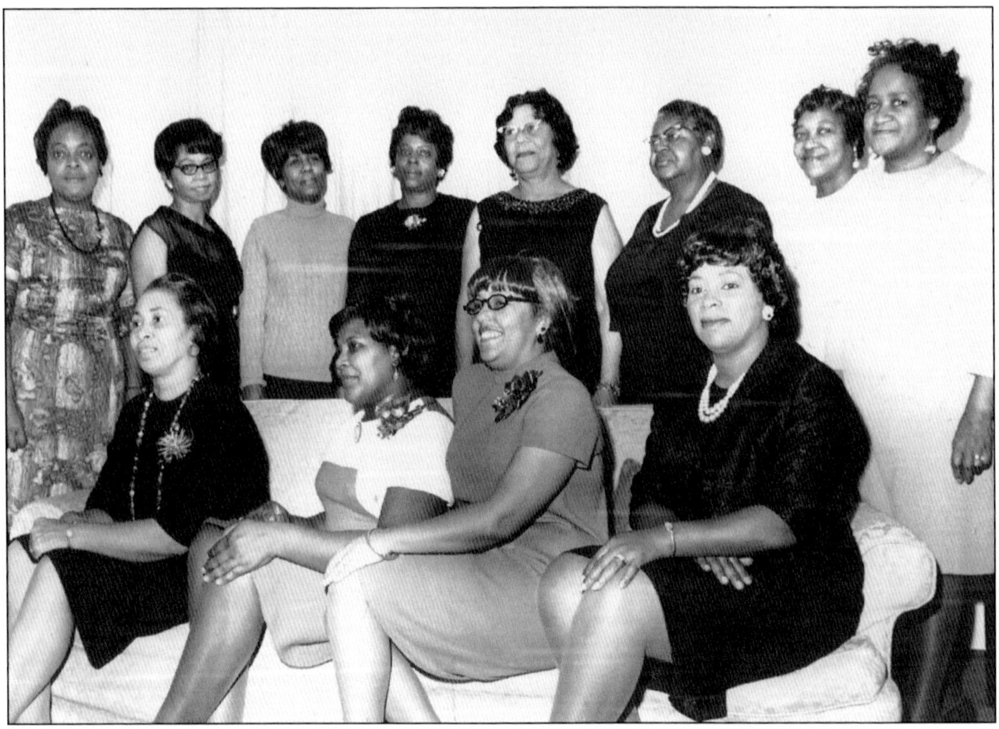

This is the Royal Duchess Club—a civic and charitable organization—of the Quioccasin, Zion Town, and Westwood communities. Pictured are the following members, from left to right: (first row) Martha B. Fountain Lyles, Sally Jackson Talley, Emily Moss, and Matilda Cauthorne; (second row) Susie Truman, Marie Taylor Pryor, Yvonne Taylor, Everlina King, Lucy Bryant Carter, Mary "Maidie" Fountain, Lavinia H. Dabney, and Mary Frances Warden Lambert, the last surviving member, who turned 97 years old in July 2009. (Ernest Dabney.)

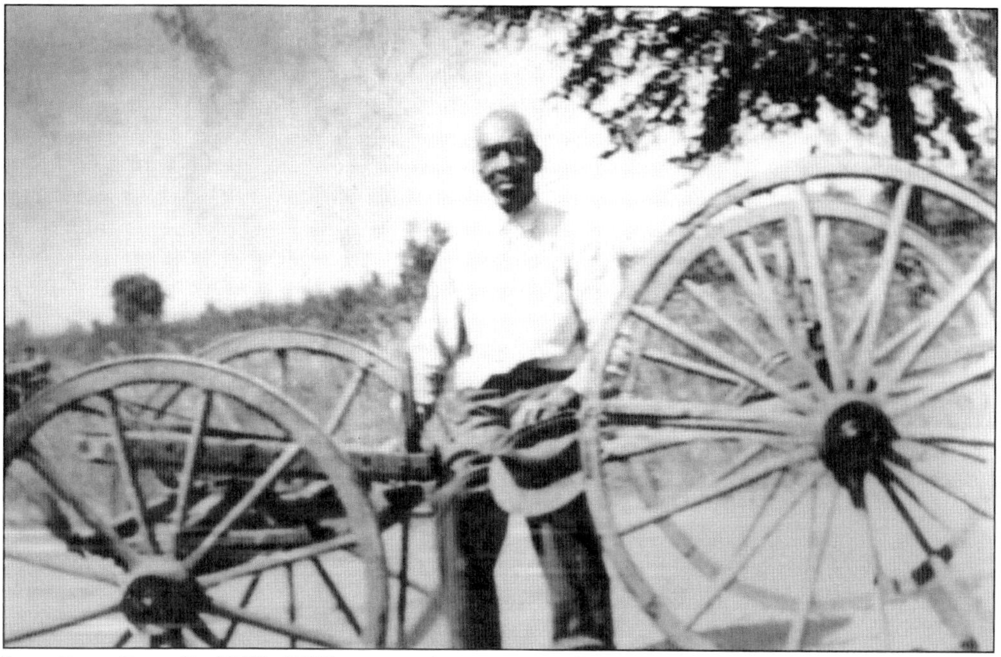

Jesse Scott Pryor Sr. (1855–1939) sits on a horse cart on Patterson Avenue, which was a dirt road, around 1920. Jesse was the son of Henry and Panola "Piney" Thomas Pryor, former enslaved people and founders of Zion Town. He married Eliza Jane Moss (1864–1914) in 1887, and they had seven children, Carrie Ollie, Blanche Irene, Jesse Jr., Edward Forest, Emit, Malennis Adolphus, and Ellsworth Reddington. Jesse worked for the railroad, the Higginbotham farm, and the Hancock family of Patterson. He purchased 14 acres in 1905 on Ridge Road (now Eastridge Road) and built the family home named Pryor's Court, where he had a large farm and garden. He was the first person to be buried in Pryor Memorial, the cemetery named after him. (Blanche P. Dabney.)

Bibliography

Fairfax, Colita Nichols. *Hampton, Virginia*. Charleston, SC: Arcadia Publishing, 2005.

Harlan, Howard, *Zion Town—A Study in Human Ecology*. Charlottesville, VA: University of Virginia, 1935.

Kern, M. Ethel Kelley. *The Trail of the Three Notched Road*. Richmond, VA: William Byrd Press, 1929.

Manarin, Louis H., and Clifford Dowdey. *The History of Henrico County*. Charlottesville, VA: University of Virginia, 1984.

Parks, Mary Thompson. *Forget Me Not: Memories of Rio Vista, Virginia*. Richmond, VA: Old Dominion Press, 1972.

Picott, J. Rupert. *History of the Virginia Teachers Association*. Washington, D.C.: National Education Association, 1975.

Richardson, Selden. *Built by Blacks: African American Architecture and Neighborhoods in Richmond, VA*. Richmond, VA: Dietz Press, 2007.